SOVEREIGN EQUALITY AMONG STATES:
THE HISTORY OF AN IDEA

The rise of the concept that all nations are equal has transformed international relations in the twentieth century, setting radically new terms for the conduct of war and peace, for economic relations, and for the organization of international society. It is Dr Klein's belief that uncritical adherence to this concept is a major stumbling block to the reorganization of the world community.

This book is the first study of the historical antecedents and philosophical foundations of the concept of sovereign equality. The older concept of great-power primacy pictures states as abstract entities with a fictitious personality. Increasingly challenged since Alexis de Tocqueville, it has been supplanted by the opposing concept of sovereign equality, which was brought to world attention at the Second Hague Peace Conference in 1907. This view endows states with human personality and transfers to them the political principle of individual equality. Dr Klein concentrates on the tension between these two concepts in the New World, particularly as the idea of equality underwent its principal development in the sphere of American relations with the Latin American republics.

Neither concept is adequate, Dr Klein maintains, although each conforms in varying degrees to the international reality; yet any suggested deviation from the concept of sovereign equality is rejected, and thus the development of a more effective international system is inhibited. Essentially the problem is philosophical: to prevent too great a gap between the real and conceptual worlds that man inhabits.

ROBERT A. KLEIN is an independent researcher in the field of international relations in the archives of the League of Nations at the UN Library in Geneva.

ROBERT A. KLEIN

Sovereign equality among states: the history of an idea

UNIVERSITY OF TORONTO PRESS

© University of Toronto Press 1974
Toronto and Buffalo
Reprinted in paperback 2017
ISBN 978-0-8020-5297-1 (cloth)
ISBN 978-1-4875-9239-4 (paper)
LC 73-82582

To
Johnny and Jimmy
equally

Contents

Foreword

International relations are determined by the myths that, as surrogates for realities beyond our comprehension, dominate our minds. The myths may represent the realities more or less truly, more or less falsely, with corresponding consequences, for good or evil, when action is taken on the bases they provide.

For example, until the end of the nineteenth century Chinese policy was determined by the myth that there was no civilization outside China, that those who lived outside were barbarians, and that the Chinese emperor had sovereign jurisdiction over the entire world, over Chinese and barbarians alike, by virtue of Heaven's Mandate. Because this myth was remote from the reality, it misled the Chinese in their efforts to cope with the reality. The consequence was a century of agony for China, from the 1840s to the 1940s, during which its misconceived efforts to deal with the incursions of Western civilization produced successive disasters.

The American and British people fought World War II on the mythical premise that the world was divided between two species of nations, the peace-loving nations and the aggressor nations. On this premise they were unable, after victory, to make a proper peace with Germany, regarded as an aggressor nation, or to limit the expansion of Russia, regarded as a peace-loving nation. The result was the Cold War, which entailed the replacement of the old myth by a new one according to which the world was the scene of an irreducible conflict between freedom-lovers and Communists. (Franco's Spain was a freedom-lover.)

Nations, themselves, are mythical concepts that may correspond roughly to realities or may have virtually no correspondence to them. The corporate personality with which we endow them in our minds is metaphoric and convenient rather than real. Closely related to the concept of the nation is that of the people as a single sovereign – if, indeed, it is not simply a particular formulation of the national concept. When the president of the United States speaks in the name of the American people or when the ruler of Russia speaks in the name of the Russian people he is acting out a myth that represents a reality, more or less well, more or less badly.

In its representation of reality, then, the concept of the nation is less strained in some cases, more so in others. The concept of France, having become established over centuries (although not over nearly as many centuries as the myth would have it), and representing a certain linguistic, cultural, and geographical coherence, is less strained than the concept of Yugoslavia, artificially created as late as 1918, which lumps together as one nation Serbs, Croats, and Slovenes, Christians and Muslims, those who speak Servo-Croatian, those who speak Slovenian, and those who speak the Macedonian language.

There had never been an Indian nation, and there had never been a Philippine nation, but the withdrawal of colonial rule from the Indian subcontinent and from the myriad Philippine Islands in the 1940s was regarded as the restoration of a national independence that had been temporarily lost. Even the most scholarly studies described the respective events in these terms.

After World War II, upon the withdrawal of European rule from black Africa, with its primitive tribal societies, a number of nations were simply declared into existence. Their boundaries were, for the most part, determined by lines of artificial demarcation, drawn originally merely to define the respective colonial spheres of European powers, and the populations living within them were largely without ethnological, religious, or linguistic coherence. Zaïre is an example. Today, when the ruler of Zaïre speaks for the people of Zaïre, reporting their views and their wishes, he is speaking for a mythical entity that has virtually no relation to any human reality. I have seen literature issued in Ghana that recounts the achievements of the Ghanese nation in mathematics and science as long ago as the fifth century B.C. (Where a myth cannot come to birth naturally, the use of forceps may be necessary.)

Another recently declared nation is Qatar, with an Arab and Persian population of some 60,000 indistinguishable from the neighbouring Arabs and Persians, its borders permeable to the pastoral nomads who, moving back and forth across them, thereby confound the census-taker. Qatar, founded in 1971, is equal to China in the General Assembly of the United Nations.

If Long Island, New York, with a hundred times the population of Qatar, should become independent of the United States, it would in its newly realized national dignity be entitled to equal weight with the United States.

Because international relations are determined primarily by the concepts that dominate men's minds, the most fundamental changes in the historical evolution of international relations are those that result from the replacement of old concepts by new. No change has been more radical than that brought about by the recent rise of the concept that all nations are equal, which has transformed international relations in our century.

Alexis de Tocqueville, in the Introduction to his *Democracy in America*, called attention to the fact that Western civilization since the eleventh century had been increasingly swayed by the concept of human equality. The concept that all natural persons are created equal – equal in the eyes of God or, as a matter of natural justice, equal before the law – had gradually risen to primacy by the time he wrote, in the 1830s. But it had not yet been extended from the natural person to the mythical person which is a nation-state. No one, in his day, would have suggested any kind of equality between San Marino, which was never more than a village with surrounding fields, and the Russian Empire, on the grounds that both were persons and that all persons are created equal. No one would have suggested that San Marino should have an equal voice with Russia in managing the Concert of Europe. The concept that still prevailed in Tocqueville's day was that of great-power primacy, according to which their very greatness gave the great powers a commensurate responsibility and a paternalistic authority over small or weak states.

The concept of great-power primacy was one item in a mythical complex, corresponding more or less well, more or less badly, to the realities for which it stood. It was to be increasingly challenged, after Tocqueville's day, by the new concept of the sovereign equality of all states great and small, which also corresponded more or less well, more or less badly, to the realities for which it stood. The new concept was to be increasingly entangled in other mythical concepts, such as the concept that every state, speaking with the voice of its ruling authority, represented its population as one people – a concept that made it acceptable for the agent of Generalissimo Rafael Leonidas Trujillo Molina, absolute dictator of the Dominican Republic, to sign in San Francisco on 26 June 1945 a document that began:

'We, the peoples of the United Nations ...' Under the sway of the myth, Generalissimo Trujillo was accepted as the spokesman for the views and wishes of the Dominican people. How many were heartened, in that day, by the spectacle of virtually all the world's peoples, over two thousand million, agreeing on the principles set forth in the Charter of United Nations! But how few of the world's people knew that they had subscribed to it!

If it is true that the most basic changes in international relations are changes in the minds of men, then the rise to supremacy of the concept of sovereign equality is the most important development of modern times. It has set radically new terms for the making of war and peace, for economic relations – and, indeed, for the whole organization and conduct of international society. The French Revolution was not more radical in its impact. Yet this transformation has not until now been subjected to historical research and critical examination. Despite all the activity of our universities in the study of international relations, despite their thousands upon thousands of research projects every year, and despite the voluminous annual literature on virtually every aspect of international relations, this single most important development in the evolution of international relations has remained unexamined – presumably because the concept of sovereign equality has been as accepted without question by the members of academic communities as by everyone else.

In my own view, the mission of scholarship is to comprehend reality, and this requires an element of Voltairean scepticism that has diminished in our intellectual life as ideological thinking has grown. To comprehend the reality of social relationships, scholarship must condition itself to recognize what is mythic as such. It follows that the mission of scholarship cannot be carried out by those who accept the myths of the day as literal truths or as representing an authority not to be questioned. Today, in fulfilment of Tocqueville's prophecy, the very word 'equality' has acquired a sanctity in our thinking, like the sanctity we attach to the words 'peace' (which we so rarely try to define) and 'justice,' so that, I suspect, if someone proclaimed the equality of all sticks and stones, we would hesitate to question it as we would hesitate to question virtue itself. Even though the questioner should, in the end, conclude that the doctrine of the sovereign equality of all states, great and small, alone represented justice, that the moral and material progress of mankind alike depended on it, the very fact of examining that doctrine critically would seem to almost all of us as dangerous as the first critical examination of Holy Scripture by the historians of the nineteenth century seemed to their orthodox contemporaries.

If I may be allowed to speak in personal terms, now that a critical examination of this historic change is at last publicly available – in the form of the book to which these words are introductory – I am at last relieved of a long-standing frustration. From now on, in such lecturing and writing as I do on the subject of international politics, I can fill the great gap in the bibliography of international relations by referring my auditors or readers to a text indispensable for the understanding of international relations in our time.

Dr Klein's work is historical and philosophical. It recounts the history of the conflict, in the minds of men, between two rival concepts, a conflict on the outcome of which the whole nature of international relations would depend. Both concepts were mythical, both had their points of greater and of lesser correspondence to reality, both had elements of justice and injustice alike. The supremacy of either was bound to entail difficulties as well as advantages.

At the same time that Dr Klein has traced the history of this epoch-making conflict he has raised the philosophical questions fundamental to it. He has shown that the justification for the doctrine that all natural persons are equal is not automatically transferable to the doctrine that all states are equal, so that we are not exempted from giving the matter thought.

I have said enough, now, to show why I regard this as one of the most important books on international politics of our times. But I have no idea whether it will be received as such. I have no idea whether our common resistance to any critical examination of the myths by which we live will allow it to be so received. For those minds to which it is accessible, however, it provides an indispensable key to the understanding of international relations in the twentieth century. Whether it is used or not, the key has now been made available. All I can do is to advocate that it be used, to advocate that this book be read and pondered by all who strive for an understanding of modern international relations, to advocate that its contents be made part of the curriculum wherever international relations are studied or taught.

LOUIS J. HALLE

Preface

The international system is in deep trouble because of the pressure exerted by two conflicting concepts: sovereign equality and great-power primacy.

In his study of the Peloponnesian War, Thucydides records a judgment implicit in the latter idea. It was always a rule, said the Athenians, that the weak should be subject to the strong. More then 2000 years later at the Congress of Vienna, the Great Powers refined that rule. They declared themselves responsible for peace because they were the strongest. Growing disillusion with such arrogance parallels the rise of the nation-state. In the opinion of Kurt Waldheim, Secretary-General of the United Nations, the concept of great-power primacy obviously cannot be acceptable to 'the peoples of the world.' Indeed, with the increasing democratization of political life the structure of international society has come to rest, virtually unnoticed, on the opposing idea of sovereign equality.

This book is, I believe, the first attempt to write a history of the idea of sovereign equality, to uncover its philosophical roots, and to consider the confusion inherent in pressing reality to conform to contradictory concepts, both of which are more or less inadequate.

The words 'sovereign equality' caught the fancy of Latin American diplomats at inter-American and early international conferences. Officials of the Department of State picked up the term and through their efforts it was introduced into the UN Charter. For the first time this complete subsidiary history is also told.

One of the major problems in a study spanning close to a century and a half is the awesome mass of material available. I have had to wrestle continually with the problem of what to include and what to omit, what to stress and what to note in passing. All this affected the structure of the work. Roughly, it is organized as follows: the first chapter sets the conceptual framework for the historical material. The second chapter discusses the rise of the concept of great-power primacy to a controlling position in world affairs. The next three chapters, except for references to the Second Hague Peace Conference (where the philosophical basis of the concept of sovereign equality was first expounded) and the Paris Peace Conference (1919), draw heavily on inter-American affairs. The idea of equality underwent its principal development in the relations between the United States and the twenty Latin American republics. The repercussions were worldwide. This is the justification for concentrating on the tension between the two concepts in the New World. Chapter 6 examines the conceptual struggle between great and small states in the period immediately before and after World War II. The last chapter explains how our thinking is dominated by the concept of sovereign equality.

To come to grips with a history of opposing ideas, I scrutinized the speeches of statesmen, the notes and memoranda they prepared, and the agreements they drafted. Some of this material is contained in personal memoirs, but by far the largest part is found in the minutes and proceedings of international and regional conferences, the reports of delegations, and the publications of official government documents. These are the primary sources on which the work is based.

To Louis J. Halle I owe a special debt for suggesting the topic of this book, and for giving me the benefit of his impeccable counsel. Professor Halle possesses an invaluable gift: treating people not as they are but as they may potentially be. Working with this inspiring teacher made me feel as if my insight had been raised to a higher power. I am grateful also to Professor Jacques Freymond, the distinguished Director of the Graduate Institute of International Studies where much of the work on my book was done.

At the United Nations Library, M. Arthur Breycha-Vauthier granted me numerous favours. In particular, he let me use his office to consult D.H. Miller's *My Diary at the Conference of Paris* – one of the only copies of this twenty-volume set available in Europe. Mr Norman S. Field, associate chief librarian, was extremely generous. He gave me access to the stacks and either ordered or borrowed source material not otherwise available. The co-operation extended by this outstanding librarian made my task considerably easier. The librarians of the Graduate Institute of International Studies: M. Pierre Pagneux, Mme Lydia Anhöck, and Mlle Irène Sauvin deserve special mention for their gracious assistance.

My appreciation is extended to the University of Toronto Press. Publication of this book has been made possible by a grant from its Publication Fund. I also profited from the suggestions of Mr R.I.K. Davidson, editor (social sciences), University of Toronto Press, and from the expert editorial advice of Mrs Gertrude Stevenson, assistant editor.

To the unknown officials in the Contrôle de l'Habitant, who permitted me to do my research these many years in the beautiful city of Geneva, Switzerland, a word of thanks is also in order. Finally, an affectionate acknowledgment to my wife Lucette for typing, translating, and tender loving care.

Abbreviations

Malta Yalta: United States, Department of State, *The Conferences at Malta and Yalta*, 1945, Washington, D.C., 1955

Metternich *Mémoires, Documents et Ecrits Divers, laissés par le Prince de Metternich*, publiés par son fils, Le Prince Richard de Metternich, Paris 1880, vol. 4

Miller Diary: Miller, D.H. *My Diary at the Conference of Paris*, set No. 23 printed by the author, New York, 1924

Miller Drafting: Miller, D.H. *The Drafting of the Covenant*, New York, 1928

Minutes *Seventh International Conference of American States*, 'Minutes and Antecedents,' Montevideo, 1937

Peace Handbooks: Great Britain, Foreign Office, *Peace Handbooks*, No. 153, 'The Congress of Vienna,' London, 1920

Proceedings *The Proceedings of the Hague Peace Conferences*, 'The Conference of 1907,' New York, 1920, 1921

Proceedings 1936 *Inter-American Conference for the Maintenance of Peace*, 'Proceedings,' 1936, Buenos Aires, 1937

PWFPP United States, Department of State, *Postwar Foreign Policy Preparation, 1939–1945*, Washington, D.C., 1949

Report 1945 *Report of the Delegation of the United States of America to the Inter-American Conference on Problems of War and Peace*, Mexico City, 1945, Washington, D.C., 1946

Reports *The Reports of the Hague Conferences of 1899 and 1907*, edited, with an introduction by J.B. Scott, Oxford, 1917

Secretary-General *Second Pan American Scientific Congress*, 'The Report of the Secretary-General,' Washington, D.C., 1917

Talleyrand: *Mémoires du Prince Talleyrand* publiés avec une préface et des notes par le Duc de Broglie, Paris, 1891, vol. 2

UNCIO *United Nations Conference on International Organization*. United Nations Information Organization, New York, 1945

WSD *Wellington, Supplementary Despatches, Correspondence and Memoranda of Arthur Duke of*, London, 1862

War and Peace *The Public Papers of Woodrow Wilson*, 'War and Peace,' 1917–1924, edited by R.S. Baker and W. Dodd, New York, 1927

SOVEREIGN EQUALITY AMONG STATES:
THE HISTORY OF AN IDEA

Lupin, pour chaque Etat, mit deux tables au monde: l'adroit, le vigilant, et le fort sont assis à la première, et les petits mangeant leur reste à la seconde.
LA FONTAINE

A wretched, pitiable creature is man with his craving for positive solutions. For centuries men have been struggling and laboring to put the *good* on one side, the *evil* on the other. Centuries will pass, and no matter how much the unprejudiced mind may strive the scales will refuse to tip the beam, and there will always be equal quantities of the *good* and the *evil* on each scale. If only man would learn to form judgments, and not indulge in rash and arbitrary thoughts! If only he would learn that every thought is both a lie and a truth!
TOLSTOY

I
Corporate and real persons

This study of the concept of sovereign equality reflects a particular view of international political society. The ideas set forth below about the state and the individual serve as a touchstone for the main body of research.

The state is a political artifact. It is imitable and alterable. It is thought into existence and can be thought out of existence. So complex, however, is the task of establishing and maintaining order that, in dealing with the problem, men are forced to provide a basis of myth and legend.

Myths stir the mind and spirit. They evoke visions of political harmony. By attracting popular loyalites they are able to secure men's allegiance to the state so that it can operate. In a real sense myths are indispensable to making community life work. But some of them are so far out of tune with reality that, in trying ro realise them, the quest for political order may actually be defeated. In the long run, then, the problem men face is a choice of myths: selecting those that will enable society to function effectively.

Central to the never-ending search for order among states is the concept of corporate personality. International relations are based on this fiction. And it is, therefore, on the conceptual level of a world of corporate persons that we intend to examine the concept of sovereign equality.

To understand the mythical nature of the personality of the state, let us recall that man conceives the world by creating analogical relations. For reasons that lie deep in man's nature, analogies drawn from individual human beings are often irresistible.

The ancient Romans found it particularly convenient to deal with an association of human beings as if it were a real person. This permitted the group to carry on transactions individuals might hesitate or be unable to undertake. In the nominal world of the law, a group of individuals acting together was said to have a single legal personality. Roman legists, however, never lost sight of the fictitious nature of this creation. They were far too realistic to believe that by attributing legal personality to a group of men they had thereby created a real person.

Hobbes was among the first to apply the concept of personality to the territorial state. And a useful concept it proved to be, for it permitted pinning on these new political entities rights and duties towards each other. In those days, and up to the rise of the nation-state, there was a certain surface plausibility in this extension of the concept of personality. For whatever the diversity of governmental systems of Europe, the state was, for the most part, identified with the real personality of the ruler. Louis xiv expressed the idea succinctly in his famous equation of the state with himself.

With the rise of the nation-state the concept of corporate personality continued to dominate legal and political philosophy. Only now the myth was even wider from the mark of reality. Reliance on it posed new obstacles to clear thinking about ordering international life, for sovereignty was no longer embodied in a flesh-and-blood ruler. Instead, it was lodged in a political abstraction called 'The People.'

Under the influence of Rousseau and Hegel the fictitious nature of corporate personality was often forgotten. Men came to identify 'The People' as a real if not superior individual. Thus Rousseau, called by Bergson the most powerful influence which the human mind has experienced since Descartes, found sovereign power in a 'moral person' with a 'general will.' Here was the first step in the idealization of the state; for the general will was only precariously identified with the wills of human beings. It was not any will but a higher will.

When we come to Hegel the state is no longer an artificial creation but the result of a natural organic development – a world process. He found a spiritual principle inherent in political communities. This *Volkgeist*, invested with reality and identified with the state, Hegel sublimated into a superorganism above that of ordinary mortals. According to the German philosopher, all the worth a human being possessed he possessed only through the state.

It was left to Mazzini, whose theory of nationalism has had an incalculable effect on statesmen far into this century, to find that God had divided mankind into distinct national groups. According to him, God intended the general purposes of the world to be carried on through the medium of nations, each with a separate tone of thought and each with a separate part to fulfil.

While the concept of corporate personality has, no doubt, proved indispensable for relations among sovereign states, the capacity of political leaders to view the state in the Rousseau-Hegel-Mazzini tradition, makes it imperative to underscore what to some may seem axiomatic: the state is a person only metaphorically; its will is a term of art. As opposed to the state, individual human beings are real. It is as human beings that we are endowed with the power of will and a spark of responsibility. Intimately linked with the assertion that the only real actions, feelings, and thoughts are those of human beings, is the conviction that in some fundamental sense they are equal.

This is not to deny the important differences of every kind: age, colour, sex, religion, race. Nor that men are unequal in every measurable ability. Rather it is to assert an ideal concept of man that can be said to support Western civilization: in ultimate terms, all human beings share in the divine character – each is a God in miniature. One human being of infinite worth is neither greater nor less than another human being of infinite worth.

The origin of this ethical insight is lost in the unrecorded past. Roots extend back to Biblical times and to the teachings of Jewish sages; to Stoic thinking in ancient Greece and Rome; and to the early Church Fathers and the belief in each man's immortal soul under the Fatherhood of God.

Until modern times, the idea of individual equality in organized political society remained strictly limited to a ruling élite. One reason is that the inevitability of social conflict in man's collective life places a premium on power in ordering group relations. At the same time that the use of power serves to guaranty peace in society it makes for individual inequality. Those who control the instruments of power not only tend to take the rewards and privileges their power commands, but to monopolize the legal and political process as well. By the end of the eighteenth century, however, men began to translate their consciousness of the infinite value of human personality into a new sense of justice. Henceforth the object of government would be to secure the general happiness of all members of the community and to protect such natural rights as equal legal and political treatment.

To understand the idea of individual legal equality, let us recall an inescapable element in human feeling to which it is almost impossible to admit exceptions – the feeling of justice and injustice. For ages past the idea of justice and the idea of equality were intimately connected. Both Plato and Aristotle, in their analysis of justice, included the requirement that like should be treated in like manner. Justinian's idea of justice was expressed in terms of *suum cuique* – to each his due. In more recent times Mortimer Adler defined justice in this way: 'Treat equals equally, and unequals unequally in accordance with their inequality.'

This hardly explains what is just or who is entitled to equal treatment. In the creation of early legal systems only members of the élite in society were granted legal status; that is, only a special class was the subject of legal rights and duties. The rest of the population was excluded. According to the modern Western democratic tradition, when the law attaches a disproportionate consequence to an individual's colour, sex, religion, class, and the like to deny him equal legal and political status, it is arbitrary and does violence to his essential worth.

Today legal equality means that, as far as the law is concerned, all adult citizens have the same status: they can make contracts, transfer property, inherit estates, institute legal proceedings; in short, do all the acts the law permits. The concept of legal equality, of course, embraces the notion of equality before the law; i.e., in its application to all legal subjects it will be equally administered. In spite of the wide differences among individuals, few will deny that the myth of legal equality has proved vital for the development of democratic society.

When we turn to politics, we find the seventeenth century English Puritans, steeped in the religious significance of man's uniqueness, developing the idea of the individual as the essential political unit in society. By the time of the American and French revolutions the idea had taken deep hold. No longer was government created to benefit a particular class. Instead, it encompassed the entire community of free and equal citizens. In practice, it took considerable time to gain acceptance for the idea of all men sharing equally in the decision-making process. The belief persisted that economic power should determine political power. For individuals to hold political power disproportionate to their stake in the country, went the argument, would give the poor power to destroy the rich.

But in time, and for a variety of reasons, suffrage was widened to include all adult citizens. By the twentieth century, government came to rest on the notion 'that each man is more likely to be right than to be wrong, and that one man's opinion must be treated as equally good with another's ...'[1] Today political equality means that an individual's economic power, race, sex, etc. are no longer accepted criteria for deciding who has the right to sanction the political management of the community. The utilitarian

1 Bryce J. *The American Commonwealth*, New York, 1937, vol. 2, 350

formula: every man to count for one, no man to count for more than one, has been transferred to the ballot box. Here the vote of each citizen is entitled to the same weight and the principle of majority rule prevails.

In man's search for order in community life the nominal world holds out to individuals of every conceivable difference the possibility of enjoying legal and political equality. However imperfect the myth may be, few will deny that it is vital for the development of democratic society.

The concept of man possessing an inviolable essence envisages a political society characterized by an equality of concern for all its members. To safeguard the individual's legal and political rights, to create an atmosphere in which man's highest potentialities may flourish, is regarded as a primary objective of political society. As already suggested, to further these ends the myth of state personality may, at certain times and for certain purposes, play an important role. The great risk is the tendency of all but those with the most disciplined minds to forget that what we call the will of the state is, and often must be, the agreement of a more or less limited group of public officials. When this happens, the personality of the state may come to have greater value than the personality of the individual.

Alexander Hamilton showed a nice appreciation of this problem when he wrote about the inadequacies of the Articles of Confederation. Writing in *The Federalist*, Hamilton declared: 'The great and radical vice in the construction of the existing Confederation is in the principle of LEGISLATION for STATES or GOVERNMENTS, in their CORPORATE or COLLECTIVE CAPACITIES, and as contradistinguished from the INDIVIDUALS of which they consist.' James Madison thoroughly agreed. He explained how some delegates to the Constitutional Convention had gone so far as to demand a bill of rights 'declaratory, not of the personal rights of individuals, but of the rights reserved to the States in their political capacity.' To men like Hamilton and Madison this idea was intolerable. Effective government had 'to address itself immediately to the hopes and fears of individuals.' Legislation for communities, as distinguished from individuals, was theoretically improper and, in practice, subverted the order and ends of political society.[2]

In the years that followed, many political leaders cultivated the myth of state personality. In Italy, Mussolini's 'Charter of Liberty,' which set forth the principles of Italian fascism, begins with this statement: 'The Italian nation ... is an organism with a being, and ends and means of action,

---

2 *The Federalist*, Henry Cabot Lodge (ed.), New York, 1888, no. xv, 86; xxxviii, 227; xvi, 95; xx, 119

superior to those of the individuals ... of which it is composed ...' Nazi Press Chief Dr Otto Dietrich said, 'There is no freedom of the individual. There is only freedom of peoples, nations, or races, for these are the only material and historical realities through which the life of the individual exists.' And in the same vein, Stalin exhorted: 'Be devoted to the working class, to its party, to its state. This is necessary and good. But do not mix it with devotion to persons, with this hollow and superfluous prattle of the intelligentsia.'[3]

With all of this in mind, we are in a position to gauge the concept of sovereign equality. This concept finds its ultimate expression in the Charter of the United Nations. The Preamble equates faith 'in the equal rights of men and women and of nations large and small.' Article 1 (2) declares the purpose of developing friendly relations based on respect for the principle of equal rights of peoples. Article 2 (1) reads: 'The Organization is based on the principle of the sovereign equality of all its Members.' And according to Articles 9 and 18 the General Assembly shall consist of all members of the United Nations, each shall have one vote, and decisions shall be made by a majority of the members present.

Implicit in the idea of the sovereign equality of members of the United Nations is the myth that each state is an indivisible entity – a single corporate person with a single, coherent will. By the slippery shorthand of analogy, the same standard of justice that applies to individual persons in domestic society is held to apply to corporate persons in international society.

Frequently, the concept of sovereign equality is based on an alleged metaphysical essence said to be inherent in the state. Equality is regarded as an inalienable natural right, possessed by the state as a creature of nature. This claim draws sustenance from the field of law as well as from political philosophy. It was part of the mythology permeating the development of a law of nations that states were analogous to individuals in a state of nature. Drawing on this legend, Rousseau's contemporary, Emerich de Vattel, found nations equal by Nature and, consequently, enjoying the same rights, the same obligations – a perfect equality. In applying the idea of Natural Law to legal relations among states, Vattel simply followed the intellectual fashion set by men like Hobbes, Grotius, and Pufendorf. He was well aware of having created an ideal legal standard likely to collapse under the realities of international life. He knew that men, particularly

---

3 *International Conciliation*, New York, 1937, 476; Snyder, L.L., *The World in the Twentieth century*, Princeton, 1955, p. 167; the *New York Times*, 10 Dec. 1937, p. 8

those in positions of power, were not likely to follow the prescriptions of natural laws. Yet he refused to give up hope of making some impression on them. To do otherwise was to despair of the human race.

It may be worthwhile to touch briefly on the legal fiction of equality of states. For, in spite of the broad, generous language of Vattel, its meaning is far from being precise. Charles G. Fenwick has noted how firmly the principle of equality is established in international law. Still, he could find little agreement as to the basis on which it rests, the scope of its application, or the inferences to be drawn from it in matters of international concern.[4]

To be a legal subject is to be the subject of rights and duties. And to confer legal rights and to impose legal duties is to confer legal personality. In the creation of a legal system among territorial states, all sovereign princes, from the outset, acquired legal personality. Here was recognition that each sovereign possessed supreme power internally and bowed to no superior externally. In these circumstances, legal equality meant all sovereign princes, regardless of wealth or military might, enjoyed the same legal status – the same right, as sovereign rulers, to lead an independent existence. As time passed the concept of legal equality was extended to cover the nation-state as a corporate person.

Obviously, the concept of legal equality embraces the notion of equality before the law. This is implicit in the creation of a true international legal order. It means that the law will be applied to all legal subjects irrespective of real differences in power. It does not mean that every legal subject has identical rights and duties. There has never been such a legal system. States are legally equal insofar as general international law treats them so. The insight of Oliver Wendell Holmes is apropos: 'Of relative justice the law may know something, of expediency it knows much; with absolute justice it does not concern itself.'[5]

A great deal of confusion on the subject of legal equality arises because of muddled thinking over the rights which a state may assert in law and the degree of political influence it possesses. International law offers no guarantee against inequitable results arising from inequality of power. Yet, with the development of international organizations, publicists found in the concept of legal equality a political principle of equality. It corresponded to the electoral rights all citizens enjoyed domestically – rights, we recall, that had been derived from their essential dignity as human beings. Accordingly, whatever their real inequalities, in the nominal world of indivisible

4 *International Law*, New York, 1948, 3rd ed., 218
5 Quoted in 'The Editor's Scrap Book,' *New York Law J.* 28 September 1959

corporate persons with a unified will, all states were politically equal. Each was entitled to one vote and each vote was entitled to the same weight.

During the nineteenth century, the Great Powers never lost sight of the entities they were dealing with. As far as they were concerned, the possession of preponderant power and the role of leadership went hand in hand. Higher rank and special privilege were the attributes of superior responsibility. The Great Powers, therefore, simply took it upon themselves to create a new European order and to make it work. And they excluded the lesser states from any meaningful participation in their arrangements. Except insofar as it contributed to maintaining an equilibrium among themselves, the Great Powers ignored any principle of equality. James Lorimer expressed the prevailing view when he wrote: 'All states are equally entitled to be recognized as states, on the simple ground that they are states; but all states are *not* entitled to be recognized as *equal* states, simply because they are not equal states.'[6]

Another scholar, T.J. Lawrence, reviewed the continuing activities of what had become known as the Concert of Europe. In his opinion the concert had been acknowledged so constantly for the greater part of a century as to have become part of the public order of Europe. Great Powers enjoyed what could hardly be distinguished from a legal right to settle certain questions as they pleased. When they acted collectively, small states were obliged to obey. Ultimately, he concluded, the European Concert enjoyed a 'superintending authority' recognized by the tacit consent of other states.[7]

Whatever merit there may be in the argument, the idea of a concert of Great Powers having primary responsibility for the maintenance of peace and security has never lost its hold on men's imagination. Thus, in 1945, when the Great Powers put themselves under the United Nations organization, small states expressly consented to their superior status. As long as the Great Powers duly acted in concert the principle of equality expressed in Article 2(1) of the Charter was not pertinent. Nor, in the event, would any question arise as to the legitimate authority of the organization for international peacekeeping.

The dilemma arose when the cold war destroyed the facade of great-power unity. In place of the idea of a concert, the contradictory concept of sovereign equality was raised to eminence. To fill the vacuum left by an impotent Security Council, all members of the General Assembly were

6 *The Institutes of the Law of Nations*, 1885, Vol. 2, 260
7 Hicks, F.C. 'The Equality of States and the Hague Conferences,' *AJIL*, 1908, vol. 2, 547–9

now said to share equally in the decision-making process. Each of their votes, completely divorced from military strength and other sources of power, had the same weight. And the decision of the majority, even when the means to implement it were absent, prevailed.

Questions immediately arise. Are these democratic principles applicable to international politics? Are they suitable for calling great powers to account? How we answer, it is submitted, depends largely on our conceptual thinking. Do we picture governments as representing indivisible entities, each with a single will, like men of flesh and bone? Or do we recognize the contingent nature of the will of the state, and the existence of these corporate persons on an entirely different level of being?

We become increasingly aware here of man as an actor in two worlds. At the same time that he lives in the real, existential world, he is compelled by his nature to live in a realm of artificially created, mythically rooted communities. Ambiguity and paradox are his constant companions – inherent in the human predicament of having to live in two worlds that do not correspond. On the basis of this duality we may hope to come to terms with the concept of sovereign equality.[8]

In the text that follows I shall try to bring historical insights to bear on the tension existing between the two worlds – a tension that finds expression in opposing concepts. According to one concept, responsibility for international peace and security is proportioned to power. This leads its proponents to declare that the Great Powers enjoy something in the nature of a mandate to police the international community. Opposed to the idea of great-power primacy is the concept of sovereign equality. According to its adherents, all states are corporate persons with a single will, and the same qualities or attributes philosophically applicable to human personality apply to them. In arriving at decisions affecting world order, therefore, inequality of power is irrelevant: all states have an equal voice, none entitled to a greater weight than another, which strongly implies that the will of the majority must prevail.

8 For a profound exposition of the dual philosophy applied to the study of international
   relations, see Halle, L. J., *Men and Nations*, Princeton, 1962

2
The rise of the concept
of great-power primacy

After the defeat of Napoleon, in the spring of 1814, the principal allied powers assumed the task of restoring peace and order in Europe. At the Congress of Vienna the four most powerful states, Britain, Russia, Prussia, and Austria, assumed the responsibility for European security. This chapter describes the development of the concept of great-power primacy in international politics, and the friction that arose with those who sought to join the councils of the great.

In 1814, at the time of the congress, there was a wondrous world where all states were in law perfectly equal. But in the real world it was the disposal of national power that ordered their relations. Measured in terms of military strength, Britain, Russia, Prussia, Austria, and defeated France ranked at the top of the European power hierarchy. Below them came Spain, Sweden, Portugal, The Netherlands, and Denmark. While at the base of the pyramid were more than seventy 'wee' states, including the nineteen Swiss cantons and at least fifty states ruled by either German or Italian princes.

Let us consider briefly some of these small states. The nineteen autonomous Swiss cantons were former members of a confederation under Napoleon's domination. In no more than five of them did the population exceed 100,000. In almost one third of the rest it numbered less than 30,000. (The king of France, on the other hand, ruled close to 29,000,000 subjects.) All the independent Swiss cantons planned to send delegates to the congress to protect their sovereign rights.

In addition, there were the thirty-seven German sovereigns. Their domains ranged in size from the Kingdom of Bavaria (three and a half million people, 1600 square miles) to the principality of Leyen (4500 inhabitants, less than three square miles). The vast majority of these German princes ruled less than 70,000 inhabitants each. Added to them were mediatized German princes, and free cities. Altogether, Germany consisted of 360 more or less independent territories. For the most part they had been absorbed in the Confederation of the Rhine under Napoleon's domination. Now these German rulers looked to the Congress of Vienna to restore their former status.

Finally, there were the Italian states, ranging in size from the Kingdom of Sardinia (population 4,000,000) to duchies like Modena and Parma (average population 30,000), to such nutshell republics as Lucca and San Marino. Napoleon had consolidated them either into separate Italian kingdoms or directly into the French empire. Similarly, all these former rulers counted on the congress to permit them to recover their prior sovereignty.

One other observation. In every Great Power except England, and in almost all small ones, supreme authority resided in an individual ruler. Nation-states either did not exist or were inchoate. 'The People,' the 'Nation,' was used primarily as a figure of speech to describe large masses of individuals who lived in a particular territory. International relations remained the exclusive business of sovereigns and a small ruling class.

By the Treaty of Paris, 30 May 1814, every European power engaged on either side during the Napoleonic wars was invited to attend a congress at Vienna. The purpose was couched in equivocal terms: to regulate the arrangements necessary to complete the treaty of peace. Vague and ambiguous as the invitation was, the idea of a congress open to all powers, large and small, created an impression that a new relationship among states was about to begin. But the representatives of Britain, Russia, Prussia, and Austria, the four allies primarily responsible for Napoleon's defeat, did not intend to be entrapped by any illusion which the word 'congress' might generate. From the outset, they recognized themselves as the only parties among the states of Europe qualified to make and keep the peace.[1]

Three months before the Treaty of Paris, the Four laid the groundwork

---

[1] Among the Great Powers, Alexander I directed Russian policy; King Frederick William authorized Chancellor Hardenberg, assisted because of age by Baron Humboldt, to speak for Prussia – though more often than not they were under Alexander's domination. With the emperor's approval, Metternich virtually controlled Austrian foreign policy. Talleyrand directed French affairs with the full confidence of Louis XVIII. Viscount Castlereagh, sole representative of a constitutional monarchy, acted more or less autonomously, although under the sovereign authority of Parliament.

for their claim to pre-eminence over the secondary states of Europe. At Châtillon, where they had agreed to meet with Napoleon's representatives to discuss ending the war, they stated their position. The Four formally declared themselves responsible for the peace negotiations with France. They were acting, they said, in the name of Europe, which formed but a single entity. The idea of Europe forming but a single entity will be considered later. What is noteworthy at this point is that already the Four were acting on behalf of Europe. Castlereagh best expressed the Four's sentiments: 'The alternative then practically is whether this tentative for peace shall be made by four Powers or by four and twenty. In the latter case, any hope of secrecy is at an end; and it is impossible to foresee the variety of questions which may be put forward to embarrass these preliminary proceedings.'[2]

After peace talks with France collapsed, the Four concluded an alliance at Chaumont. The treaty, signed 1 March 1814, expressed their determination to consult together when peace with France was concluded. Their purpose: to work out the most appropriate way to guaranty European order. Further, they resolved to procure a general peace which would assure the freedom of all nations. The Treaty of Chaumont is important because it marks a key step in the evolution of the distinction between great and small powers. From here on the term 'Great Powers' begins to be used as a current diplomatic expression.

After the treaty was signed, Castlereagh added a paternal note implicit in the concept of great-power primacy. He intended the treaty, he said, as a refuge under which small states could look for their security. Thus, when the provisional government at Brussels asked what were the Allies' intention with respect to its future, Castlereagh did not hesitate. For the people of Flanders to be free, he wrote, they had to be strong. And to be strong, they had to be incorporated into a large unit, like Holland. Flanders could then count on its security being backed up by the Great Powers.

Once the war ended, the idea that the Four occupied a special position became more marked. In a secret article to the Treaty of Paris, the Great Powers reserved to themselves the solution of the major problems involved in a peace settlement. 'The disposal of the Territories given up by His Most Christian Majesty,' read Article 1, '... and the relations from whence a system of real and permanent Balance of Power in Europe is to be derived, shall be regulated at the Congress upon the principles determined upon by the Allied Powers among themselves ...'[3]

2 *CC*, vol. IX, 294
3 *Hertslet*, p. 18

During September, a month before the Congress was due to open, the Four met privately to discuss the nature of the coming conference. Previous treaties had referred to an entity called 'Europe.' At Châtillon, the allied protocol stated that the Four met in the name of Europe forming but a single unit. It was important to clarify this point. Did Europe have an existence separate and apart from the individual delegates to the congress? The answer was no. 'Europe forms only an ideal whole,' said Humboldt. The Europe assembled at Vienna was to be found in the personal characteristics of the different delegates. Europe was not a constitutional unit. It was impossible, according to the baron, to create a European republic. Consequently, the coming European congress was not a deliberative assembly. In his opinion, European politics could not be bound by constitutional norms. Both Castlereagh and Metternich agreed. The idea of all the states invited to the congress arriving at decisions affecting European security by a 'plurality of voices' was simply unthinkable.[4]

What was the congress then? Chancellor Hardenberg was said to have such a terrible fear of the word 'congress' that the Prussians took pains to deny it was even a peace congress. The furthest Humboldt would go was to call it a complex of different negotiations in the general interest of European security. But no matter what it was called, there was little doubt that the Four considered it no more than a device to ratify their decisions. Thus, on 13 April 1814, Castlereagh expressed the hope that the great monarchs – Alexander I, Frederick William, Francis Joseph, and the Prince Regent, whose armies, he said, had saved Europe – could confer together in England. Afterwards, they would be joined by their respective ministers for foreign affairs. In this way all the essential points requiring discussion could be agreed upon. Nothing would be left for the congress except to ratify the settlement. Humboldt's view was similar. The only way the European states could effectively act together, he thought, was for the Great Powers to take the lead, agree among themselves, giving the small states a right to express their views.

Castlereagh, described as a man contemptuous of abstractions, who approached international problems from the point of view of practical common sense, suggested that France and Spain join the Four to form a directing committee of the congress. Together they were the most competent to work out a settlement. They were the six European powers 'most considerable in population and weight.' They were what he called 'Powers of the first order.' To include any more states, said Castlereagh, would require an invidious selection, opening the door to a whole group of powers

4 *Peace Handbooks*, App. IV, pp. 156–7, App. V, p. 164; *BD*, p. 203; *Talleyrand*, p. 427

of nearly equal size. To all this he had the strongest objection, though he did not elaborate. C.K. Webster finds the idea of Great Powers, possessing rights as such, distinct from those derived from treaties, as probably dating from this period in September 1814, when the Four were exchanging ideas on the nature of the Congress of Vienna.[5]

Castlereagh's proposal was accepted. But the Four still intended to retain absolute control. Their decision was founded on several reasons. It was the result of their former relations during the war. It was expedient. They were the most qualified, had the greatest right to do so, and were the most impartial. Humboldt claimed that with regard to certain postwar problems, such as the distribution of the German states, they were the only ones who were capable of keeping a strictly European point of view. Of course, there were some matters, like the abolition of slavery, and the free navigation of rivers, which concerned all states. But did this mean that all powers had an equal right to take part in the negotiations? Not at all. According to Humboldt, treating all states as perfectly equal was impossible. It was up to the Four, plus France and Spain, to determine the principles of negotiation. As for the lesser states, the Six would be willing to listen to their views. Naturally, when the time came to enter into treaty arrangements all the European powers had to approve. Even at this point, however, every single state in Europe was not included. Humboldt could find only sixteen qualified; his criteria: a state's degree of power and independence.[6]

There was a difference of opinion among the Four about how to tell the other delegates that the Great Powers had assumed full responsibility for all vital decisions. Humboldt preferred to say so directly without mincing words, whereas Castlereagh favoured a more subtle approach, particularly with respect to France and Spain. In the relations among the Four, France, and Spain he wanted to avoid any distinction. In the long run, this would facilitate their negotiations. Most important, it would not appear as if the Four were acting dictatorially. With regard to the rest of the smaller powers, Castlereagh uttered a word of caution: 'a feeble government uneasy at being excluded from what it holds to be its due share of influence in the greater politics of Europe, is not unlikely to endeavour to ferment disunion

---

5 *Cambridge History of British Foreign Policy, 1783–1919*, London, 1923, vol. 2, 49–50; *Peace Handbooks*, p. 61, App. II, pp. 151–2

6 *CC*, vol. x, 76; *Talleyrand*, p. 322; *BFSP*, p. 555; *Peace Handbooks*, App. IV, pp. 158, 161–2. The sixteen were Britain, Russia, Prussia, Austria, France, Bavaria, Denmark, Holland, Portugal, Sardinia, Sicily, Spain, Sweden, Switzerland, Wurtemberg, and the Vatican.

amongst the Powers whose existing connection diminishes its influence.' But this was not a serious consideration. The Four had to avoid the appearance of throwing their weight around. They must, at all times, act courteously, respectfully. They must be wary of trying openly to assume authority. If opposition to the concept of great-power responsibility nevertheless continued to exist, Castlereagh said, it should be compelled to show itself openly. In that way it could be met and suppressed before it got out of hand. Humboldt agreed, stressing the importance of doing nothing to undermine the self-respect of the delegates of the small states.[7]

Tsar Alexander I, who took an active part in these preliminary discussions, has been described as one of the great enigmas of history. Unlike his allies, his gift for abstraction rivalled his capacity for realistic thinking. This quality may have had its roots in his early training. Alexander was raised by men who worshipped Rousseau. In the early part of his rule he came under the sway of aristocrats who had been seduced by the new ideas. Later, under exalted religious and mystical influences, he came to dread them. At home in two worlds – the world of ideas and the real world around him – he was, nevertheless, unaware of the need for some consistency between them. This may account for his vigorous support of the concept of great-power primacy at the same time that he called for the application of broad principles of equality.

If we go back to the early years of the Napoleonic wars, we find Alexander, in 1804, insisting on an Anglo-Russian concert as the best means of preserving peace. The two Great Powers would form a league which all the lesser states of Europe would be invited to join. Under the auspices of the Great Powers, he said, a new era of stability would be assured. To him, Russia and Britain possessed special qualities not to be found among the smaller states which justified their predominance: they were the only ones invariably concerned with the rule of order and justice; the only ones capable of maintaining such rule; the only ones who, because they were free from conflicting desires, would never disturb the peace of Europe. But only a year later Alexander reversed himself. In 1805, he called for a general congress after Napoleon's defeat in order to establish more precisely the precepts of international law. And to ensure the primacy of law in settling European disputes he urged the establishment of 'a federal system.'

Two years before the Congress of Vienna, Alexander appeared to

7 *Peace Handbooks*, App. III, pp. 153–5, App. IV, p. 155; *FPC 1815*, p. 65

support even broader principles of equality than may be implied in a federal system. Now he called on men to develop more magnanimous feelings towards each other. Once this came about he could visualize all 'peoples' united to make their freedom secure. Like brothers, they would be ready to give each other all the assistance they needed, motivated by a single purpose: the common welfare of all. By 1814, however, at the private meetings which took place among the Four prior to the opening of the Congress, Alexander acquiesced fully in the primary role they had arrogated to themselves. This conviction did not deter him from declaring that the pacification of Europe must be founded on 'the solid and unshakeable bases of the independence of peoples and the sacred rights of nations.' Nor did it deter him at the Congress from proposing a great-power intervention in Turkey to protect persecuted Christians. Why? Because there was an unwritten, fully operative book of international rules which guaranteed equal rights to all nations.[8] As we shall have occasion to see, Alexander was constantly torn between his ideals and the reality of international politics.

Metternich, like Castlereagh, also prided himself on his practical approach. In 1813, when he wrote the tsar that Austria would be found on the side of the allies, but at a time of its own choosing, he revealed something about the nature of his thinking. 'Little given to abstract ideas,' he wrote, 'we accept things as they are and we attempt to the maximum of our ability to protect ourselves against delusions about realities.' It goes without saying that the Austrian chancellor supported the concept of great-power primacy. Nor did he have any doubt about the true nature of the congress. As Talleyrand recorded it, he said the congress was not really a congress. Its opening was not a true opening. The comissions chosen to look into certain matters were not actually commissions. And since there were two sides to every question, in trying to establish European order either the Great Powers would remain in agreement or they would not.[9]

On 22 September 1814, the Four drafted a protocol which declared that they alone would decide the questions relating to the conquered territories. They agreed to permit France and Spain to give their 'opinions' and 'objections.' But this involved no right to enter the discussion on a footing of equality. In fact, the Four watered down the role of the French and Spanish plenipotentiaries to the point where they were permitted to speak

---

8 Bourquin, M. *Histoire de la Sainte Alliance*, Genève, 1954, p. 139; *WSD*, vol. IX, 442; Treitschke, H. von, *History of Germany in the 19th Century*, London, 1916, vol. 2, 79; Kissinger, H. A., *A World Restored*, Boston, 1957, pp. 68–9
9 *Talleyrand*, p. 420

only after the Four had come to a firm decision. The protocol suggested there were questions of another nature which all six powers would have the right to discuss as principals, but gave no further details.

TALLEYRAND'S VIEW OF EQUALITY

The only statesman capable of effectively challenging the concept of great-power responsibility was Talleyrand. His aim was to upset that part of the secret treaty of peace which gave the Four the exclusive right to dispose of the conquered territories. He could not support the idea of France simply approving and ratifying the Four's decisions. He wanted France to participate in them on the same basis as the other Great Powers. If the Congress of Vienna could be made into a wide general assembly, if he could become spokesman for the smaller states, he might be able to use the congress as a lever to accomplish his purpose. In such a situation he did not hesitate to call up principles of justice and equality. Accordingly, in the summer of 1814, at least a month before the Four had begun their private meetings, Talleyrand set down his ideas about the nature of the Congress of Vienna. In a memorandum of instructions 'For the King's Ambassadors to the Congress,' he touched on various aspects of the tension between the concept of great-power primacy and the concept of equality.[10]

No assembly, he wrote, could act legitimately if it was not formed legitimately. He backed the right of all states, large and small, to be represented at the congress entirely independent of their comparative force. Even the smallest, the very ones most likely to be excluded because of their weakness, had a right to attend. Why? Because, for example, one problem at the congress would be to create a German confederation, and there were a great number of weak states in Germany. To create a new Germany without all the interested parties present would be unjust and would violate their 'natural independence.' To this he added that the nations of Europe live under moral or natural law as well as under international law (*le droit public*). In the absence of a sovereign's consent, conquered territory could not be transferred from one power to another without the 'sanction of Europe.'

Appeals to principles of justice, to international law, to the sanction of Europe, to a state's natural independence were in sharp contrast to the concept of great-power primacy held by the Four. But deference to these ideas was not the only reason for opposing the Great Powers. Talleyrand

10 Ibid. pp. 214–18, 235–6

explained the practical considerations. French policy had to be based on protecting the small states because their interest and the interest of France coincided. By obtaining their support, France would add to its influence with the Four. But for the small states to attend the congress, said Talleyrand, was one thing. To have their voices counted without regard to their size or power was another.

Talleyrand reasoned as follows: there were about one hundred and seventy million people in Europe. Roughly one hundred and ten million 'belonged' to the eight states which signed the Treaty of Paris (the Four plus France, Spain, Sweden, and Portugal). Half of the balance, around thirty million, were in conquered lands. Not having engaged in the war they would not be represented at the congress. The remaining thirty million were spread out among more than forty states, some of which were barely one hundredth the size of Portugal. Even if these forty states were united into one state, they still would not be equal to any of the Great Powers. This raised a series of questions: to what extent did the small states have the right to participate meaningfully in the congress? What role would they have in the deliberations? Would they have a right to vote equal to the Great Powers? Then he answered his questions with this simple reply: to treat the small states as if they were equal to the Great Powers would 'shock the nature of things.'

But why should it shock the nature of things? Talleyrand had already said states possess a natural independence. As a logical corollary, did not states possess a natural equality as well? That far he would not go, but he pursued the problem in his memo, asking and answering questions in this vein: 'Will they have only a single voice in common? They would never succeed in forming it. Will they have none at all? Better then not to admit them. But who will we exclude? The Ministers of the Pope, of Sicily, of Sardinia? or the one of Holland, or the one of Saxony or only those who are not monarchs? But who will yield for those Princes, if they must give way? Who will consent for them ... if they must do so?' Finally, Talleyrand found a way to reconcile both 'law and expediency.' The role of the small states in the congress should be measured not on the scale of power, but on their interest. They had the right to participate in matters only directly concerning them. For example, the Italian states would participate in the arrangements regarding Italy and the German states would participate in the arrangements regarding Germany. It was the task of the Great Powers to see that all the parts were fitted into place.

The key question, however, remained unanswered. How would this lesser order of states take an effective part in the deliberations? They had no individual vote. They had no collective vote. Apparently, law and expediency were served merely by permitting them to be present when matters concerning them were settled. Talleyrand elaborated no further. He had come into contact with reality. For him there was nothing in the real world which gave a state the right to participate actively in politics except the scale of power. And Talleyrand's mental discipline would not permit him to ignore it. This did not mean, however, that he would surrender to the Four without a struggle.

THE CLASH OF OPPOSING CONCEPTS

At Vienna Talleyrand met with the Four and read their protocol on the conduct of the congress. It confirmed his worst fears. They meant to stick by the provisions of the secret treaty, to make all vital decisions, and to exclude France from participating in the European settlement. As he wrote Louis XVIII, the Four admitted, in effect, that they had agreed among themselves to take charge as the supreme arbitrators of Europe.

At once, Talleyrand began his attack on the concept of great-power primacy. When Metternich and Hardenberg referred in their conversation to the intentions of the 'allied powers,' he jumped on the term. The word 'allies,' he said, had no place at a congress of European states. If the Four were going to think of themselves in this way, they would have to get along without him. The invitation to the congress had been extended to all the powers of Europe engaged in the war. When was the conference going to begin? That was the important question. As for the congress itself, it consisted of all the delegates. Neither the Four nor any other group of powers, including those who had signed the peace treaty, were qualified to do more than prepare and propose; they could not decide. They were not the congress but only a part of it. If they were to attribute to themselves a power which belonged to the conference as a whole, it would be a usurpation and Talleyrand would be extremely embarrassed, if he were to concur in it, to reconcile it with his responsibility.[11]

The first task, he continued, was to draw up rules and regulations for the congress. Once drafted, the rules had to be submitted to the entire membership for approval. Considering the way the Four had been acting up till now, it was their individual will alone which had become the law of Europe. According to Talleyrand, Castlereagh admitted the force of his argument but wondered if what Talleyrand wanted was practicable. That is like

11 Ibid. pp. 280-1, 324-5, 331

asking, Talleyrand wrote his king, if the Great Powers could avoid arrogating to themselves a power over Europe that Europe had never given them.[12]

The French minister further criticized that part of the protocol which invited France and Spain to join the Four in directing the peace settlement. At first blush, it did constitute a kind of recognition of France's status as a Great Power. But the terms were too harsh, for it excluded France from all vital matters until the Four were in complete agreement. As Talleyrand was quick to observe, even supposing that France and Spain would always agree on all questions, they would still be only two against four.

Finally, Talleyrand urged the Four not to fear the presence of so many small states. He did not believe that all the states invited to the congress had to take a hand in all the problems that would be discussed. He doubted they even wanted to. Metternich became furious at Talleyrand's attempts to tell the Four how to run the congress. He made it quite clear that he would much prefer to have the Four handle everything in their own way.[13] But for several reasons the Four did not care to risk an open breach with France. After all, from every point of view France was still a great power, and to make the sitation more troublesome, Talleyrand now exercised enough influence over the secondary states at Vienna to embarrass the Four's plans.

At one point Metternich tried to soften Talleyrand's attitude by explaining that France had its own special interests which the Four recognized. He pointed out the matter of Naples and said it 'is honourably yours.' Talleyrand, who kept calling for the revival of the sacred principle of legitimacy, was not to be taken in. 'No more mine,' he replied, 'than everyone else's.' If the Four disposed of the conquered territories and created a balance of power in Europe as they saw fit, said Talleyrand, Europe would not abide by the arrangements. Then he added a new note: the only settlements that will last will be those in response to 'the general will.'[14]

The concept of the general will was drawn from revolutionary ideology. It implied the existence of a separate European entity with a personality and a will capable of being expressed. As an egalitarian concept it could mean that, in determining the general will, each state had an equal voice and a majority decision was decisive. Even Talleyrand would never have pushed the idea that far. The Four, of course, could have used his reference

12 *BFSP*, pp. 561–2, *Talleyrand*, p. 337
13 *BFSP*, pp. 559, 562; *Talleyrand*, p. 338
14 *Talleyrand*, 281, 343; *BFSP*, p. 561

to the general will to suit their own purposes. They could have claimed, and made it stick, that only they knew what the general will of Europe was, that only they had the right to speak on behalf of Europe. In a sense, this is part of the rationale behind the concept of great-power primacy. But the Four were wary of such abstractions. To them, Europe had no personality. It was a geographical term. As for the congress, it was simply a diplomatic device. Neither one could have a will. The Four dominated the proceedings because in terms of population, resources and military might, they had the power to do so.

Talleyrand's tactics left the Four little choice. They decided to delay the opening of the congress until 1 November. After a long argument, Talleyrand agreed on condition that to the protocol of postponement these words were added: 'the proposals presented to the Congress will conform to international law and the legitimate expectations of Europe.' The manoeuvre only succeed in infuriating the Prussians. The idea of applying to the territorial settlement of Europe abstract legal principles was so foreign to Humboldt's concept of responsibility that he asked outright, 'What is international law doing here?'[15]

Ultimately, Talleyrand won a meaningless victory. The Great Powers framed a protocol paying lip-service to the ideas of justice and equality. It referred to the interest of all the parties to postpone the opening until the deliberations of the Four were in harmony with three norms: principles of international law, the common wish of Europe, and the honourable expectations of their contemporaries. In the intellectual climate of the time, however, concepts which failed to take into consideration the reality of power were not likely to have any great effect on the actions of the Four. And Talleyrand knew it. It was clear, said the French report sent to Louis XVIII, that the Four want to arrange a settlement among themselves, rather than conform to principles of reason and justice.

With the congress postponed, the Four decided to ignore Talleyrand and to apply themselves to the business at hand. We shall touch briefly on the conquered territories of Poland and Saxony. As part of the fruits of victory, Alexander demanded all of the Duchy of Warsaw, and Hardenberg demanded all of the Kingdom of Saxony. Each, in general, supported the other's claim. Castlereagh and Metternich opposed what they considered a dangerous increase in Russian and Prussian power. Deep rivalries split the Four, threatening to make unworkable the concept of great-power responsibility for the peace of Europe.

15 *Talleyrand*, pp. 334, 346

The British government favoured the principle of Polish independence, but the reality confronting Castlereagh was the Russian army in complete control of the disputed land. 'I have 200,000 soldiers in the Duchy of Warsaw,' the tsar told Talleyrand, 'let them try and drive me from it.' Given the cast of his mind, Castlereagh did not dwell on the rights of the Polish people. Unable to envisage them as an indivisible entity with a single will, he was ready to offer Alexander a liberal and important addition on his Polish frontier. Only it must not be excessive. How secondary were a million Poles more or less, he wrote the tsar, compared to the qualities of generosity and moderation. Alexander was in no mood to compromise. Before the deadlock was broken, both sides had alternated between opposing concepts. Alexander, for example, told Castlereagh not to plead the cause of international law. Rather he should be practical. In other words, the British foreign secretary would do better to assure the victors those advantages to which they were rightfully entitled. Only in this way could one more reasonably hope for a peace likely to be maintained by the Four. Yet at the same time the tsar kept referring to his concern for the happiness of the Poles. The settlement of Europe, he insisted, had to conform to twin concepts: 'the independence of peoples and the sacred rights of nations.'[16]

For his part, Castlereagh explained how moved he was by a public duty owed to Europe. The tsar, he explained, had a similar duty. In fact, none of the Four had a right to increase its power 'to the unnecessary prejudice' of weaker states. In what may have been desperation at Alexander's stubbornness, Castlereagh was ready 'to make an appeal to Europe.' He called on Austria and Prussia to send official notes to Russia exposing their views. Copies of these documents were to be placed before the congress. And the rest of the states of Europe were to be asked to tell the tsar to what extent and under what conditions 'Europe in Congress' would admit His Majesty's claim to an aggrandizement in Poland.

When the tsar learned about these plans from Metternich he said frankly that he had no respect for the congress and reportedly challenged Metternich to a duel. Castlereagh's idea was soon dropped.[17] Considering the basic conceptual thinking of the parties, it is difficult to imagine any of them making an appeal to something called 'Europe in Congress,' and of far greater importance, abiding by the result.

16 *BD*, pp. 210–11, 207; Mowat, R.B., *A History of European Diplomacy, 1815–1914*, London, 1927, p. 10; *WSD*, vol. IX, 329–30, 442, 445, *BFSP*, pp. 642–3
17 *WSD*, vol. IX, 330; Chodzko, L.J.B., *Le Congrès de Vienne et les traités de 1815*, Paris, 1863, vol. 2, 270, 291, 293; *BD*, pp. 213–15; *Peace Handbooks*, pp. 69, n. 2, 70; Kissinger, n. 8, p. 159

While negotiations over Poland remained stalled, the Four considered Prussia's claim to all of Saxony. The problem was similar to the dispute over Poland. Castlereagh believed Saxony should not be totally absorbed into Prussia. But again he was faced with the presence of Russian troops ready to ensure Prussia's claim. And again he was prepared to compromise. Saxony was not an immutable organism. The principle of legitimacy was far from being sacred. The controlling idea was not to 'sacrifice the peace of Europe for two or three hundred thousand subjects more or less,' if a reasonable solution could be found. Castlereagh hoped both France and the Saxon King would give the Prussians a liberal share of Saxony. This would contribute to the territorial equilibrium necessary for peace. Conceptual thinking about the personality of states had not yet stigmatized such a solution as unethical or unworthy. This is why Castlereagh could feel no moral or political repugnance to the idea.[18] Still, Prussia held out for the entire country. The impasse was only broken after France had been admitted as an equal into the councils of the Four, and cast its considerable weight with Britain and Austria against Russia and Prussia.

Five months before the Congress of Vienna was to open, Talleyrand expressed his confidence that France would keep the same status it always enjoyed. He was counting, in the words of Charles Dupuis, 'on the force of law to impede every attempt to exclude France from the decisive deliberations.'[19] But depending on more than abstract principles of law, Talleyrand sought to achieve equal status as a great power by making French military support invaluable to Britain and Austria. As early as the summer of 1814, France was said to have proposed a military alliance with Britain. During the Polish-Saxon talks, from which Talleyrand had been excluded, he let it be known that France would support Britain against the excessive demands of Russia and Prussia.

Talleyrand's insight was sound. The deadlock among the Four over Poland and Saxony deteriorated to the point where Prussia mobilized its troops. War between Britain and Austria on one side and Russia and Prussia on the other appeared imminent. Castlereagh knew he had to form a defensive alliance with Austria, and France, with a potential army of over half a million men, would have to included. The threat of war produced immediate action. By 3 January 1815, Britain, Austria, and France had signed a treaty of defensive alliance. Now Castlereagh and Metternich refused to continue negotiations with Russia and Prussia unless France

18 BD, p. 279; Peace Handbooks, p. 118; WSD, vol. IX, 339–40, 511
19 Le Ministère de Talleyrand en 1814, Paris, 1920, vol. 2, 155, 157

participated in the discussions. Castlereagh impressed the tsar with the importance of treating Talleyrand with the consideration to which the representative of a great power was entitled.

The tsar was no fool. He was aware of the alliance with France and fully appreciated its significance. He knew France was a great power. On 4 October of the preceding year he had asked Talleyrand about the French army. Talleyrand told him of its complete loyalty to the king: one hundred and thirty thousand Frenchmen, he said, were under orders; three hundred thousand more, at the very first call, would be able to join them. 'I do not know,' said Talleyrand, 'if your Majesty counts France in the rank of the [Great] Powers.' With an army of that size there could only be one answer. 'Yes, certainly,' Alexander replied.[20]

How was it possible after Napoleon's defeat for the Four to have left French military power intact? One answer lies in the conceptual thinking of the parties. None of the Four conceived of punishing a political abstraction known as 'the French nation' or 'the French people.' The concept of corporate personality was widely recognized as no more than a legal fiction. Napoleon, even after his escape from Elba, was considered the 'Enemy and World Trouble-Maker.' As Castlereagh explained, he was the only obstacle to an honourable peace. Never in question was the power of France; only the time when, after Napoleon's removal and the restoration of the Bourbon dynasty, it would regain its equal rank with the Four.

In a limited way that time had come. Neither Russia nor Prussia was prepared to go to war over the conquered territories. By the nature of things it had become impossible to exclude France from the conversations regarding Poland and Saxony. Up to this moment Talleyrand had opposed the concept of great-power primacy advocated by the Four. He had harried them with demands to turn the Congress of Vienna into a general congress. He had insisted all legitimate sovereigns had an equal right to remain as sovereigns. He had called for something known as 'the sanction of Europe' to approve contested transfers of conquered territory. On the basis of these principles Talleyrand had supported the re-establishment of the independent Kingdom of Poland. With regard to Saxony, he assured the King that he could count on France's support. Prussia's all-inclusive demand to the entire territory, he wrote Metternich, could only be justified by holding 'that peoples have no rights distinct from their sovereigns and can be compared to the cattle of a rural farm ...'[21]

20 *Talleyrand*, pp. 326–7
21 Dupuis, n. 19, p. 161

Now, however, with France about to participate in the conversations on Poland and Saxony on an equal footing with the Four, Talleyrand adopted a different approach. The idea of an independent Polish kingdom gave way to the need for empirical adjustments. Belief in the integrity of Saxony gave way to deciding what proportion of the country should be incorporated into Prussia, and how to induce the Saxon king to make the necessary cession.

After Talleyrand had been accepted as an equal, writes the German historian Heinrich G. von Treitschke, 'not a word did he ... utter of the fine-sounding reasons with which, at the beginning of the congress, he had defended the equal rights of all the states of Europe.' This may have reflected Talleyrand's hypocrisy, but it also underlines a truism so well expressed by Reinhold Niebuhr. 'Politics,' said the Protestant theologian, 'will, to the end of history, be an area where conscience and power meet, where the ethical and coercive factors of human life will interpenetrate and work out their tentative and uneasy compromises.'[22]

THE NATURE OF SMALL-POWER PROTESTS

The small powers, excluded from a share in the principal decisions at Vienna, had little choice of action. Some were content to protest what was primarily an affront to their dignity. Thus, the Portuguese delegate described his country's rejection from great-power councils as unjust and humiliating, while the failure to consult with the king of Bavaria and the king of Denmark left both monarchs insulted.

Other powers demanded equal participation in the negotiations, based upon the principle of legal equality. Among them there was a certain amount of conceptual confusion. Consider the view of Ferdinand vii of Spain. When the Great Powers asked him to join the second military alliance against Napoleon, the king refused unless they recognized the true rank of Spain at the congress. He invoked 'the perfect and absolute equality' inherent in independent governments. But the perfect equality the king really wanted was equal status with the Four – not equal status with the lesser powers. Spain belonged in the first rank, the king said, because of its size, dignity, and military weight.

Baron de Haske of Baden reacted similarly. He denied the right of the Great Powers to exclude him from the Committee on German Affairs. According to the baron, the principles of international law prohibited

22 Treitschke, n. 8, p. 72; Niebuhr, R., *Moral Man and Immoral Society*, New York, 1932, p. 4

unequal treatment. This did not mean, however, that every German prince was entitled to committee representation. The baron made an exception for himself because even among the most powerful German sovereigns he always enjoyed the highest rank.

The idea of using force to protest against great-power domination may have occurred to some small states. Castlereagh referred to a meeting of thirteen German princes who appealed to Bavaria to join them in resisting the usurpation by the Four. But in the long run, against the overwhelming might of the Great Powers, the small states were in no position to alter the secondary part they were forced to play.

Perhaps the Abbé de Pradt, whose book on the Congress of Vienna appeared in 1815, offers an insight into the general attitude towards the preponderant role assumed by the Great Powers. When peace finally came after the Thirty Years War, he wrote, and the Powers had met at Westphalia, small states did not ask the congress where it obtained the right to dispose of this or that territory. Rather they thanked the congress for having ensured peace for them and their descendants. By the same token, the small powers at the Congress of Vienna did not ask about the use the Four intended to make of a particular fraction of sovereignty. What they did ask was whether, after so many storms, there would finally be a period of calm and stability for Europe.[23]

Eventually, the Great Powers disposed of the conquered territories as *they* saw fit, and created to their own satisfaction the relations out of which a real, permanent balance of power could be derived. The work ended when no Great Power felt its security menaced. As Humboldt wrote, the 'real' Congress of Vienna consisted of Russia, Prussia, Austria, Britain, and France.[24] Their authority to act was a consequence of their overwhelming power. However noble the ideal of the perfect and absolute equality of all independent states, to permit some seventy-five sovereigns to share with them the responsibility for peace and security, was too far out of contact with reality to be tolerated.

THE HOLY ALLIANCE, QUADRUPLE ALLIANCE, AND EQUALITY

In the aftermath of Napoleon's escape from Elba and defeat at Waterloo, Alexander experienced a period of religious exaltation. In the fall of 1815, the tsar originated the Holy Alliance. It symbolized in his mind the dawn of

23 De Pradt, Abbé Dominique, *Du Congrès de Vienne*, Paris, 1815, vol. 1, 149
24 Treitschke, n. 8, p. 72

a new era in international relations. Only a few months after having received the greater share of the spoils of war at Vienna, the tsar apparently had second thoughts about the different status of great and small powers. In sharp contrast to the idea that the most powerful states must play the primary role in maintaining international order, Alexander now sought to introduce religious precepts that implied the equality of all states, large and small.

On 14 September 1815 the king of Prussia and the emperor of Austria joined Alexander in solemnly declaring their unshakable resolve to conduct both domestic and international relations in accordance with the religious commandments of justice, love, and peace. They saw themselves as members of one and the same Christian nation, each having been delegated by Providence to govern a single branch of the same family. Every Christian monarch, without regard to power, was invited to join the alliance, to consider himself a member of the same Christian nation, to act towards the other members as brothers, and to follow the principles of the Christian religion in their mutual relations. Those who agreed were to be received 'with equal ardor and affection' into the alliance. Originally, Alexander wanted the pledge to cover not only all Christian sovereigns but their subjects as well. He wanted all men to agree to regard one another as brothers. He wanted all soldiers to agree to act in accordance with Christian principles. He wanted all armies to consider themselves part of one army. Only the firm editorial hand of Metternich limited the signatories of the Holy Alliance to Christian monarchs.[25]

Considering all Christian nations as a single family under the sovereignty of God was a noble idea, but how was this to be given effect? The Holy Alliance contained no binding military obligation. It called for no general disarmament. It contained no precise political promises. As Castlereagh was quick to point out, the Holy Alliance did not provide for the usual diplomatic obligations which bind states. Metternich agreed. An 'empty and sonorous document' could not be the subject of a treaty between sovereigns. For all these reasons, no doubt, plus the unwillingness of most rulers to offend the tsar, almost every Christian monarch in Europe agreed to become a party to its high sounding phrases.

The tendency to think about international relations in abstract terms, to find by the hook of analogy that political relations among states can be governed by principles philosophically applicable to individuals, will become a recurring temptation. Particularly will this be so, as sovereign

25 *Hertslet*, pp. 317–18; Kissinger, n. 8, p. 189

power passes from individual monarchs to an abstraction called 'The People.'

At the time of the Holy Alliance no attempt was made to force political reality to conform to nominal religious ideals. Alexander soon realized the wide gap between the world as it was and his visional expectations. The reality for the Tsar was still the threat posed by France to European order. If, as was generally believed, France harboured latent aggressive designs even with Napoleon gone, more concrete steps than a pledge of brotherhood had to be taken to ensure European security. Alexander had the capacity to face the demands of practical politics, but he did not entirely dismiss the possibility of realizing his religiously inspired dream.

One month after the publication of the Holy Alliance, Alexander joined his allies in a military alliance directed primarily against France. According to the new Quadruple Alliance, each of the Four undertook a specific military obligation in the event of renewed French aggression. In addition, the Four extended the concept of great-power responsibility developed at Vienna. Article VI provided for meetings among Britain, Russia, Prussia, and Austria to consider the measures necessary for maintaining the peace of Europe. France was excluded from these great-power reunions.

But by now a subtle change had occurred. Castlereagh felt impelled to justify the paternal role assumed by the Four. In a circular letter to British ministers in foreign courts (1 January 1816), he first defended the concept of great-power primacy. He linked the responsibility of the Four for the peace of Europe with the major part they had played in defeating Napoleon. He thought small states should cherish the union of the Four as the best form of security against a resurgent France. They should consider the association of the Great Powers, he wrote his ministers, without distrust or jealousy. For if the small states reviewed past great-power decisions, they would be found 'unstained by a single act of injustice.'[26]

Castlereagh continued to view the demand of small states to participate in the deliberations of the Great Powers as a natural disposition on their part to oppose exclusive engagements. Even the most friendly Courts reacted in this way because, at bottom, it affected their dignity. For this reason he urged British ministers to do everything possible to conciliate the small states. Above all, he wrote, make them feel 'that in so large a Confederation [as Europe] an equality and community of council is utterly incompatible with the march of business ...'[27]

26 FPC-1815, App. A, pp. 509–11
27 Ibid.

THE ADMISSION OF FRANCE TO GREAT-POWER STATUS

On 30 September 1818, at Aix-la-Chapelle, the Four held their first
peacetime meeting to consider ending the military occupation of France
(undertaken by them after Napoleon's defeat at Waterloo). They were
concerned, however, over the way the small states would interpret the
meeting. They made a special point to notify all European sovereigns that
there would be no congress at Aix. The Four were meeting merely to
discuss their particular relations with France. Alexander assured the small
states that the Four would not act on general European problems. If they
did so, said the Tsar, they would be faced with the invidious charge of
setting themselves up as a higher authority to control the affairs of other
nations. Metternich agreed. He was prepared to pledge never to deal with
any question involving the interest of a third party without the latter's
direct participation.

Meanwhile, Castlereagh, who considered great-power reunions as
among the best instruments for securing peace in Europe, was engaged in
quieting the fears of members of the British Cabinet. Minister George
Canning, for one, described the periodical meetings among the Four to
consider the general concerns of Europe as highly questionable policy. He
felt all other states must object; for here was an attempt to place the rest of
the nations of Europe under great-power domination. But Castlereagh
argued against conferences open to all states, regardless of size and power.
Such meetings were unwieldy. Indeed, small states were more than likely
to use them to make demands intolerable to the Four. Great-power conferences, he told the Cabinet, were a new discovery in European government.
He had only praise for their efficiency in assuring European stability. The
opposition gave in. Even so, aware of the distrust they aroused, Castlereagh warned the other Great Powers to be particularly careful what they
said and did, so as not to provoke the small states.

On 4 November 1818, after having found 'the order of things' established in France, the Four agreed to pull out their occupation troops. More
important, by inviting King Louis XVIII to take full part in future deliberations among the Four, they confirmed the equal status of France as a Great
Power. In England, Lord Bathurst, a member of the Cabinet, was one of
the first to protest. He feared the invitation to the French King would
arouse the jealousy of the other powers. And he said they would be right to
complain about their exclusion. Once again, Castlereagh successfully defended the course of action. Adding France to the system of great-power
consultations, he argued, enhanced its moral weight. Moreover, the pres-

ence of one more country would not hinder the efficiency of the proceedings as would an open invitation to all the states of Europe.

The meeting at Aix-la-Chapelle put the final touch on the primacy of the Great Powers. On 15 November the Five issued a protocol. They pledged never to depart, in future meetings, from the principles of 'the Right of Nations.' No attempt was made to define this abstraction, but one thing was sure: it did not include the right of small states to share the responsibility that goes with power. The Four did, however, vouchsafe an invitation to participate in discussions to all small states whose interests were directly involved. There was a good deal of grumbling and protesting, but in the long run the small states accepted the preponderant role of the Great Powers for maintaining order in Europe.

FOUR REVOLUTIONS UNDERMINE THE
CONCEPT OF GREAT-POWER PRIMACY

At Aix-la-Chapelle the Great Powers became more fully aware of the tension between the concept of great-power primacy and the idea of equality implicit in the right of all states to lead an independent existence. On one side, we find Russia, Prussia, and Austria, ready to intervene in any state to crush revolutionary movements. On the other side, we find the British, with serious reservations about such an extension of great-power responsibility.

The first inkling of a split among the Great Powers appeared at Aix when the tsar suggested a security pact open to every European state. He visualized all the countries of Europe as members of a league guaranteeing to each other the maintenance of the status quo in thrones as well as in territories. As usual, Alexander did not go into details. Castlereagh was struck by the plan's sweeping generalities. He did not believe an unqualified guarantee by each state to support from attack the type of government of its allies could be achieved. Nothing could be more humiliating for a state, he said, than to be bound to its neighbours to preserve their domestic political system. The only prudent principle was expressed in the law of nations: no state had a right to endanger other states by its internal policies. If it did, provided sound discretion was used, the aggrieved party had a clear right to intervene. The tsar was trying to create a universal alliance for the peace and happiness of the world, said Castlereagh, and in his opinion it could not be done.

Matters came to a head over the problem of intervention after a series of revolutions broke out in Europe. The first erupted in Spain (January 1820) against King Ferdinand VII. Originating in the army and fed by general discontent with the king's misgovernment, the revolution spread throughout the country. Eventually, Ferdinand was forced to readopt the Spanish Constitution of 1812.

Alexander's first reaction to the revolt was to view it as a threat to European peace. He was ready to join with the other Great Powers, under the broad provisions of the Quadruple Alliance, to crush the uprising. Castlereagh did not agree. On 5 May 1820 he defined British policy with regard to Spain. Later he had his ideas circulated to the principal governments of Europe. Intervention by the five Great Powers, he warned, had the air of dictation and of threat. Intervention by force of arms in the domestic affairs of another state in order to enforce obedience to the governing authority involved questions of great moral and political delicacy. The concept of great-power primacy as Castlereagh understood it was not intended either as a means of governing the world or of supervising the internal affairs of other states. Then he revealed the precarious assumption on which the concept of great-power primacy was based. Great Powers could not possibly feel alike upon all subjects. The institutions, habits of thinking, national prejudices all contributed to render them essentially different. Consequently, the right of intervention could not be generalized; it could not be reduced to a system; it could not be imposed as an obligation.[28]

As to the immediate problem, Castlereagh tried to show that the Spanish revolution was a local affair. There was no real danger to Europe, no real menace to peace and security. He pledged his country to fight against an actual threat, but he refused to let it act on 'abstract and speculative Principles of Precaution.' Castlereagh had no difficulty convincing Metternich. The Austrian chancellor was far from ready to see Russian troops moving across Europe into Spain. Neither was he ready to jeopardize British friendship. He persuaded Alexander not to press for collective intervention.

Six months later revolution broke out in Naples. King Ferdinand IV was forced to concede to the demands of the insurgents for a constitution establishing a parliamentary system of government. This was a more delicate affair. The interests of Austria were directly involved. Ferdinand had bound himself by treaty not to permit political changes inconsistent with the principles adopted by the Austrian emperor. Alexander, of course,

28 Temperley, H., *The Foreign Policy of Canning*, London, 1925, p. 12; *Cambridge History of British Foreign Policy*, n. 5, App. A, pp. 627–9; 631

pressed for a conference of Great Powers. This time he had Metternich's support. Again Castlereagh opposed collective action. The danger stemming from revolution in Italy, he said, affected the different allied states very unequally. If Austria felt itself immediately threatened, then it was up to Austria to decide what to do, and to do it in her own name, not in the name of the Great Powers. He suggested Austria first get allied approval before taking drastic steps. He felt sure she would get it if going into Naples was a matter self-defence and not a means of aggrandizement.

Russia, Prussia, and Austria, however, insisted on holding a conference at Troppau. Britain and France attended, represented only by observers. On 19 November 1820, the three Courts issued the Troppau protocol, formally widening the concept of great-power primacy to include the general right to use coercive power to suppress revolutionary changes of government. Rumours concerning their intentions reached such extravagant proportions that the three Courts issued a special circular dispatch. They insisted their only motive was to deliver Europe from the scourge of revolution, which violated all principles of order and morals

Castlereagh asked Russian Ambassador Lieven to justify the creation of a system so threatening to the right of all nations to be free from external control. His answer was simple. Russia, Prussia, and Austria could not be expected to look on while a sovereign was being deprived of his authority. Castlereagh acknowledged the point. What he was against was the means the three powers were ready to use. Only the strongest necessity justified intervention. Its exercise was an exception to the general rule.[29]

Castlereagh's arguments were wasted. Determined to intervene in Naples, the three Courts adjourned their conference to the town of Laibach. With tactics still very much in fashion, they summoned King Ferdinand. Under the influence of Metternich and the tsar, the king repudiated his solemn oath to support the new constitution – an oath sworn to in church, and in the presence of his Court and his ministers. Thereafter, with Russian and Prussian consent, Austria moved 50,000 troops into Naples, crushed the revolt, and restored Ferdinand to his former authority. According to the three Courts, the people of Naples never considered the action as an attack on their independence. Rather, they welcomed the Great Powers as the guardians of their liberty.

Great-power unity was restored momentarily later in the year when the Greeks revolted against their Turkish oppressors. Castlereagh's discussion of the pros and cons of intervention – a problem that continues to

29 *FPC 1815*, App. F, p. 570

bemuse statesmen to the present day – may be worth setting out in detail. Let us recall, first, how the Greeks had long suffered intense religious persecution at the hands of the Turks. Now they yearned to be free. Throughout Europe their struggle aroused overwhelming sympathy. In England, particularly, pressure mounted on the government to intervene in their behalf. In this atmosphere the British foreign secretary weighed the alternatives: whether to respect the principle of non-intervention or to make an exception on the basis of a widely felt compassion for a persecuted minority.

Castlereagh asked: 'Ought the Turkish yoke to be forever rivetted upon the necks of their suffering Christian subjects; and shall the descendants of those, in admiration of whom we have been educated, be doomed in this fine country to drag out, for all time to come, the miserable existence to which circumstances have reduced them? It is impossible not to feel the appeal ...' But, continued the foreign secretary, '... if a statesman were permitted to regulate his conduct by the counsels of his heart instead of his understanding, I really see no limits to the impulse, which might be given to his conduct ... [W]e must always recollect that his is the grave task of providing for the peace and security of those interests immediately committed to his care; that he must not endanger the fate of the present generation in a speculative endeavour to improve the lot of that which is to come.'[30]

Today, when the equal right of all peoples to govern themselves is accepted as a basic premise of international life, Castlereagh's next observation has a special significance. It was difficult for him to believe, he said, even if the Turks were miraculously to be withdrawn from the country (and he refused to consider what it would cost in blood and suffering to throw them out by force), that the Greek population could create a system of government less defective than the one they were under. He refused, therefore, to come to the aid of the rebels on the chance that out of a revolutionary war a responsible government would emerge. Once the fighting started, he argued, the way would be open for every political fanatic in Europe to move into the troubled area and jeopardize the European system so recently created. Was there, then, nothing to be done to aid the Greeks? Castlereagh's mind, undistorted by the concept of all peoples enjoying an unqualified right to sovereign independence, placed reliance on 'the hand of Providence' to work out, slowly and steadily, the future of the Greek population.

30 Ibid. pp. 376 et seq.

For Alexander the dilemma was especially cruel. As protector of the Greek Orthodox Church and as arch foe of the Turks, he longed to assist the Greek insurgents. Yet was he not at the same time the uncompromising foe of revolutionary movements? Metternich feared the tsar might be pulled in the direction of a war against Turkey, thus enabling him to get a foothold in the Balkans. Clearly, the British were right this time. No one must intervene. He helped the tsar make up his mind by insisting that the principles set forth at Troppau take precedence over all other considerations. Alexander was won over. The Great Powers did nothing to prevent Turkey from crushing the Greek revolt.

Such unity of purpose was not to last. In the spring of 1822, Spain was again the scene of revolution. This time France massed an army near the Spanish border, ready to intervene with or without great-power approval. Alexander had his heart set on an international army, but the thought of a Russian army marching across Europe haunted Metternich. He, therefore, supported French intervention, acting as the agent of the Five. Predictably, Britain rejected any interference in Spanish affairs. In an attempt to arrive at a common understanding, the Great Powers agreed to confer together at Verona in the fall.

Before they met, Foreign Secretary Canning (Castlereagh had died in August) set forth British policy. Intervention in Spain by force of arms or menace, he wrote the Duke of Wellington, British plenipotentiary to the great-power conference, was dangerous, objectionable in principle, and completely impracticable in execution. But the other powers were prepared to act without Britain. When France solicited support for armed intervention in Spain, Russia, Prussia, and Austria agreed. Wellington protested. By assuming responsibility for the government of another state, he said, the Great Powers were exceeding the limits of their authority. Unable to win them over he quit Verona. On 14 December 1822, the three Courts issued a circular dispatch, citing the revolutionary disturbances in Spain as a sad example of what inevitably occurred when 'the eternal laws of the moral order' were outraged. Having apparently become privy to these laws, they confirmed in the broadest language so far used the extended range of their responsibility first announced at Troppau. The three monarchs had decided to repel the principle of revolt, wherever and in whatever form it showed itself.[31]

In sum, Canning followed in the tradition of Castlereagh, basing British policy on the equal right of all nations, large and small, to set up the form of

31 *BFSP 1822–1823*, pp. 4–6, 9, 922–3

government they thought best, and to be left free to manage their own affairs so long as they left other nations alone. For Metternich and the tsar, such a view was dangerous. Only legitimate sovereigns enjoyed the right to lead an independent existence. In a showdown, it was the duty of the Great Powers to pass upon questions of legitimacy and, if necessary, to back up their judgment by force of arms. France alternated between the two views, tending to follow whatever policy suited its interest at the moment. Notwithstanding the division among the Great Powers, none of them considered calling in the small states to achieve a wider consensus. The idea of the weak and the small participating in international political decisions on an equal basis with the Five was rejected categorically as unworkable. But as we shall soon see, this possibility was, in a way of speaking, already in the atmosphere.

A HINT OF CONCEPTUAL CHANGE: 1823

Shortly after the conference at Verona, Metternich sensed a shift in conceptual thinking. If the revolutionary principle of individual equality were applied to states, how could one defend the supremacy of great powers? The problem came to the fore as a result of a communiqué from the king of Würtemberg. Officially, the king had first heard of the great-power reunion at Verona after it had ended. On 2 January 1823, he circulated among several European countries his views on great-power conferences. His opening remarks were cautious enough. He did not contest the right of the Great Powers to watch over the well-being of Europe. What troubled him was the means. As far as the king was concerned the Great Powers had violated inalienable rights of independent states. They had met without giving less powerful states the opportunity to present their point of view. They had concluded treaties among themselves which affected the entire European family. Such diplomatic innovations, said the king, were acceptable only with profound reservations. The cause of peace was common to all states. It was objectionable to treat second-class powers as strangers to the problem.[32]

In the marginal comments made on the copy he received, Metternich denied any intention to treat other independent states as wards or to act as their guardian. Surely, he wrote, the Great Powers did not need the consent or help of the lesser powers just to get together to proclaim the principles which guided them in Europe's interest. Metternich believed the king of

Würtemberg was hinting at the introduction of democratic procedures in the conduct of international relations. For the Austrian chancellor the entire democratic philosophy was anathema. For example, the mind little given to abstract ideas, except when revolutions violated the eternal laws of the moral order, deeply distrusted the dogma of the sovereignty of the people. Popular sovereignty, he wrote, could only be a fictitious idea. Sovereignty meant supreme power. Since that power was incapable of being exercised by 'the people,' it had to be delegated by them to some authority. The only reality for Metternich was the flesh-and-blood ruler, the true and visible head of the empire. Any other concept was pure invention.[33]

Similarly, Metternich had no patience with such terms as the 'Greeks' or the 'Italians.' What are 'Greeks,' he asked, a people, a country, a religion? If they are said to be a people or a country, where are the dynastic and geographical limits? And if they are a religion, over fifty million men would have to be recognized as Greeks. Long experience had taught him the danger inherent in racial denominations, particularly when used by those seeking to overthrow the existing order.[34]

Metternich's basic political philosophy was revealed in his reaction to the king of Würtemberg's criticism of the *form* of the Verona conference. Anticipating the General Assembly of the United Nations, Metternich asked the king what other suggestions he had. Did he want to substitute for great-power reunions a system of representative diplomacy where forty to fifty minister-representatives met in one assembly? Did the king prefer a system of deciding the most complicated international matters by majority vote, often problematical and often inadmissible, when even three or four Great Powers, with the best will in the world, had so much difficulty in arriving at satisfactory arrangements? What man, he concluded, wise in the way European problems were handled, would have to think twice before protesting against such an innovation?[35]

The king of Würtemberg was not ready to step out of the intellectual climate of the time. He quickly placed a retraction in the *Gazette de Stuttgart*, acknowledging his complete acceptance of the principles proclaimed at Verona.

As the years passed, two dynamic forces gathered momentum: one moved

33 Bertier de Sauvigny, G. de, *Metternich and His Times*, London, 1962, p. 41; Kissinger, n. 8, pp. 208–9
34 Bertier de Sauvigny, n. 33, p. 35
35 *Metternich*, vol. IV, p. 31

towards constitutional reform and political democracy; the other moved towards national independence. A revolutionary pattern of thought was proving irresistible: no individual or group of individuals in domestic society had the right to dominate others by virtue of privilege or power. Why was not the same idea relevant to the corporate persons engaged in international relations?

Mazzini stands out for having vivified the transcendental nature of the 'peoples' of the world and their inherent equality with each other. We believe in 'the HOLY ALLIANCE OF THE PEOPLES,' he wrote, 'as the broadest formula of association possible in our age – in the *liberty* and *equality* of the peoples, without which association has no true life ...'[36]

In the summer of 1907, Ruy Barbosa of Brazil followed the same logic to confound the Great Powers at the Second Hague Peace Conference. In doing so, he gave the concept of equality new direction, launching it on its way to acceptance as a basic principle of world politics. But aside from that limited experience, discussed in chapter 3, the concept of great-power primacy continued to dominate the European continent up to World War I. Imperfectly, and intermittently, the Great Powers acted together to maintain peace simply by arrogating the responsibility to themselves. Yet as Castlereagh so well understood, institutions, habits of thinking, national prejudices, all contributed to making the Great Powers essentially different. For forty years after 1815 a semblance of unity was preserved owing to their fear of revolution. But for forty years after 1871 they became increasingly fearful of each other. By 1914 disunity among the Great Powers – Germany and Austria on one side, Britain, France, and Russia on the other – had made a mockery of the idea that they could preserve peace. As World War I engulfed mankind, the lack of correspondence between the concept of great-power primacy and existential reality had become abysmal.

Winston Churchill observed the 'pervading mutability of all human affairs. Combinations long abhorred,' he said, 'become the order of the day. Ideas last year deemed inadmissible, form the pavement of daily routine ... the passage of even a few years enables – nay, compels – men and peoples to think, feel, and act quite differently without any insincerity or baseness.'[37] It is important to recall this when we consider the change in thinking that occurred in the mid-twentieth century, when to deny the nation-state an equal share in international political decisions because of an inferior power position, will appear to impugn the very foundation of liberal

36 Mazzini, J. *The Duties of Man and Other Essays*, London, 1907, p. 176
37 *Marlborough, His Life and His Times*, London, 1947, vol. 1, p. 296

democratic society. To examine some of the forces at work destined to change 'an innovation,' Metternich's term, into a commonplace, is the task of the following chapters.

3
Conflicting concepts
in the Western Hemisphere and in Europe
1881–1913

In the relations between Latin America and the United States, the conflict between the concept of equality and the concept of great-power primacy had implications unsuspected by most statesmen. This chapter discusses the alternative ideas in the Western Hemisphere, and a singular contribution made by a Latin American delegate at the Second Hague International Peace Conference.

THE IDEA OF EQUALITY IN THE WESTERN HEMISPHERE

In 1881 there were nineteen independent states in the Western Hemisphere: the United States and the eighteen Latin American republics. (Cuba became independent in 1902 and Panama in 1903 to bring the number of the original Latin American states to its present total of twenty.) The United States had not yet become a world power, but it far surpassed the other American states in wealth, military might, and political stability. Measured against it, the Latin American group was, in varying degrees, politically immature and economically underdeveloped.

The Latin American states had a somewhat ambivalent relationship with each other. Those in South America felt drawn together by their common struggle for independence from Spain. Many of them, in fact, attempted to confederate. At the same time they were beset by intense rivalries. Border disputes, often leading to war, and acts of aggression by the more powerful among them (Chile and Argentina, for example), were a recurring feature of their history. Similarly, the Caribbean states were drawn together and drawn apart. There was the same feeling of kinship, the same intense rivalries, the same fear of domination, particularly that posed by Mexico. With regard to the United States, Latin American ties were primarily commercial. Even though the Latin American republics were influenced by the ideals of the American revolution, mutuality of interest was difficult to establish.

We have selected 1881 as a starting point because in that year Secretary of State James G. Blaine inaugurated a series of inter-American conferences. In effect, he started the inter-American system. Blaine had two principal objectives, of which the first was to maintain hemisphere order. Chile, Peru, and Bolivia were at war. Chile and Argentina, Guatemala and Mexico, Colombia and Costa Rica, were all close to open conflict. Continued turmoil undoubtedly would lead to European intervention. Anticipating elements of the Good Neighbor Policy of fifty years later, Blaine was disposed to join with the other American republics to settle disputes amicably. His second objective was to promote inter-American trade. The idea of a customs union among the American states was particularly appealing.

From the start Blaine recognized the importance of basing the conference on the principle of formal equality. The concept had no political overtones. To meet with representatives of the other American states on an equal footing accorded with accepted diplomatic practice. In exchange, it was hoped, United States leadership in the hemisphere would be accepted more readily. The invitation to the first conference played down United States superiority. It was not the intention of the United States, Blaine wrote, to appear before the delegates as the protector of its neighbours and the arbiter of their disputes. On the contrary, according to the invitation, the United States would enter into the deliberations of the congress on the same condition as the other powers, 'a single member among many coordinate and co-equal States.'[1]

There was nothing exceptional about these statements. It was hardly likely that the Latin American states would have attended on any other basis. In Latin America the idea of equality was beginning to signify something more than a corollary of sovereign independence. Men were starting to think of it as an attribute inherent in the state, in the same manner, as one Latin American expressed it some years back, 'as heat and light are inherent in fire.' The notion dates from their early history. Ever since they won their independence from Spain, Latin Americans, particu-

1 *HA*, p. 257

larly in the South American republics, tended to see themselves as members of a single family of nations. Implicit in this kindred analogy was an idea of equality similar to what was believed to exist among brothers and sisters. Common language, common background, common aspirations all gave currency to the idea.

We can readily understand their thinking when, for example, we read an extract from the Peruvian archives written in 1826: 'Colombians and Argentines completed the war of independence for Peru. An Argentine army freed Chile ... Bolivar exercises supreme command in five republics and no one thinks of branding him a foreigner ... A Venezuelan governs Bolivia ... an Argentine governs Peru. A Mexican ... is the first plenipotentiary of Colombia in Mexico ... The first diplomatic representation of Peru in a foreign country is entrusted to an Argentine ...' The anonymous author of the foregoing statement found among the various South American chancelleries the same feeling of 'brotherhood' as reigns among individuals. Bolivar dreamed of creating a society of 'sister nations.' Almost all plans for confederation referred to the idea of organizing the Latin American states into 'one family.' Even when the plans failed, according to one authority, it did not destroy the consciousness of their special, intimate relationship.[2]

The tendency of statesmen to think and speak about the Latin American republics as close relatives carried a grain of truth. But the disposition to conceive the state in human terms tended to become, as we shall see in the discussion of the Second Hague Peace Conference, a camouflage for loose thinking.

Two answers to Blaine's invitation indicate an early Latin American preoccupation with the concept of equality. Venezuelan Minister for Foreign Affairs Rafael Seijas, for example, was gratified to be invited, but his pleasure was increased, he said, when he noted how the United States respected the concept of equality. Mexican Foreign Minister Ignacio Mariscal thought the United States deserved special praise for making no distinction between 'the feeble and the strong.' He, too, noted with satisfaction that all states would meet on a footing of 'perfect equality.'[3]

By the time the invitations to the conference went out in 1884, there was a new president of the United States, Chester A. Arthur, and a new secretary of state, F.T. Frelinghuysen. The latter did not like the idea of a

2 Quintanilla, L. *A Latin American Speaks*, New York, 1934, pp. 94–5, 97; Alvarez, A. 'Latin American and International Law,' *AJIL*, 1909, vol. 3, 293–4. 300–1
3 *HA*, pp. 260, 270–1

meeting with the other American states where the smallest of them would have a voice equal to that of his country. It was not that Washington would necessarily be bound by the conclusions reached, but if the United States felt forced to reject measures adopted by the conference it would weaken rather than strengthen its influence. If there was to be a reunion of American states, he told the Senate Foreign Relations Committee, it should be limited to negotiating reciprocal commercial treaties.

When Congress finally authorized an inter-American conference, all questions directly affecting United States security were excluded from the agenda. The main topics for discussion were the creation of a customs union and the arbitration of disputes. The concept of perfect equality was recognized by giving each state the right to one vote. But, to avoid any misunderstanding, the United States underscored the consultative and recommendatory nature of the meeting. According to the express wording of the invitation, the conference was wholly without power to bind any of the parties.

On 2 October 1889, the First International Conference of American States opened in Washington, D.C. Once again Blaine was secretary of state. In his welcoming address he was disposed to gratify Latin American feelings about their status in the hemisphere. You are showing the world, he told the delegates, a conference in which all American powers, great and small, are meeting together on terms of 'absolute equality.'[4]

When the conference got down to business, it became evident that the concept of absolute equality was not necessarily conducive to constructive achievement. All the American states, for example, were anxious to promote a greater flow of trade. One suggestion was to form a customs union: member states would be required to interchange their own commodities on a basis of free trade, to adopt substantially the same tariff laws, and to divide the revenue thus collected in a fixed proportion. According to the majority Report of the committee on a Customs Union, the establishment of such a union would pose almost insuperable difficulties. Among them was the creation of an international assembly empowered to frame a common tariff. This assembly would have to allot each state its proportionate share of revenue. On what basis would this be done? Above all, how was representation to be fixed in the assembly?

In the nominal world all the American republics were equal. But in the real world, to quote the majority report, they 'differ so much in territorial extent, in population, and in national wealth, that, if these things should be

4 *IAC*, p. 40

taken as the basis of representation in such assembly, the small States would not be in a position adequately to protect their interests ...' Then why not stick to the nominal world and disregard the differences? Because if all nations were to be admitted on an equal footing, according to the same report, 'the interests of the larger nations would not be adequately guaranteed.'[5]

A little more than a century earlier, the American states that had revolted from Britain faced a similar dilemma. The context was different, for the former colonies were seeking to create a federal-type government rather than to promote trade. But the discussion at the Constitutional Convention in 1787, and the comments on the new charter of government appearing in *The Federalist*, are worth recalling.

The original thirteen American states were members of a confederation. Regardless of size or power their perfect equality in its Congress was recognized. At the Constitutional Convention they struggled to create a legislative assembly representative of the real disproportion of power among them. The 'great powers' (like New York, Pennsylvania, Virginia, Massachusetts) favoured a national legislature with members apportioned according to population. The small states (like New Jersey, Delaware, Maryland) insisted on the principle of absolute equality. They wanted a single legislative body in which each state, regardless of power, had one vote.

Alexander Hamilton of New York, writing in *The Federalist*, attacked the conceptual outlook of the small states. 'Every idea of proportion,' he wrote, 'and every rule of fair representation conspire to condemn a principle which gives to Rhode Island an equal weight in the scale of power with Massachusetts, or Connecticut, or New York ...' To claim that all states were equal was, for Hamilton, a kind of logical legerdemain. To expect large states to give up their rank in the political scale was to be, in his opinion, insensible to the love of power and, therefore, irrational. The small states knew their welfare depended upon union with the larger ones, he said. And for that reason they should be ready to renounce their pretension to equality.[6]

At the convention, James Wilson of Pennsylvania argued for proportional representation. If all authority was derived from the people, he said, then equal numbers of people should have equal representation. As he viewed the problem of equality, by granting equal votes to all states the

5 Ibid. p. 103
6 *The Federalist*, ed. Henry Cabot Lodge, New York, 1888, no. XXII, 128–9

articles of confederation had actually violated the principle. His reasoning is interesting. First he traced the equality of states to their sovereignty, and the natural equality of men to each one being sovereign over himself. Then he argued that no man could retain his natural equality when he became a member of civil government. Consequently, neither could a state when it became a member of a federal government.[7]

A lot depended, though, on how one viewed the state. Luther Martin of Maryland took a different approach to defend the position that all states retain equal votes. The new government, he believed, was meant to preserve states and not to govern individuals. The thirteen states had entered the confederation from a state of nature on a footing of perfect equality. Now, at the convention, they were back in a state of nature. They therefore could not give up their equality without giving up their liberty. For these reasons, he could never agree to a plan, he said, whereby an inequality of votes placed small states at the mercy of large ones.

Small states, like Delaware and New Jersey, supported an equal vote for all states regardless of size or power, out of fear of being 'swallowed up' by the large states. William Paterson of New Jersey expressed his distrust of submitting the welfare of New Jersey, with five votes, to a council where Virginia, say, had sixteen. To him this was autocracy. His fellow delegate, David Brearly, believed all sovereign states should have an equal vote, no matter how large or populous some might be. Yet he was forced to admit it was unfair, even unjust, for a small state like Georgia to have an equal vote with powerful Virginia. He did, however, find an answer. What it may have lacked in practicability was surely counterbalanced by its logic. Take a map of the United States, he suggested, erase all the boundaries, and divide the whole country into thirteen equal parts.

Men like Franklin and Madison knew a compromise was the only solution. The government had to be founded on a mixture of the principles of proportional representation and equal representation. And this is exactly what happened. To reduce as far as possible the gap between the real world of unequal states and the nominal world where either the strong must predominate or all are absolutely equal, the delegates created two chambers: a House of Representatives and a Senate. The small states gave up their claim to equal representation in the House. The large states gave up their claim to proportional representation in the Senate. The House de-

---

7 For the views of James Wilson, and those that follow: Luther Martin, William Paterson, and David Brearly, see Van Doren, C. *The Great Rehearsal*, New York, 1948, pp. 73–5, 95, 99

rived its powers from the people. The Senate derived its powers from the states, all of which, regardless of size, were to be represented on the principle of equality.

We return now to the First International Conference of American States. Faced with the problem of creating an international assembly representative of the United States and the Latin American republics, members of the Committee on a Customs Union recalled the solution reached at the Constitutional Convention. They made a similar suggestion: create two bodies. In one, all the American states, large and small, would be represented equally. In the other, representation would take into consideration the vast differences in population and wealth among the members. The suggestion fell on deaf ears. What troubled the delegates was getting over the conceptual hurdle. To create an assembly of great and small states based on a mixture of proportional and equal representation did violence to the purity of the concept of equality as they conceived it. According to the majority report the delegates were unwilling to make even a partial sacrifice of their national sovereignty. In such an atmosphere compromise was impossible. Hostages to their conceptual thinking, the delegates were forced to abandon the customs union they universally favoured.

The other major object of the conference was to make compulsory the arbitration of disputes threatening inter-American peace. In the discussion that followed, the words of Manuel Quintana of Argentina set the mood: 'To the eye of international law,' he said, 'there are on the continent neither great nor small nations. All are equally sovereign and independent; all are equally worthy of consideration and respect.' Out of deference to this nominal world it was important not to create a 'council of Amphictyons.' He opposed any agreement whereby a majority of American states either could compel other states to carry out their obligations or could render moral judgments.[8]

With this idea in mind the delegates agreed on a 'compulsory' arbitration convention with an important escape clause. According to Article IV, matters which in the judgment of one of the parties might imperil its independence were excluded. J.M. Hurtado of Colombia criticized the exception. It made no practical sense, whatever its cogency in theory, to argue that an adverse decision by an arbitration tribunal might impair the independent rights of a state. It was one thing for states to preserve their equal sovereignty and equal independence, but were not the delegates

8 *IAC*, vol. 2, 961

overlooking the real inequality among them? In any dispute, he argued, one state will always be weaker than the other. If the weaker could refuse to arbitrate it would then have no recourse but to accept the conditions imposed by the more powerful. If the stronger could refuse to arbitrate, the weaker would have no means of redress.

But cogency in theory was not to be lightly tossed aside. Quintana knew Article IV defeated the idea of compulsory arbitration. But the equal sovereignty and independence of states was at stake. All other considerations had to give way – even the possibility of avoiding armed conflict. Here was his reasoning. Suppose arbitration should be unduly declined. Suppose war then broke out between the dissenting nations. The only thing left to the other American nations, Quintana assured the delegates, was to deplore the downfall of a noble human aspiration. Quintana spoke for the vast majority of American states. The convention was passed with the escape clause and the principle of equality as a corollary of sovereignty and independence remained inviolate.

At the First International Conference of American States neither of the two basic objectives was fulfilled. In spite of this, Salvador de Medonca of Brazil undoubtedly reflected the views of the other Latin American delegates when he stressed what seemed like a key accomplishment. On 18 April 1890, during the closing ceremonies, he said to the delegates, 'Well it is an honor to us to assert that there never prevailed around this table any other measure of respect for opinion, liberty of speech, or the value of a vote, than that of the most perfect equality among sovereign States.'[9]

The Second Conference of American States was held in Mexico City in 1901 and the third met at Rio de Janeiro in 1906. On both occasions the United States and the Latin American republics met on the basis of their most perfect equality. On both occasions the United States made the nominal concession because of the restricted nature of the topics on the agenda: no political questions could be discussed; no controversies could be settled; no judgment could be passed on the conduct of any state.

But what about the vital problems affecting the peace and security of the hemisphere? At this point the United States was ready to act on an entirely different conceptual level. Gone was the idea of perfect equality. In its place was the idea of a special status for those enjoying superior power. This meant that primary responsibility for hemisphere order belonged uniquely to the United States. Among the representatives of the other American states, however, the constant repetition of the perfect equality of

9 Ibid. p. 1154

the hemisphere republics had its own force of seduction. It contributed to a belief in what was not but what they would like to be so. Before we consider the tension arising over the contradictory ideas, a word on the concept of great-power primacy.

THE CONCEPT OF GREAT-POWER PRIMACY IN THE WESTERN HEMISPHERE

In his famous message, President James Monroe declared to the world that the United States assumed full responsibility for keeping non-American powers out of the hemisphere. The United States consulted no Latin American states beforehand, and made no attempt to get Latin American support afterwards. On the contrary, it rejected Latin American offers to co-operate. The primary concern of the United States was its own security. While it may not have intended to assert superiority over the other American states, the unilateralism of the Monroe Doctrine was bound to come into conflict with the concept of their perfect equality.

Less than fifty years later, the United States had clearly become the major power in the hemisphere. The extent to which this fact had impressed itself on some influential members of the administration may be seen in the view of Secretary of State Hamilton Fish. In 1870 he set forth the rationale behind the concept of great-power primacy:

The United States, by the priority of their independence, by the stability of their institutions, by the regard of their people for the forms of law, by their resources as a government, by their naval power, by their commercial enterprise, by the attractions which they offer to European immigration, by the prodigious internal development of their resources and wealth, and by the intellectual life of their population, occupy of necessity a prominent position on this continent which they neither can nor should abdicate, which entitles them to a leading voice, and which imposes on them duties of right and honor regarding American questions, whether those questions affect emancipated colonies, or colonies still subject to European dominion.[10]

Twenty years later another secretary of state, Richard Olney, went far beyond the implications in Hamilton Fish's modest catalogue of American virtues. This was the famous statement of 20 July 1895, when Olney found the United States practically sovereign on the continent, and practically

10 Lockey, J.B. 'The Meaning of Pan Americanism,' *AJIL*, 1925, 106–7

invulnerable against any other power. Subsequently, Olney developed the point to its ultimate extent. We may recall the Declaration of Independence proclaimed the right of the thirteen American colonies to assume a separate and equal station among the powers of the earth. Now Olney found it fitting to accept 'the commanding position' that it occupied among the powers of the earth.[11]

Behind Olney's claim to primacy for the United States may be seen the views of an American naval officer, Captain Alfred Thayer Mahan. During the 1890s Captain Mahan had begun a series of magazine articles designed to indoctrinate Americans with a new sense of national power and national destiny. He had a prophetic vision of the United States as a world power. He predicted the United States would soon be engaged not only with rival European powers, but with Oriental powers as well. He underlined the crucial importance of strategic bases in the Pacific and Caribbean areas. And he urged the creation of a powerful fighting fleet. By 1895 Mahan had become a leading figure in American political life and his ideas had widespread support in congressional circles.

In the same year Congress became the centre of heated debates over American commercial rights in South America, and over British encroachments in Venezuela. It is not surprising, therefore, to find Representative Leonidas F. Livingston of Georgia declaring that the British claim in Venezuela related to a matter 'on our continent.' Eventually, Great Britain admitted the superior position of the United States in the Western Hemisphere. But for our purpose, it is the relationship with Venezuela that deserves further attention.

At the time, Venezuela was ruled by General Cipriano Castro, a strong-arm dictator known as the 'lion of the Andes.' Dexter Perkins, in a model of understatement, described him as 'unlovely.' All during the preliminary Anglo-American conversations, the United States studiously ignored the General. When the United States and Great Britain finally agreed to arbitrate their differences, Olney went so far as to oppose any representative from Venezuela on the arbitration board. He did not see why Venezuela had to be consulted at every step. Ultimately, Venezuela was permitted to name an arbiter, but forbidden to name a Venezuelan. (It chose a justice of the United States Supreme Court.) By the terms of the award Venezuela was forced to accept a treaty made by foreign powers, concerning the limits of its own frontier, and concerning the right of navigation on its principal river.

11 La Feber, W. 'The Background of Cleveland's Venezuelan Policy,' *Amer. Hist. Rev.*, 1961, 962

Under the standard of international justice as interpreted by the United States and Britain, any claim that the rights of some abstract entity called 'Venezuela' had thus been violated, would have been rejected summarily. The reality for the two Great Powers, we can be sure, was that Venezuela was none other than General Cipriano Castro, the unlovely dictator. In the circumstances, justice required the United States and Britain, as Great Powers, to assume responsibility for ending the dispute – Venezuela's interests having been adequately safeguarded by the presence of its chosen arbiter.

By the twentieth century, Captain Mahan's vision of the United States as a world power was adopted by Theodore Roosevelt. As Assistant Secretary of the Navy to President William McKinley in 1897, Roosevelt advocated a big navy, armed intervention in Cuba if necessary, territorial expansion overseas, and an aggressive foreign policy. If anyone was ready to put the capstone on the concept of great-power responsibility in inter-American relations it was President Roosevelt. And he did. In him we find its classic expression.

THEODORE ROOSEVELT (1901–1909)

When President Theodore Roosevelt took office in 1901, the United States was committed to defend the entire Western Hemisphere against European encroachment, and to defend Guam and the Philippines (ceded by Spain after the Spanish-American War). This territory, coveted by Germany, was almost 7000 miles from the California coast, in an area adjacent to British, Dutch, and French spheres of influence. By the acquisition of the Philippines the United States found itself at the strategic crossroads of the empires of Eastern Asia.

With the United States now involved in two oceans, an east-west canal offering speedy transit to American fighting ships appeared vital to American interests. The most practical area for the construction and operation of an interoceanic canal was either Central America or the Isthmus of Panama. Clearly, the entire Caribbean was a strategic area vital to the security of the United States.

Within a thousand-mile radius of the Isthmus was a mosaic of a dozen-odd Central and South American states. All of them had enjoyed at least fifty years of independence. The original leaders of these petty republics may have been inspired by the ideals of the American Revolution but, for the most part, the states remained long-time hosts to civil war and brutal, tyrannical government.

President Roosevelt made a clear distinction between 'civilized' and 'non-civilized' nations. Only civilized nations could participate in international affairs. What characterized highly civilized nations were their power and energy to expand and their ability to govern themselves. Imperialist expansion was limited by one criterion: the interest of civilization in general. German expansion in 1914, for example, did not meet this test. That is why it had to be contained. But the United States in the Philippines, England in India and Egypt, France in Algeria, Russia in Turkestan, Japan in China, each showed the expansive energies of a superior people. By the same token, the inability of other nations to govern themselves marked their inferiority among the powers of the world. Sophisticated nations, therefore, were required to intervene and care for these callow specimens until they had matured.

Throughout the world powerful and stable governments bore the responsibility for the maintenance of international order. Roosevelt did not envisage them acting in concert as Castlereagh and Metternich had. Instead, each great power had its own special sphere. Britain had special duties in Egypt and India; the job of policing the Orient fell to Japan; and, of course, the stability of the Western Hemisphere was the special province of the United States. Any notion of collective responsibility for hemisphere order, based on the perfect equality of all American states, would have been dismissed as unthinkable.

Consider, in this respect, his description of Colombia as 'a corrupt pithecoid community.' To think of it in the same terms as such responsible powers as Holland, Belgium, or Switzerland was absurd. Roosevelt compared Colombia's leaders with a group of Sicilian or Calabrian bandits. You could no more make a valid agreement with the rulers of Colombia, said Roosevelt, 'than you could nail currant jelly to a wall ...' Even more brutal was his comment on Mexico and Venezuela. To ask either of them to join with the United States in guaranteeing the Monroe Doctrine was 'like asking the Apaches or Utes to guarantee it.'[12]

When order broke down in the hemisphere, regardless of formal rules of equality applied in inter-American conferences, Roosevelt acted on the idea that the United States had to protect these little states. His denial of their perfect equality with the United States, together with the assertion of responsibility for the uncivilized ones, conformed to the missionary spirit of the times. Men like Senator Albert J. Beveridge were proclaiming ties with Providence. 'God has made us the master organizer of the world to

[12] Hill, H.C. *Roosevelt and the Caribbean*, Chicago, 1927, p. 208; Burton, D.H. 'Theodore Roosevelt: Confident Imperialist,' *Rev. Pol.* 1961, 365

establish system where chaos reigns,' he told his colleagues. 'This is the definite mission of America.'[13]

Such sentiments were not limited to the American continent. In Europe, French statesman Jules Ferry wrote: 'the superior races have a right as regards inferior races. They have a right because they have a duty. They have a duty of civilizing the inferior races.' In Germany, the Kaiser said, 'God has created us to civilize the world.' While from England came the voice of Cecil Rhodes: 'I contend that we are the first race in the world, and the more of the world we inhabit the better it is for the human race.'[14]

Roosevelt's position on actual intervention in the internal affairs of the other American states was, essentially, in the tradition of Castlereagh. Intervention was to be considered only in the last resort; only if the vital interests of the United States were involved; only if there was danger of foreign interference. In these circumstances the United States would unhesitatingly exercise an international police power.

When revolution broke out in Santo Domingo – in debt to European creditors for over $30,000,000 – Roosevelt had the power to act out his well-known metaphor: 'I want to do nothing but what a policeman has to do in Santo Domingo.' Nevertheless, he acted reluctantly. He had been hoping and praying that the Santo Domingans would behave so that he could avoid interfering. But the government of Santo Domingo had been 'bedeviling' the United States to establish a protectorate over the island and to take charge of its finances. By 1905, completely bedeviled, the United States did intervene, took over the custom house, and assigned part of the income received to pay off overseas creditors.

One Latin American statesmen, Foreign Minister Luis Maria Drago of Argentina, was evidently not impressed by the modest appraisals of great-power worth that came so easily to the lips of its leaders. For some time he had sought to bar all paternal interventions to collect debts, for he saw defaulting Latin American countries being taken over by their great-power creditors. Enlarging the scope of the Latin American family to cover a continental brotherhood, he appealed to an alternative concept: multilateral not unilateral action. The United States and Latin America should, he said, join in upholding a principle that 'humanity' had consecrated: all states, regardless of the force at their disposal, were entities in law, 'perfectly equal to one another.'[15]

13 Welles, S. *Naboth's Vineyard*, New York, 1928, vol. 2, 916
14 Moon, P.T. *Imperialism and World Politics*, New York, 1926, p. 43; Page, K. *National Defense*, New York, 1931, pp. 5–6
15 *FR* 1903, pp. 1, 2, 5

Roosevelt faced a different reality. Default on an international obligation made foreign intervention practically inescapable. If the United States
did not move first on behalf of all the parties, a non-American power might
conceivably get a foothold in a strategically vital area. So far out of
correspondence with the real circumstances was the nominal idea of a
continental brotherhood of perfectly equal states that Roosevelt ignored it.
He substituted for it the concept of great-power paternalism. In his conception of the world, the United States, with an overwhelming preponderance
of power, had a duty to assume primary responsibility for preserving order.
'In international matters,' he said, 'to make believe that nations are equal
when they are not equal is as productive of far-reaching harm as to make
the same pretense about individuals in a community.'[16]

THE THIRD INTERNATIONAL CONFERENCE OF AMERICAN STATES

The utterances of President Roosevelt heaping scorn on uncivilized governments, his description of the United States as a hemisphere policeman,
and the interventions in states bordering the Caribbean had caused grave
concern among many Latin Americans. It fell to Secretary of State Elihu
Root to dispel the bad impression, and to deny that the United States policy
implied an assumption of superiority over the Latin American republics.

At the Third International Conference of American States, held in Rio
de Janeiro in 1906, Root was Honorary President. In his opening address he
contributed a broad definition of the concept of equality underlying inter-
American relations. On its face, it appeared to herald a complete reversal of
United States policy. It certainly seemed inconsistent with the principle of
international conduct on which the United States acted.

The words of the secretary of state, on behalf of the greatest power in the
hemisphere, struck a harmonious note with the delegates. The equal rights
of the smallest and weakest state, he said, were entitled to as much respect
as those of the greatest power. The United States claimed not a single right,
privilege, or power that it did not freely concede to every other American
republic. Here, indeed, was a definition of equality that any Latin American could understand. But did this mean the United States was ready to
abandon the concept of great-power primacy? Not at all. Neither Root nor
President Roosevelt, who heartily approved Root's words in his annual
message to Congress, had any such intention. Neither of them believed the
other American states were qualified to participate in the principal political

16 Burton, n. 12, p. 374, n. 48

decisions affecting hemisphere security. To show how far such a thought was from the President's mind, in the very same speech in which he approved Root's expression of equality, Roosevelt told how the United States had 'assumed sponsorship before the civilized world for Cuba's career as a nation ...' If the Cuban elections should degenerate and become a farce, he continued, if insurrections should become a habit on the island, the United States would unquestionably intervene. Under such conditions, it would not permit Cuba to continue as an independent nation.[17]

How do we reconcile the right of the United States to intervene with its professed respect for the independence and equal rights of all sovereign states? One way to explain the paradox is to recall that in civil society the *sine qua non* for the enjoyment of individual civil rights is conformity to generally accepted standards of community behaviour. Individual equality is not violated by punishing the drunk and the disorderly. If a parallel is drawn with international society, we may say the rights of states are enjoyed by those conforming to international standards of behaviour. The equality of states, therefore, is not necessarily violated by intervening in the domestic affairs of those states indulging in farcical elections or exhibiting insurrectionary habits.

But the parallel breaks down in one important respect. In civil society, for the most part, standards of behaviour are the result of a general consensus in which the entire community presumably participates. Also, it is the community as a whole that metes out punishment. In international society, on the other hand, the will of the great powers, in general, prevails. They determine what constitutes acceptable behaviour, and how violators should be punished. At this point, the judgment of the great powers fails to achieve that legitimacy attributed to the judgment of the community as a whole. The day did come, though, in Franklin D. Roosevelt's administration, when the United States in quest of this legitimacy renounced the concept of great-power primacy in favour of multilateral action by the entire community of American states.

Returning now to Root's speech, there is another reason for recognizing its importance. Throughout Latin America it elicited a deep emotional response. Did it not signify the end of such unilateral acts as the seizure of the Santo Domingo custom house? Did it not suggest the exceptional nature of United States involvement in the Panama revolt from Colombia (1903)? Did it not presage the diminution of tension between the contradictory concepts of equality and great-power primacy? Senor Mariano Cor-

17 *FR* 1906, p. xlv

nejo of Peru reacted to the secretary of state's words in fairly typical style. Here was a speech which 'not only defined the interests, but ... also stirred in the soul of America all her memories, all her dreams, and all her ideals.' Ruy Barbosa of Brazil described Root's message as having 'reverberated through the length and breadth of our continent, as the American evangel of peace and justice.'[18] By 1907, the substance of Root's remarks was being referred to constantly by Latin American delegates attending the Hague Peace Conference. There, joined by the representatives of other small states, they were ready to extend the idea of equality far beyond its original meaning. Barbosa supplied the rationale. As it turned out, the consequences were comparatively minor, but he set in motion a trend with far-reaching consequences for international political relations.

THE SECOND HAGUE PEACE CONFERENCE
AND THE CONCEPT OF SOVEREIGN EQUALITY, 1907

The peace conferences at The Hague in 1899 and 1907 were the first international peace-time reunions for the purpose of preserving peace. Both endeavoured to humanize the stringencies of war, and to provide for the pacific settlement of disputes.

Forty-four states from all over the world attended the 1907 conference. Among them were the eighteen Latin American republics. Largely through the efforts of the United States, they were making their first appearance at an international assembly. As Root had urged, they were attending with the rights of equal sovereign states. From the very beginning the atmosphere at The Hague was unrealistic. The controlling devices and jargon of a democratic assembly of individual legislators were lifted from domestic political practice and applied to a conference of states. Provision was made for presidents, vice-presidents, chairmen, and reporters; for committees, sub-committees, and drafting committees; for roll-calls, speeches, and votes; for majority and minority reports; for full sittings and plenary sessions. Some delegates sensed the incongruity of the proceedings. Said J.B. Scott, member of the United States delegation, 'It seemed extraordinary to those not accustomed to it to see Governments, as ordinary individuals, responding to a roll-call.'[19]

In his welcoming address to the delegates (15 June 1907), Russian Ambassador S.E.M. Nelidow, president of the conference, kept up the

18 Root, E. *Latin America and the United States*, Cambridge, Mass., 1917, pp. 3, 12
19 *Reports*, p. xxxi

equation of state and individual. He cautioned the delegates not to be too ambitious, reminding them that 'nations are living beings, just like the individuals of which they are composed; that they have the same impulses ...'[20] But in spite of similar remarks, in spite of the democratic trappings, in spite of the rules which permitted each state to place itself on as many committees as it chose and to have an equal voice in all matters, the Great Powers dominated the proceedings. They either forced their views upon the conference or used other methods to prevent unacceptable conventions from being adopted. They were not prepared, however, for the revolutionary deduction that was drawn from the concept of equality. Nor did any Great Power seriously try to refute its logic.

First a word on the background. In order to settle international disputes, the First Hague Conference had created a 'phantom court' – so called because it was not really a court at all, but only a framework for the selection of arbitrators. Many states were reluctant to use the arbitrators, notwithstanding their unimpeachable integrity, for they were considered to be acting as diplomatic agents rather than judicial officers. Secretary of State Elihu Root backed a permanent tribunal composed of judges with a judicial sense of responsibility and 'nothing else.' He hoped the innovation would inaugurate the widespread use of the new court to settle disputes that would otherwise lead to war.

The principal difficulty in creating the court centred around the question: How do you fix the number of judges among forty-four equal states? Clearly, a court of forty-four judges could not perform effectively. One plan, favoured by the Great Powers, was to create a court composed of seventeen judges, for a twelve-year period, and to give each state the right to appoint one judge. But, as United States delegate Scott explained, there was a close tie between population, wealth, and industry on the one hand, and law suits on the other. Judges coming from states with greater population, wealth, and industry were, therefore, entitled to greater participation on the court. According to him, judges from first-class powers should serve the full twelve years; judges from second-class powers, ten years; judges from third-class powers, four years; and so on down to states like Monaco and Lichtenstein whose judges would serve for one year.

To the small states, with the Latin American delegates showing the way, the plan was unacceptable. To permit the Great Powers to classify or grade states according to rank violated the principle of perfect equality. This principle meant much more than equality before the law, much more than

20 *Proceedings*, vol. 1, 48

equality of rights and obligations. According to T.J. Lawrence, it meant 'equality of influence, equality in council, equality therefore on the judicial bench.'[21]

Ruy Barbosa of Brazil led the fight of the small states. He was not only the most distinguished delegate of his country but truly representative of Latin America. During the concluding weeks of the conference he had become a dominating personality. Two rights were involved, as far as Barbosa was concerned: the right to appoint judges and the right to sit. The right to appoint was freely admitted: the great-power proposal would respect the perfect equality of all states. But the right of sitting in the court was a different matter: the small states 'would be absolutely unequals. And it is this inequality which violates the equality of States.' He rejected the argument, made by the United States delegate Joseph H. Choate that the principle of absolute equality was met by giving each state the right to appoint a judge. He dismissed his argument that the mere length of tenure did not compromise the principle. He was unmoved by the thought that his own suggestion would result in the creation of an international tribunal unable to operate effectively. What was involved was the distribution of judgeships according to a state's influence and power. This, he insisted, was a principle of inequality. There was no right more worthy of being called vital than that of the equality of sovereign states. And he cited Root's famous speech at the Rio conference when the secretary of state said that the United States neither claimed nor desired any rights, privileges, or powers that it did not freely concede to the other American republics regardless of their size and power.

But the burden of Barbosa's argument went deeper than a play on words. He was incensed by a press report about the small states demanding equal representation on the tribunal with Britain, France, Germany, and the United States, regardless of their material, moral, or intellectual condition. The newspaper article agreed that the deductions Latin American statesmen made from the premise of absolute equality were irrefutable. Perhaps, the author intimated, the premise needed reformulation, for there was no sense to the conclusion. The article ended with this comment: 'Hence, in view of the fact that the Great Powers are not at all disposed to put over them, as their judges, the most corrupt and the most backward States of Asia and of South America, we shall not yet have the arbitral court.' Barbosa read the entire article into the record. Then he rose to the challenge. Of course there were diversities of wealth, power, culture,

21 Lawrence, T.J. *International Problems and Hague Conferences*, London, 1908, p. 74

honesty, and the like between states even as between individuals. But was this enough to create differences with regard to their essential rights? Of course not.[22]

Then he drove home the point by appealing to the logic on which the concept of sovereign equality has come to rest. 'Civil rights,' he said, 'are the same for men everywhere. Political rights are the same for all citizens. Lord Kelvin or Mr John Morley have the same vote in electing the august and sovereign Parliament of Great Britain as the ordinary workman dulled by work and misery.' With the equation suggested Barbosa was ready to clinch it. In terms reminiscent of Mazzini, he declared: 'We have demanded equality of right for the peoples.' By the hook of analogy Barbosa had transferred to an abstract political concept the equal political rights heretofore applicable to individual human beings. Ever since the American and French revolutions governments had gradually been extending equal civil and political rights to all citizens. It was widely recognized as unjust to attribute to the personality of the Lord Kelvins and the John Morleys a greater political value than to the personality of the ordinary workman dulled by work and misery. Each had one vote; and each vote had exactly the same weight. Now Barbosa found the delegates of the Great Powers persisting in a most abominable mistake: 'teaching the peoples that rank between the States must be measured in accordance with their military situation.'[23]

Barbosa had struck a first blow at the idea that in a world of sovereign states with no international superior, responsibility for international order falls on those with preponderant power. If the corporate personality of the state can be equated with the real personality of the individual, as Barbosa had equated it, how could one logically deny it equal civil and political rights in international affairs? As to the immediate problem, the distribution of judgeships according to a state's influence and power, here was a clear violation of the ideal world where all states, like individuals, were perfectly equal.

After Barbosa had finished, José Tible Machado of Guatemala contributed a phrase destined to assume growing importance as a catchword in international affairs. He based his opposition to the composition of the arbitral court on its violation of 'the fixed principle of the sovereign equality of the States as political entities ...'[24] As we shall see, the so-called fixed

22 *Proceedings*, vol. 2, 149–50
23 Ibid. 150, 153, 155
24 Ibid. 159

principle of sovereign equality soon took on the property of a political incantation. Incidentally, students looking for the origin of the wording in Article 2(1) of the Charter of the United Nations might very well take Machado's contribution as a logical starting point.

No Great Power cared to, or dared to, attack the basic conceptual thinking of Barbosa and his supporters. All of them opposed the ultimate conclusion. Some, like British delegate Sir Edward Fry, hinted that this would be the last international reunion of great and small powers. On 16 October 1907, in a private despatch to his government, he wrote: 'The claim of many of the smaller states to equality as regards not only their independence, but their share in all institutions ... is one which ... may perhaps drive the greater powers to act in many cases by themselves.'[25] Notwithstanding this prophetic warning, neither he nor any other representative of the Great Powers struck at the heart of the matter. They permitted the analogy between the equal rights of individual human beings and the equal rights of corporate person to go unchallenged.

Oddly enough, one of the Latin American delegates raised the point. José Batlle y Ordoñez of Uruguay was conscious of the delegates having 'entered upon the wrong road.' He knew they had become confused and spotted the fundamental philosophical error in their thinking: the tendency to think of nations in the same terms as individual human beings. Thus, in trying to create a judicial organization for states, the delegates set up a tribunal fashioned after the ones used in domestic society for resolving individual disputes.[26]

It is necessary to go outside the conference for the most outspoken criticism of the concept of equality. On 19 October 1907 the London *Times* denounced the gross violation of the law on which the conference was based. It conceded that for certain limited purposes the concept of equality was useful. Basically, however, the idea was a fiction, 'and a very absurd fiction at that.' Everybody knew states were not equal. Why did the delegates persist in ignoring this essential truth? Because of the pretence, according to the article, the conference had condemned itself to impotence. The *Times* supported the concept of great-power primacy by appealing to what common sense teaches us. The Great Powers 'will not, and can not, in any circumstances ... [allow small states] to have an equal right with themselves in laying down the law by which their fleets, their armies, their diplomatists, and their jurists are to be guided on matters of the supremest

25 Hicks, F.C. 'The Equality of States and the Hague Conferences,' *AJIL*, 1908, 542–3
26 *Proceedings*, vol. 2, 156

moment.' Any other suggestion was 'fatuous.' The criticism ended by dismissing Barbosa's logic in these terms. To place certain small states on an equal footing with the Great Powers 'would involve the subjugation of the higher civilization by the lower, and would inevitably condemn the more advanced peoples to moral and intellectual regression.'

The small states did not see it that way. They hoped to eliminate power as the principal means of influence in world affairs. In domestic society each citizen counts for one and no more than one in the decision-making process. In international society each people must also count for one and no more than one. Drawing an analogy between the rights of individuals and the rights of peoples created no conceptual difficulty for them. In the final analysis what other recourse did they have?

The attempt to realise the concept, however, revealed the wide gap between the ideal and the reality. An effective tribunal simply could not be created on the basis of Barbosa's reasoning. But this was much less important than complete loyalty to principle. Evidently, the Great Powers were not sufficiently concerned about creating the court to impose their will on the small states. The tension between the incompatible concepts remained unresolved. In the end, it prevented the creation of a permanent arbitral court of justice.

One other matter decided at the conference is relevant to the idea of equality: the right to collect debts by force. The problem was a carryover from the Third International Conference of American States. That re-union, held in Rio de Janeiro in 1906, was redolent with memories of the unilateral intervention by the United States in Santo Domingo. To forestall future violations of the perfect equality of the American states, Drago of Argentina wanted the delegates to subscribe to the formula: no state has the right to intervene in another state to collect unpaid public debts. The view of the Latin American republics at Rio was unanimous. If debt default was sufficient reason for intervention, they would be at the mercy of the Great Powers from whom they were heavy borrowers. The right to intervene to collect debts was discriminatory. It was a right only the strong could enjoy, and only at the expense of the weak. It violated the principle, as Drago had earlier pointed out, that all states, whatever the military power at their disposal, were entities in law, perfectly equal to one another. After discussion, the delegates to the Rio Conference decided to seek a ruling from the Second Hague Peace Conference. This is how the matter came to arise at The Hague.

The problem of debt collection was of vastly greater concern to the Great Powers than creating an international arbitration court. None of them was prepared to permit valid debts to go by default for the sake of any abstract legal principle. As for the small states, in spite of their apparent success in preventing the creation of the court because it violated the principle of equality, they did not have the power to frame conventions as they willed. Nevertheless, their plea to outlaw intervention as a collection device did not go unheeded. Since the nineteenth century, Castlereagh's point of view had acquired greater respectability. Intervention was deemed permissible only when the vital interests of a state were at stake. In the case of unpaid debts, the United States was prepared to place limits on the concept of great-power primacy. Root had decided to renounce the use of the army and navy for collection purposes – provided the debtor acted in good faith. The other Great Powers agreed. They supported a resolution permitting intervention only in the event a defaulting state refused to arbitrate, or prevented a *compromis* from being agreed on, or failed to abide by an arbitration award.

For the majority of Latin American republics, the obligation to arbitrate, and the right to intervene in case of refusal, violated the concept of perfect equality, but it conformed to the standard of justice set by the Great Powers, and there was little they could do about it. Still, as a result of the new approach to debt collection, part of the tension arising over intervention by the United States in Latin America had diminished. Only time would tell if one day the United States would renounce all intervention in their affairs.

At the close of a conference it was customary for the delegates to say a few words about the progress they thought had been made. The extent to which the concept of equality had metamorphosed in the minds of some delegates may be judged by the remarks of Roque Sáenz Peña. 'Henceforth,' said the delegate from Argentina, 'we are able to state that the political equality of States has ceased to be a fiction and is established as an evident reality.'[27] Senor Sáenz Peña's remarks were pure rhetoric. But as Whitehead observed, words and phrases carry with them 'an enveloping suggestiveness.' Ultimately, some statesmen will cease to distinguish between words and things. Words will take on an importance quite apart from the reality they are supposed to represent. They will develop unpredictable authority. When this happens major difficulties of perspective will be unavoidable.

For the moment we are not concerned with the usefulness of some words and phrases or whether they are sensible or realistic. What we wish

27 Ibid. vol I, 587

to stress is Barbosa's contribution. In the tradition of Rousseau and Mazzini he supplied the rationale for the present-day concept of sovereign equality. By equating the equal civil and political rights of individual persons with the equal civil and political rights of corporate persons, the notion that each state has an equal voice in international affairs, entitled to the same weight, appears irrefutable.

After the Hague conference ended, it did not take long for the Latin American republics to realise the fictional nature of their political equality with the United States. During the administration of President William Howard Taft (1909–13), the concept of great-power primacy entered what Sumner Welles called its 'pernicious phase.' According to Welles, United States policy now consisted in a series of attempted interventions in the internal affairs of the Caribbean republics. The purpose: 'to force on the inhabitants of those countries, governments considered by the State Department in Washington suited to their requirements, regardless of whether or not the people of the nations concerned had a real voice in their selection.'[28]

Consider two examples of what came to be known as 'dollar diplomacy.' When revolution broke out in Nicaragua, the United States intervened, forced General José Santos Zelaya out of office, and installed in his place a new chief of state. In the opinion of Samuel F. Bemis, the intervention and occupation of Nicaragua was totally uncalled for. In Santo Domingo, a treaty negotiated by the previous Roosevelt administration gave the United States a limited right to intervene to protect the receiver of customs. The State Department (Philander C. Knox was secretary of state) insisted on the government instituting certain domestic reforms. When they were not forthcoming, the United States forced President Eladro Victoria to resign. By using its power of recognition, writes Bemis, the United States was able to get rid of a constitutional but unruly government.

Welles has described what he considered the fatal, but by no means uncommon, error lying at the root of United States foreign policy. It was typified by a way of thinking all too common to this very day: that standards of government which are successfully applied in the United States must necessarily be relevant to all peoples, wherever they may be, even those alien in every sense to American traditions. In denouncing the State Department's activities under Secretary of State Knox, Welles criticized a basic ingredient of the concept of great-power primacy. United States

28 Welles, n. 13, p. 919

policy in the Caribbean, he wrote (and his words have special significance today) was 'due in great part to a patronizing sense of superiority, which utterly ignored that another inheritance and other standards might possess their own excellence.'[29]

By 1911 Latin American public opinion, already exasperated by United States interventions in the Caribbean, was further irritated by a Senate resolution. This was the so-called Lodge corollary to the Monroe Doctrine. It declared that if non-American powers purchased or gained control of potentially strategic territory on any part of North or South America, the United States would regard it as an unfriendly act. To the other American republics, here was an example of a high-handed, unilateral pronouncement by the United States. The resolution concerned the entire Western Hemisphere, a vast part of which was under the sovereign jurisdiction of Latin American governments. Yet the unchanging concept of great-power paternalism continued to relegate them to a secondary position, even in matters affecting their own security.

29 Ibid. p. 920

4
Woodrow Wilson and the idea of equality

It has been well said that the gap between what you want and what circumstances require constitutes the dilemma and paradox of American foreign policy. This definition offers a basis for understanding President Wilson. For the chief of state (like all of us) faced the unavoidable predicament of inhabiting at the same time two opposing worlds: the real and the nominal. This chapter discusses the influence of those two worlds as they relate to inter-American affairs and the Paris Peace Conference.

INTER-AMERICAN AFFAIRS

On 27 October 1913, seven months after he took office as president of the United States, Woodrow Wilson promised a new policy towards the Latin American republics. At first glance it implied a complete renunciation of the concept of great-power primacy. In Mobile, Alabama, Wilson said the future for the hemisphere was going to be very different from the past. The United States had to prove itself the friend and champion of the other American states 'upon terms of equality and honor.' And, he added later, not on the idea that 'we are going to be your big brother whether you want us to be or not.'[1]

By January 1916 these ideas were embodied in a proposed Pan American

1 Wilson, W. *The Public Papers of Woodrow Wilson*, 'The New Democracy,' 1913–1917, Baker, R.S. and Dodd, W. (eds.), New York, 1926, vol. 1, 64, 67; Wilson to Mexican Editors, White House, cited by Miller, D.H. *My Diary at the Conference of Paris*, set no. 23, printed by the author, New York, 1924, vol. xx, 137

treaty and brought to the attention of delegates from all twenty-one American states at the Second Pan American Scientific Congress. The provisions of the treaty, Wilson told the gathering, were 'based upon the principles of absolute political equality among the States, equality of right, not equality of indulgence.'[2] By referring to 'absolute political equality' Wilson touched the right chord. But what did it mean? In domestic society all citizens had general political rights identical with each other. But in international society states might be said to be politically equal insofar as they had the right to lead an independent existence free from outside interference in their internal affairs. If states could be said to 'vote' and if their 'votes' were said to have equal weight, it was only because in international conferences an independent sovereign state could not be bound against its will. Surely, Wilson's use of the term was no more than a Pickwickian reference to the right of the American states to independence and territorial integrity. But the phrase served to lend greater credibility to the nominal world invoked by Ruy Barbosa, where all peoples enjoyed equal political rights.

The purpose of the treaty, according to the president, was that 'if any of us, the United States included, violates the political independence or the territorial integrity of any of the others, all the others will jump on her.' The treaty would mean the end of American guardianship over its sister republics and the beginning of a partnership. As it turned out, treaty negotiations never really got off the ground; for in spite of Wilson's offer of friendship to the Latin American republics on terms of equality, the United States retained its patronizing sense of superiority.

When Aldous Huxley wrote that the co-existence of incompatibilities is a commonplace of daily experience, he was not thinking of the concepts of equality and great-power primacy. But he could have been, for all during the period in which Wilson and members of his administration were solemnly proclaiming the absolute equality of the American republics, Washington based its Latin American policy on a distinction between great and responsible powers on the one hand, and small, irresponsible powers on the other. When order broke down in the Dominican Republic, Wilson ordered its military occupation. When trouble arose in Haiti, Wilson sent in the Marines. By the terms of a treaty dictated by the State Department, the United States retained control over the Haitian government until 1930. Wilson found the Marines in Nicaragua when he took office, and kept them there. Later, Secretary of State William Bryan negotiated a treaty with the Nicaraguan government so seriously infringing on its sovereignty that it was denounced by the Central American Court of Justice.

2 *Secretary General*, 94, 97, 98

Above all others, the intervention in Mexico raised the most striking contradictions. In 1913 General Victoriana Huerta overthrew the Mexican government and had himself chosen as president. Accepted international practice was to grant diplomatic recognition to a revolutionary government as soon as it had shown itself able to maintain law and order and willing to fulfil its international obligations. Wilson departed from this practice, introducing a moral judgment as a basis for recognition. Even though Britain, France, Italy, Germany, and at least thirteen other foreign powers recognized his government, Wilson called Huerta a 'traitor,' a 'scoundrel,' and refused to recognize his 'government of butchers.'[3]

With the principle of non-recognition as a weapon, Wilson decided to strike a blow at governments not chosen by popular vote. He advised the British that he would force Huerta from power and use every influence to get Mexicans a better government. To the charge that they were not fitted for self-government, he insisted that every people was fitted and that he would teach members of the South American republics how to elect good men. Under such circumstances the concept of the absolute equality of all American states gave way to the responsibilities of the US to Mexico as its neighbour and as the nation of 'paramount influence' in the hemisphere.

By 1914 the use of the armed forces of the United States appeared to be the only way for Wilson to impose on an obstinate reality his ideal of representative government for the Mexican people. The situation in Mexico had deteriorated after Huerta had arrested several American sailors who had landed in Tampico without permission. Wilson ordered the North Atlantic and Pacific fleets to proceed to Mexico at once. When Washington learned that a German ship was bringing arms and ammunition to Huerta at Vera Cruz, US troops landed at the port and after bloody fighting, seized the custom house and impounded the arms shipment. In a wave of anti-American feeling, mobs and troops looted and pillaged American property, and riots spread to Costa Rica, Guatemala, Ecuador, and as far away as Chile and Uruguay.

Unable to obtain arms or credit in the United States or Europe, and cut off by US troops from the revenue of the Mexican ports of Vera Cruz and Tampico, Huerta was finally forced out of office. His principal rival, Venustino Carranza, leader of the Constitutional Party, took over as provisional president. Within six months Wilson was ready to forget the past. In his Jackson Day address to the American people (8 January 1915) he reaffirmed the fundamental principle that every people has the right to determine its own form of government. 'It is none of my business,' he told

3 Link, A.S. *Wilson, The New Freedom*, Princeton, 1956, pp. 350, 360, 379

his audience, 'and it is none of yours, how they [the people of Mexico] go about the business. The country is theirs. The Government is theirs ... And so far as my influence goes while I am President nobody shall interfere with them.'[4]

In spite of these remarks, Wilson continued trying to foist his own ideas on Carranza about the proper way to form a government. Such interference in Mexico's internal affairs, the provisional president rejected outright. Unprepared to use force a second time, and convinced at last that Carranza was in full control of the government, Wilson shifted ground. The special responsibility of the United States towards the Mexican people gave way to a willingness to consult with other American republics. As a result, on 18 October 1915, the US joined Argentina, Brazil, Chile, Uruguay, Guatemala, Colombia, and Nicaragua in recognizing Carranza as president of Mexico. The happy ending did not last. In June 1916 the Mexican bandit and revolutionary leader, Pancho Villa, raided US territory, killed a score of Americans, and retreated across the Mexican border. The US army pursued him and American soldiers soon clashed with Mexican government troops. Relations between the two countries worsened to a point just short of war. This last intervention completely disillusioned Latin America about US intentions to respect their equality as sovereign states. Whatever good-will may have been created by Wilson's acting jointly with the other republics in recognizing Carranza had now been dissipated. By 1917, when the United States entered the war against Germany, interest in the Pan American treaty and in the meaning of the absolute 'political equality' of the American states faded away.

One of Wilson's biographers, A.S. Link, wondered what Wilson and Bryan had in mind when proposing the treaty. Both men, he believed, were unwilling to do more than pay lip service to the idea of equality. Neither was prepared to renounce the right of intervention.[5] Perhaps a better way to understand them is by viewing the right to intervene and the Pan American treaty as conflicting conceptual approaches. When the United States brought its superior power to bear, not only did it prove unworkable but it left bloodshed and bitterness in its wake. When Wilson based policy on the alternative idea, he restored a measure of confidence, only to find the gap between concept and circumstance widening once more. What Wilson and Bryan experienced was the stubborness with which the world as it is

4 Note 1, supra, *The Public Papers of Woodrow Wilson*, pp. 247–8
5 Note 3, supra, pp. 328–9

seeks to prevent the nominal world from being realized. Later, in Paris, Wilson would discover again the inescapable contradictions inherent in living in two worlds that fail to correspond.

THE PARIS PEACE CONFERENCE, 1919

Mythologizing, according to Carl Jung, is a 'healing and valid activity; it gives existence a glamour which we would not like to do without. Nor is there any good reason why we should.'[6] This insight into human nature comes to mind when we consider the tremendous uplift given to large masses of men and women during World War I when the chief executive of the United States revealed his vision of a more perfect international order based upon the equality of all nation-states, large and small.

In what President Wilson called 'the new world in which we live' there appeared to be no room for the alternative concept of great-power primacy. After referring to the method of settling international political problems at the Congress of Vienna, he roundly criticized the arrogation of responsibility by the Great Powers to themselves. He promised that there would be no return to a world where peace was made by arrangements among powerful states. All the parties to the war were going to join in the settlement of every issue. The peace to be eventually arrived at was not going to be a bargain between sovereigns, but one that was right, and fair, and just.[7]

The president went on to develop an image of international relations carried on among distinct, indivisible entities called 'peoples,' each with a single will capable of being expressed. By the fall of 1918, the war 'individual statesmen may have started' had become 'a peoples' war' in which 'peoples of all sorts and races' were involved. In the tradition of Rousseau, Mazzini, and Barbosa, Wilson elevated peoples into an entity with inherent virtue. He declared a new age was beginning in which the very same standards of conduct and the very same responsibility for wrong doing would be observed among nations as were observed among individual human beings. Implicit in the equation between corporate and individual personality was the idea that each people possessed a transcendental essence. From this followed the inviolable right of all peoples, strong and weak, to enjoy liberty and equality. Here was the root basis for applying a principle of justice that, in Wilson's words, 'plays no favorites and knows no standard but the equal rights of the several peoples concerned ...'[8]

6 Jung, C.J. 'On Life After Death,' *The Atlantic*, Dec. 1962, 40
7 *War and Peace*, pp. 179–80
8 Ibid. pp. 254, 11, 257

We may ponder, at this point, an analysis of democratic principles opposed to Wilson's view. Since, at best, our concepts have only approximate validity, the question is not primarily whether what follows reveals some fatal flaw in Wilson's ideal, but rather which concept of the role of the will of the people is more closely related to reality. George F. Kennan, writing in 1956, viewed every government as representing 'the momentary product of the never-ending competition for political power within the respective national framework.' In short, government 'speaks only for a portion of the nation: for one political faction or coalition of factions. There is always another portion of the nation that is in opposition to it and either challenges its right to speak for the nation as a whole or accepts it only grudgingly and unhappily.' In Kennan's words, 'What emerges ... from the hopper of the political process in each country and proceeds to speak for the country in international affairs is always to some degree a corrupted voice ...' Unlike Wilson's vision of a world of peoples with no other standard of justice but the equal rights of all, Kennan saw a world where the relations between governments were 'largely the product of the follies and ambitions and brutalities of that minority of the human race which is always attracted by the possibility of exercising power over the remainder of it in whatever political framework the age provides.'[9]

To come back to Wilson, his logic was equally applicable to the corporate personality of Germany. The German people was not the enemy of the allied peoples. Rather the enemy was 'the power of a vast military establishment controlled by an irresponsible government ... This power is not the German people. It is the ruthless master of the German People.' Somehow the government had corrupted the people's will, but it had never succeeded in destroying its essential worth. For this reason Wilson was not concerned that the German people may have 'submitted with temporary zest' to the dominations of the Imperial government. His ability to distinguish the Kaiser's government from the German people permitted Wilson to apply to the German people the same principle of liberty and equality applicable to all other peoples. He wished for the German people 'only to accept a place of equality among the peoples of the world ...'[10]

In December 1918, Wilson left for Europe to attend the Paris Peace Conference. Some evidence of the extent to which the concept of corporate personality had impressed itself on Wilson may be seen in the notes of Dr I.

9 Kennan, G.F. 'History and Diplomacy as Viewed by a Diplomatist,' *Rev. Pol.*, 1956, 170, 173
10 *War and Peace*, pp. 94, 161

Bowman, taken at a press conference aboard the ship carrying the president to Europe. Asked about the form a new Polish government should take, Wilson said he favoured *'any government they damned pleased*, and that he was for imposing upon them *no other provision* than those which applied to individuals ...'[11]

Once in Europe Wilson travelled, among other places, to Italy. It is hardly surprising to find him before the monument to Mazzini in Genoa. Here he expressed delight to feel he was taking at least a small part in accomplishing the realisation of ideals to which Mazzini devoted his life. He paid his respects both in a 'spirit of veneration,' and, he hoped, a spirit of 'emulation.'[12]

As Prime Minister Eduard Beneš of Czechoslovakia later said, 'the League [of Nations] is the symbol of the principle of international democracy, of democracy among nations, and is *ipso facto* an attempt to introduce into international relations the principles and the methods employed in democratic States and in the mutual relations of private individuals.'[13]

THE COVENANT OF THE LEAGUE OF NATIONS

In Paris, a plenary session of the Peace Conference was held on 25 January 1919. Its purpose was to organize methods of work and to appoint various commissions, including one on reparations and another to draft the Covenant of the League of Nations. Wilson opened this session, attended by the five Great Powers (the United States, Britain, France, Italy, and Japan) and by the representatives of twenty small states, the four British Dominions, and India. '[We] are here,' he told his audience, 'to see that every people in the world shall choose its own master and govern its destinies, not as we wish but as it wishes.' When he finished, Leon Bourgeois, speaking for France, took Wilson's cue. The president has just told us, he said, 'that we do not, that you, Gentlemen, do not represent governments alone, but peoples.'[14]

After these preliminaries, M. Paul Hymans, the representative of Belgium, brought into the open the underlying tension between the conflicting ideas of equality and great-power primacy. Hymans raised the issue when he asked Wilson how the small states would be represented on the various

11 *Miller Diary*, vol. I, 370–71 and notes
12 *War and Peace*, p. 371
13 League of Nations, *Official J.* Records of the Fourth Assembly, plenary meetings, 29 September 1923, 145
14 *Miller Diary*, vol. IV, 56, 59

commissions of the Peace Conference. The five Great Powers, replied Wilson, had decided that each of them would have two delegates on the commissions, and that all the other states, including the British Dominions and India, would have a total of five delegates.[15]

These remarks struck Pandias Calogeras of Brazil as odd. He expressed surprise at constantly being told that decisions had already been made. The proper body to take decisions was the conference itself. Sir Robert Borden of Canada agreed wholeheartedly. Every one of the small states, he said, kept asking, 'By whom have those decisions been reached and by what authority?' This, of course, was precisely the same complaint made by small states a century earlier at the Congress of Vienna. They, too, wanted to know by what right the Great Powers spoke in the name of all the sovereigns of Europe whom they did not even bother to consult.

In 1919 it was left to Georges Clemenceau, president of the Plenary Session, to explain. In terms reminiscent of the Great Powers at Vienna, he said, 'Well, we have decided, as regards the Commissions, in the same way as we have decided to summon the present Conference ... The Five Great Powers whose action has to be justified before you today are in a position to justify it. The British Prime Minister just now reminded me that on the day when the war ceased the Allies had 12,000,000 men fighting on various fronts. This entitles them to consideration.' And Clemenceau, with characteristic bluntness, added 'we might have been selfish enough to consult only each other. It was our right.'[16]

This cavalier attitude toward the concept of equality, according to one authority, brought the small powers to a state of almost open revolt. Not only were they to be accorded limited representation on the various commissions, but it soon became evident that the Great Powers intended to run the League as well. The tension between conflicting concepts reached a peak during the 4 and 5 February meetings of the commission on a League of Nations. The basic issue was the composition of the executive council. Originally, the United States and Britain had not seen eye to eye. Wilson was prepared to give small states some representation on the council. The British were opposed. On 21 January 1919, Lord Robert Cecil, one of the most highly respected members of the British delegation to the conference, had a conversation with D.H. Miller, legal adviser to the United States Mission to Paris under Colonel House's direction. According to Miller, Cecil did not agree with Wilson's plan. He thought, wrote Miller, 'that the

15 Ibid. 65
16 Ibid. 77

Great Powers must run the League and that it was just as well to recognize it flatly as not.'[17]

Lord Cecil remembered the Second Hague Peace Conference. He recalled how the appeal to the principle of absolute equality made by Ruy Barbosa of Brazil had wrecked plans for a permanent arbitral court of justice. He considered Barbosa's extension of the concept as preposterous and totally incompatible with the concept of a league of nations. However appealing the ideal may have been, and Cecil believed the principle of equality had some merit, he refused to force reality into an inhospitable mould. He made it quite clear that, if the small states entered the League at all, they would have to abandon the doctrines of Barbosa. Cecil convinced Wilson. The commission continued to use as a basis for discussion a proposal for a league known as the Hurst-Miller draft. It limited membership on the council to the Great Powers and those states, if any, which the Great Powers chose to add.

Oddly enough, President Wilson's secretary of state, Robert Lansing, was one of the most vigorous supporters of the concept of equality. Indeed, by his outspoken opposition to the idea of great-power primacy he had already lost the confidence of the president and within a year was forced to resign. It all started at the time of Wilson's original draft for a covenant of a league of nations. The president conceived of a council of great powers with a minority role for the small states. Lansing attacked the plan for establishing 'an international oligarchy to direct and control world affairs.' What President Wilson was advocating, he said, was that 'the strong should, as a matter of right recognized by treaty, possess a dominant voice in international councils.' Repeatedly, the United States had declared itself in favour of the equality of independent states. Wilson's draft appeared to Lansing as a complete reversal of policy. He, for one, found it not only difficult, but impossible, to explain in a satisfactory way. The kind of organization Lansing would support would be one whose 'basic principle was equality of nations. No special privileges are granted to the major powers in the conduct of the organization. The rights and obligations of one member of the League are no more and no less than those of every other member. It is based on international democracy and denies international aristocracy.' In short, the most serious defect in President Wilson's draft was one of principle. 'It was the practical denial of the equality of nations in the regulation of international affairs ...'[18]

17 Ibid. vol I, 337
18 Lansing, R. *The Peace Negotiations*, Boston, 1921, pp. 85, 58, 164

As we know, Lansing's conceptual thinking was rarely characterized by such rigidity. In fact, when he considered the concept of self-determination he quickly spotted its basic weakness: the absence of any qualification. Self-determination, he said, was a declaration of principle which sounded true and in the abstract may have been true. It had the advantage of appealing to man's innate sense of what is morally fair, but when the time came to apply it to every case, such an unqualified right would surely become a source of domestic disorder and a cause of rebellion.[19]

Here, then, was a public servant, who appeared to recognize the dilemma involved in adjusting abstract principles to an all but unknowable reality. Yet he was unprepared to make any exception when the principle of equality was at stake. For, according to Lansing, international controversies had to be decided according to one standard: strict legal justice. If the principle of equality, 'whatever its basis in fact,' was not preserved, force not law, the power to act not the right to act, would become the basic principle of the world organization. If this happened, said Lansing, the League of Nations would simply be an imitation of all previous congresses and concerts of Great Powers.

When the small states met to select their delegates to the commission on a league of nations, the Great Powers' attempt to weaken the concept of equality was uppermost in the mind of the delegate from Brazil. He had represented his country previously at many inter-American conferences, he told the delegates, thus proving his qualifications to discuss the concept. Equality was a great ideal, he said, which the entire world supported. Merely to say 'League of Nations' was to say 'a system of equality as between all nations.' Even though discussion had not officially started among members of the commission, Calogeras believed that the principle of absolute equality as the basic premise of the League had already been completely established.[20]

As for President Wilson, his chief aim was to get a league of nations. Even if, as Wilson had said, 'no one asks or expects anything more than an equality of rights,' the primary requirement to make the league a success in the real world, was great-power support based upon a clear recognition of the difference between those that are powerful and those that are weak. For the time being, Wilson told members of the commission that the question of representation of small powers was extremely delicate. And he reminded

19 Ibid. p. 192
20 *Miller Diary*, vol. IV, 90, 92

the small states of the greater burden falling on the Great Powers if a league member were attacked. Certainly, the interest of small states was involved, he said, but not to the same extent as the interest of the great.

Hymans of Belgium then tried to equate the small powers collectively with the Great Powers collectively. Thus, if the Great Powers had five representatives on the council, the small powers should also have five. And if one day there were six or more Great Powers, the idea of equality would be met by increasing the representation of small states pari passu. But Léon Bourgeois challenged Hyman's arithmetic. When he did his sums he found the small states made an imposing group. In terms of population and power, however, they did not come near to the Great Powers. With all this Cecil concurred. If all the members, great and small, were going to be treated as equals, he said, some great powers would surely refuse to join. The real security for small states, he insisted, had to rest, in the final analysis, on the sense of justice of the Great Powers.[21]

As the delegates struggled with the task of reconciling the opposing ideas, one thing became clear. If the small powers had to recognize Cecil's warning that 'absolute equality must be set aside, as Parliaments would not accept it,' the Great Powers had to admit that whatever reality the concept of great-power primacy represented, they simply could not ignore the doctrines of Barbosa. They offered the small states two council seats. Was a compromise between the alternative concepts possible? Milenko R. Vesnitch of Serbia was disposed to bargain. He was not going to make his acceptance or rejection of the council 'hang on a question of numbers.' Originally, he had insisted on the council being composed of five small and five Great Powers. Two seats on the council for the small states were too few. Five places were perhaps too many. He would settle for four. But Hymans continued to stress equality of representation. He appealed to something called 'the world of right' and said this world would be impressed by his suggestion of equality. Finally he gave way, and agreed to settle for four seats on the council.

Cecil did not approve of this bargaining. The question of numbers was a tough one to decide. He could not bring himself to say that two were better than five or that four were better than three. He stuck to his original stand: two seats for the small states. Wilson did not see how any injustice could be suffered by the small states simply because they only had two representatives on the council. Article 10 contained a guaranty. As far as he was

21 Ibid. vol v, 97-8, 100-2

concerned the concept of collective security was 'not only a recognition of the equality of nations ... [but] a vindication of the equality of nations.'[22] What both Cecil and the president were trying to get across was that, when all was said and done, the only real security for small states rested on the sense of justice of the great ones. It was no use to accuse the Great Powers of trying to create another Holy Alliance, as Hymans did. Nor did his argument about trying to impress the world by the fairness of the covenant carry any weight. It was left to F. Larnaude of France to bring the discussion down to a less exalted level. The problem of representation on the council, he said, could not be discussed in the abstract. Sentiment had to be ruled out. What counted was cold fact. And the cold fact was that Britain, France, Japan, Italy, and the United States won the war.

As it turned out, members of the commission on a league of nations finally decided to compromise. Two organs were created: the Council and the Assembly. In theory, the Council embodied the concept of great-power primacy. The privileged position of the Great Powers, referred to in the Covenant as the Principal Allied and Associated Powers, was recognized by giving each of them a permanent seat. All other members of the League were represented by four non-permanent members. The Council had primary authority to mediate international disputes, to advise on the means by which aggression would be met and, if necessary, to recommend the military contribution of each member. The Assembly may be said to have embodied the concept of absolute equality. It consisted of all members of the League. No distinction was made between permanent and non-permanent seats. Each state had one vote, and each vote had the same weight.

Actually, the theoretical distinction between the two organs is not quite as pat as it sounds. In the Council the Great Powers ended up sharing responsibility with the representatives of the small states. Oddly enough, Hymans' idea that the Great Powers taken collectively equal the small states taken together, in effect, prevailed at first. For when the United States refused to join the League, the remaining Great Powers had a total of four seats on the Council, and the small states had exactly the same number. This equality lasted for roughly three years when the original concept of minority membership for small states collapsed. A reverse and, of course, unintended process set in. By 1933 small-state representation on the Council increased to six. In 1936 it had jumped to eleven. Only during

22 Ibid. 102–3

the early years of the League did the Great Powers have numerical equality with the small powers.

If the Great Powers could be said to have enjoyed a superior status, it was marked primarily by their right to permanent seats on the Council. For the idea of the perfect equality of states received unexpected support from the acceptance of an old principle of international relations, the concept of sovereignty, whereby the Great Powers deduced that, in a world security organization, no state could be bound against its will. Hence the rule of unanimity. Cecil, who in January had so boldly advocated a league run by the Great Powers, was trapped by the rule. Hardly a month later, when the compromise of four seats for the small states was being worked out, he proclaimed: 'All international decisions must, by the nature of things, be unanimous.'[23] None of the Great Powers questioned his pronouncement. Even assuming that by acting together they could have kept the peace, the admission of small states to the Council on an equal footing with them made it impossible for the Council to become what the originators had designed it to be: the great-power organ of a new Concert of Europe.

As it turned out, disunity plagued the relations of the Great Powers from the outset. Britain and France disagreed over how to treat Germany. An ideological barrier separated Russia from the other Great Powers. The United States refused to join the League. Germany, potentially the most powerful state in Europe was not admitted until 1926; and the Soviet Union excluded itself until 1934. By this time the Assembly had developed great authority. In particular, the settlement of disputes, previously the province of the Council, had become associated with the Assembly. This development tended to increase its reputation, so that soon the principal organ of the League was widely considered to be not the Council but the Assembly.

The League of Nations handled more than a score of serious, though relatively minor, disputes. When major problems arose, for example, Japan's seizure of Manchuria (1931), Italy's invasion of Ethiopia (1935), Italian, German, and Russian participation in the Spanish Civil War (1936–9), Hitler's occupation of the Rhineland (1936), hostilities between Japan and China (1937), and the annexation by Nazi Germany of Austria (1938), the League was helpless. Thus we find neither the concept of great-power primacy nor the concept of equality corresponded closely enough to external reality. As a result of the inadequacy of conceptual thinking, no effective means of preserving world peace was possible.

23 Ibid. 101

THE JAPANESE EQUALITY AMENDMENT

To understand the Japanese equality amendment of the Covenant of the League of Nations it is necessary to keep in mind the following facts. First, the Japanese had long been humiliated, especially in the United States and in the British Dominions, by legislation discriminating against their nationals. United States naturalization laws excluded Japanese and other Asians. The State of California, in particular, restricted the entry and limited the length of residence of all Japanese citizens. On the Pacific coast of Canada and as far away as Australia the same story was repeated. Frequently, Japanese away from home found themselves barred from employment, restricted from owning property and, at times, denied the same legal protection afforded other nationals. This discrimination, it goes without saying, struck at their essential dignity as human beings. It implied that the Japanese were not the equals of Americans and Europeans but were members of an inferior race. Second, early in 1917, the British Admiralty, being short of surface vessels to escort its war convoys through the Mediterranean, asked Japan for a flotilla of torpedo boats. Japan agreed on condition that, when Germany was defeated, she would receive all rights possessed by Germany in Kiao Chau and in the Chinese province of Shantung. In a secret treaty the British accepted this deal. Subsequently, it was ratified by the French as well.

At the fifth meeting of the Commission on a League of Nations (7 February 1919), the Japanese delegate equated the equality of nations with racial equality. Informally, Baron Makino suggested inserting in the Covenant the following provision: 'The equality of nations being a basic principle of the League of Nations, the High Contracting Parties agree to accord, as soon as possible, to all alien nationals of State members of the League, equal and just treatment in every respect, making no distinction, either in law or in fact, on account of their race or nationality.'

In his diary of the Peace Conference, D.H. Miller recorded a conversation among himself, Colonel House, and Arthur Balfour regarding the Japanese proposal. 'Colonel House handed me a pencil memorandum,' wrote Miller, 'which he showed to Mr Balfour, commencing with the proposition taken from the Declaration of Independence, that all men are created equal.'[24] Balfour told House and Miller that the concept that all men are created equal was an eighteenth-century proposition which he certainly did not believe was true. In a sense it might be true that all men of

24 *Miller Drafting*, vol. 1, 183

a particular nation were created equal, but he did not believe that a man in Central Africa was created equal to a European. Balfour realized that once the equality of nations has been proclaimed, whether intentionally or not, racial equality has also been proclaimed. This giant step he was not prepared to take.

Colonel House explained that the Japanese could not go to Africa, China, Siberia, in fact, any white country. Yet, as a growing nation, they had to be permitted to go somewhere. Balfour understood what was involved. He knew the problem for international order arising from an anti-Japanese policy. The tension between the alternative concepts of racial equality and racial hierarchy posed a real dilemma. For the moment, all Balfour could express was a great deal of sympathy for the Japanese view. Colonel House then told Miller to prepare a substitute proposal. On the basis of the instructions he received, Miller was unable to draft anything satisfactory. Whatever he wrote had no particular legal effect, he said, simply because it was not intended to have any.

Meanwhile, the Commission on a League of Nations discussed the merits of inserting a 'religious' article in the Covenant. Wilson favoured it. Its object was to proclaim for all men complete freedom of worship and conscience. However, members found the proposal troublesome. The delegates saw more clearly than Wilson the enormous difficulties it represented in any form. This led to a revised British version, a redraft by Wilson, and finally the following version to be inserted as Article XXI:

The High Contracting Parties agree that they will not prohibit or interfere with the free exercise of any creed, religion or belief whose practices are not inconsistent with public order or public morals, and that no person within their respective jurisdictions shall be molested in life, liberty or the pursuit of happiness by reason of his adherence to any such creed, religion or belief.

At the tenth meeting of the Commission, the appropriateness of Article XXI was questioned. Most of the members of the commission agreed with the article in principle but found the drafting problems so difficult it seemed better to suppress it. Then the word was spread that President Wilson strongly desired to see it included and the delegates felt they had no choice but to agree. At this point, Baron Makino seized the opportunity to push the concept of racial equality. He found racial and religious animosities a fruitless source of trouble, often leading to war. Matters of religion and race seemed to go hand in hand. Why not include in the religious article a provision on the equal treatment of all nationals regardless of race or religion? The Baron well knew how delicate was the question of racial prejudice. He did not propose, therefore, the immediate realization of the ideal of equal treatment among peoples. His suggestion, he insisted, was no more than an invitation to states to examine the question and to devise some method of breaking the deadlock confronting different peoples. Every national, he said, would 'like to feel and in fact demands that he should be placed on an equal footing with people he undertakes to defend even with his life.'[25]

There was at least one delegate, W.H. Hughes of Australia, who was prepared to fight the amendment. The problem of Japanese immigration in his country involved the play of deep human passions; so much so, that Hughes was preparing an inflammatory speech for the Plenary Session designed to keep the proposed amendment out of the Covenant. Under instructions from the British government, Chairman Cecil had no alternative but to support Hughes against Makino, whatever his own personal feelings may have been. What was involved, Cecil told the delegates, was a matter concerning serious problems within the British Empire. Indeed, it was so highly controversial that, in spite of the noble motives of the Japanese, he thought it wiser to postpone discussion. The majority of delegates sided with Cecil. When President Wilson realized what was happening he, too, opposed Article xxi and it was eliminated from the Covenant. By his racial equality amendment Baron Makino helped make a proclamation on equal rights for all religions impossible.

In the matter of the suppression of Article xxi, it is interesting to consider the comment of Abraham Lincoln on the meaning of equality in the Declaration of Independence. Said Lincoln, the Founding Fathers 'meant to set up a standard maxim for free society, which should be familiar to all, revered by all; constantly looked to, constantly labored for, and even though never perfectly attained, constantly approximated, and thereby ... augmenting the happiness and value of life to all people of all colors everywhere.'[26]

Members of the commission, however, found more at stake than merely setting up a maxim for international society. If the racial equality proposal was included in Article xxi, they feared League members would be under an obligation to pass legislation regarding the immigration of Japanese and Eastern Europeans. According to the *Washington Post*, the proposed amendment to the Covenant would lead to demands for the admission of

25 Ibid. 324–5.
26 *The Living Lincoln*, n. 33, p. 204

Japanese – including coolies – into all countries on the basis of equality.[27]

Baron Makino appreciated the full extent of the opposition in the commission. He decided to bide his time and make a new approach. On 11 April 1919, he chose the fifteenth and final meeting of the commission, with President Wilson acting as chairman, to raise the subject of racial equality. 'I think it only reasonable,' he told the delegates, 'that the principle of the equality of nations and the just treatment of their nationals should be laid down as a fundamental basis of future relations in this world organization. If this reasonable and just claim is now denied, it will, in the eyes of those peoples with reason to be keenly interested, have the significance of a reflection on their quality and status.'[28] The baron was not blind to reality. He no longer sought an amendment to the Covenant. What he wanted was simply to insert a clause in the Preamble to the Covenant, italicized below, to make it read:

In order to secure international peace and security by the acceptance of obligations not to resort to the use of armed force, by the prescription of open, just, and honorable relations between nations, *by the endorsement of the principle of the equality of Nations and the just treatment of their nationals*, by the firm establishment of the understanding of international law ... the Power signatory to this Covenant adopt the Constitution of the League of Nations.

Robert Cecil continued to interpret the italicized words as a plea for racial equality. Mindful of the immigration problem in Australia, and of the extreme position taken by its delegate Hughes, Cecil opposed the insertion even though he, personally, was in full accord with the idea advanced by the Japanese delegation. Any attempt to solve the racial question, he said, opened the door to interference in the domestic affairs of a state. This is why it was impossible to include in the Covenant principles which were unquestionably right. He reminded the delegates that Japan's permanent seat on the Council was evidence of her complete equality with the other Great Powers. This being so, the Japanese could always raise questions concerning the equality of races and the equality of nations before the Council itself.

The logic behind Cecil's view was this: a yellow nation was equal to a white nation. But the question of whether a yellow individual was equal to a white individual either was not to be answered in the affirmative, in spite of

27 *Miller Diary*, vol. VI, 441–2; vol. I, 187
28 *Miller Drafting*, vol. 2, 388

the doctrine that all men are created equal, or was to be regarded as a judgment falling within the domestic jurisdiction of each state. The parallel with the intellectual confusion that beset the United States before the Civil War is plain.

When Viscount Chinda, the other Japanese delegate, said Japan only sought to introduce the principle of equality of nations and the just treatment of nationals into the Preamble, he won over many of the delegates. V.E. Orlando of Italy and Léon Bourgeois, who had previously opposed a separate article to the Covenant, now changed their stand. They argued that simply to endorse the idea by inserting some lines in the Preamble was not objectionable. No one could interpret that as putting members under an express obligation regarding racial equality. Moreover, an indisputable principle of justice was involved; surely it belonged in the Preamble. Cecil remained unconvinced even though the Japanese proposal was as mild and inoffensive as one could wish, for he knew it would ignite the latent demagoguery in Hughes. And once Hughes started to whip up passions in Plenary Session, as he would certainly do, the creation of the League might be in jeopardy. Colonel House urged Wilson to stick with the British.

In the opinion of Harold Nicolson, a member of the British delegation, the opposition of Hughes rescued Wilson 'by the skin of his teeth.' For the equality of man, he wrote, 'implied the equality of the yellow man with the white man, might even imply the terrific theory of the equality of the white man with the black ... /and/ no American Senate would ever dream of ratifying any Covenant which enshrined so dangerous a principle.'[29]

Wilson took a double tack. First, he approached the question from the point of view of what was the wisest thing to do. No one, he said, wished to deny the equality of nations. No one wished to deny the just treatment of the nationals of any nation. The trouble was not with the members of the commission, but with the discussion that would arise in Plenary Session. Wilson was for quieting discussions that raise national differences and racial prejudices. The harmless sounding words would not be treated on their merits in Plenary Session; rather they would ignite the flames of prejudice. The sentiment of the delegates towards each other was not in question; nor was the position of the delegates with regard to the abstract principle of the equality of nations. What might very well be in question was the establishment of the League itself.[30]

With proper deference having been paid to the demands of existential

29 Nicolson, H. *Peacemaking, 1919*, London, 1933, p. 145
30 *Miller Drafting*, vol. 1, 462–3

circumstances by one on whose shoulders rested the heavy burden of responsibility, Wilson went on to clarify the concept of equality as he understood it. Leaving no doubt that the League was based on the principle of the equality of nations, he related it to the the idea of collective security. The League of Nations, he said, was 'the first serious and systematic attempt made in the world to put nations on a footing of equality with each other in their international relations.' It was an attempt to secure for the weak the protection of the strong in case of attack. This was not only a recognition of the concept of equality, it was 'a vindication of the equality of nations.' How would could anyone, therefore, question the basic principle on which the Covenant rested?[31]

When Wilson had finished, Makino insisted on putting the matter to a vote. Wilson, evidently, was not convincing, for out of the seventeen members of the commission a majority of eleven voted in favour of adding the disputed clause to the Preamble. It was a clear victory for the Japanese and the concept of equality. But Wilson had no intention of applying principles of majority rule to nation-states, even if some of his previous declarations might have led to such an inference. Undoubtedly, he saw the very institution of a league of nations threatened. As chairman of the commission, he ruled that decisions had to be unanimous. In this way the idea of equality of nations and the just treatment of nationals was kept out of the Preamble. There was nothing the majority could do. They heard Wilson assure everyone that, in view of the other provisions of the Covenant, no one could interpret the final result of the commission as a rejection of the principle of equality.

On 28 April 1919, before a plenary session of the Paris Peace Conference, Baron Makino reviewed the problem to international order posed by the existence of racial inequality. But he did no more than express his poignant regret at the failure of the commission to approve the principle he had proposed. James Shotwell, a member of President Wilson's personal staff under Colonel House, described Makino's refusal to contest the commission's decision as a very statesmanlike attitude. There is, however, more to the story than that. What Shotwell apparently overlooked was the meeting, earlier on the same day, of Wilson, Lloyd George, Clemenceau, and Balfour. According to Sir Maurice Hankey, who acted as secretary at the meeting, Baron Makino had clearly, but with great delicacy, demanded a decision on Japanese war claims. The baron said he was asked to agree to a league even though his country could not get recognition of the principle

31 Ibid. 463

of equal racial treatment. If, however, Japanese claims to Shantung were met, this omission would be overlooked. If, on the other hand, Japan regarded itself as ill-treated over Shantung, Makino could not predict what line the Japanese delegation would take.[32]

At this point, Wilson feared Japan might refuse to adhere to the League. Italy, we recall, had only recently abandoned the Peace Conference because of the refusal of the Great Powers to satisfy its territorial claims. Could Wilson afford another defection? And, if Japan quit the conference, was it not likely that she would at once conclude a military alliance with Russia and Germany? Wilson was aware of the treaties signed by Britain and France to give Japan all German rights in Shantung, treaties he was in no position to repudiate. As he was to explain later, Japan was now in physical possession of Shantung. To take it away, the United States would have to fight not only Japan but Great Britain and France as well. This explains why a few hours before the Plenary Session Balfour was directed to tell Makino that Japan's claim to Shantung had been recognized. This also explains Makino's statesmanlike attitude at the Plenary Session when he limited himself to an expression of deep regret over the defeat of his proposal for the equality of nations and the just treatment of their nationals.

Given the state of racial and religious discrimination in the world, are we not justified in calling the rejection of the Japanese proposal a realistic solution? Perhaps. But when the choice is posed between racial and religious equality and racial and religious hierarchy, mere correspondence to existential circumstances is hardly the only test of validity. Underlying this history is the premise that, in the long run, greater validity attaches to those concepts that seek to create a greater degree of harmony and order in human affairs. By withdrawing the phrase from the Preamble, it may be said that the parties implicitly frustrated the process by which idealistic principles, in their proclamation, tend to reform the world's existential reality.

Two quotations will serve to highlight the dilemma of statesmanship. Consider one from Secretary of State Lansing. He believed the Shantung settlement was no less than 'an iniquitous agreement.' On the other hand, R.S. Baker, United States press director at the conference and Wilson's authorized biographer, said Wilson knew he would be accused of violating his own principles. Even so, he still had to work for world order. The

32 *FR*, 'The Paris Peace Conference,' vol. v, 308, 317; Shotwell, J.T. *At the Paris Peace Conference*, New York, 1937, p. 297

Shantung settlement, explained Wilson, 'was the best that could be had out of a dirty past.'[33] It is clear that high ideals and sordid realities interpenetrated at Paris to work out an uneasy compromise.

DEFEATED GERMANY AND THE IDEA OF EQUALITY

On 17 May 1919 the German delegation received the Peace Treaty. Their spokesman, Count Brockdorff-Rantzau, complained of its harsh terms – a veritable death sentence for the German people. The Allies replied that the German people supported the war and shared the responsibility for government policy; at any moment they could have reversed that policy. Simply changing rulers after the war was lost did not absolve them from the consequences of their acts.

Germany, the German people, it was now clear, was not to be granted a place of equality among the peoples of the world, as Wilson had promised. The Peace Treaty barred Germany from membership in the League. Why? Because it was impossible for the victors 'to sit down immediately in equal association with those by whom they have been so grievously wronged.' The German people, according to the Allies' reply, had to prove they were no longer in favour of the aggressive policies that had caused the war. Furthermore, the other powers were waiting to judge from the acts of the German people if they could be lived with as good neighbours.[34]

The German delegates quoted in vain from Wilson's speeches in which he distinguished the German people from its ruthless masters. In vain the German delegates appealed to the principles of the equality of nations and equality of rights, without which Wilson had said there could be no lasting peace. By this time, a spirit of revenge had gripped large masses of men and women. Coming into full bloom were the irrational forces which destroy orderly human progress. Lloyd George, prime minister of Great Britain, was promising the British people to see to it that the Kaiser was hanged and to collect from Germany the costs of the war 'shilling for shilling and ton for ton.' Elihu Root, former secretary of state under Theodore Roosevelt, respected president of the American Society of International Law, was equally vindictive. He found the Germans only 'half civilized in all that makes for civilization. She [Germany] has the abnormal instincts which characterize her barbarisms and separate her from any civilized people.' Even Wilson found himself caught up in this oppressive atmosphere. In

---

33 Baker, R.S. *Woodrow Wilson and World Settlement*, New York, 1922, vol. 2, 266
34 Finch, G.A. 'The Peace Negotiations with Germany,' *AJIL*, vol. 13, pt. 2, 1919, 551

a complete about face, Wilson picked up the logic of Barbosa. The Versailles Treaty, he now said, seeks to 'punish' all the wrongs *Germany* tried to do. Therefore, Germany had to pay. If, as Barbosa believed, nations are a unitary projection of individuals, possessing the civil and political rights of individuals, did it not follow that an entire people could be found guilty of the crimes committed by its component members? Wilson seemed to think so. 'I can testify,' he told the American people on his return from Paris, 'that the men associated with me at the Peace Conference ... did think that it ought to be burned into the consciousness of men forever that no *people* ought to permit its government to do what the German Government did. In the last analysis ... as we in America would be the first to claim, a *people* are responsible for the acts of their Government.'[35] (Italics added)

Here was a fashion of thought unknown to the Great Powers at the Congress of Vienna. No one could seriously argue that the French people were less united in their support of Napoleon than the German people were in their support of the Kaiser. Yet Napoleon, not the French people, was branded as the enemy. He alone was the only obstacle to peace. Conceptual thinking about the nature of the state had not yet vivified corporate personality sufficiently to indict an entire people as the enemy. In the real world, of course, there was such an interaction between countless individuals that it was impossible to place on the German people the unqualified responsibility usually associated with an individual human being for his acts. But the opposite reasoning prevailed. The corporate personality of the German people was credited with a degree of single-mindedness it did not in fact possess. The distinction between the Kaiser's government and the German people was quickly forgotten. Long after the government had been removed, men continued to demand the punishment of some 40,000,000 Germans as though they were a single indivisible entity with a single will. In the attempt to bridge the distance between concept and fact, the victors generated forces that, when exploited, only served to make unrealizable the ultimate restoration of peace.

One is struck by the way statesmen at the Paris Peace Conference were alternately attracted and repelled by opposing concepts. Out of the tension between the contradictory ideas and the demands of contingent circumstances stemmed frustration, paradox, ambiguity. Robert Langbaum wrote: 'We have to learn all the little "realistic" truths to appreciate in the end the big truth in Wilson's remark soon before he died: "The world is *run*

35 *War and Peace*, pp. 590–1

by ideals. Only the fool thinks otherwise." '[36] To this may be added a postscript. In the final analysis, what determines *how* the world is run is the degree of correspondence between the nominal world of ideals and the world as it actually is.

With this in mind we turn to consider how an ideal was elevated into international law. This development took place when the United States, acting on the concept of absolute equality with the other American republics, signed a convention not to intervene unilaterally in matters affecting them, something the Covenant had in no way enjoined. Here was a first important breach in the concept of great-power primacy.

36 'Woodrow Wilson: Tragic Hero,' *Commentary*, Feb. 1959, 165

5
Changing concepts in inter-American relations

From 1928 until the eve of World War II the concept of the United States as a hemisphere policeman gradually gave way to the idea of twenty-one American states sharing the responsibility for continental order as sovereign equals. The following chapter discusses this historical development in terms of the contradictory ideas of equality and great-power primacy.

In 1928 Walter Lippmann referred to 'thirty military interventions [by the US in Latin America] during the last generation.'[1] How could this be squared with the continued declarations of the absolute equality of all American states? Henry Stimson, secretary of state during the administration of Herbert Hoover (1929–33), explained the paradox in terms of a conflict between the nominal world and existential reality. The basic foundation of our Latin American policy, he wrote, has always rested on the recognition of the equal rights of all the American republics. He cited past conferences as evidence of the fundamental rule of equality which had never been broken. Contrast this with European practice, he said, 'where only the great powers were admitted on a basis of equality.'[2]

But as Stimson readily admitted, the concept of equality was an ideal 'resting on postulates which are not always and consistently accurate.' In the Caribbean Sea, and in Central America, he explained, were found the countries least able to safeguard the legitimate rights and interests of

1 Lippmann, W. 'Second Thoughts on Havana,' *Foreign Affairs*, July 1928, 543
2 'The United States and the Other American Republics,' *Foreign Affairs*, Spec. Suppl. No. 3, April 1931, iii, iv

foreign nationals. Yet this was the area most vital to the safety and prosperity of the United States. 'Years and decades of alternations between arbitrary power at one time and outbreaks of violence at another,' he said, 'have pointed out again and again how different a matter it is in human affairs to have the vision and to achieve the reality.'

Stimson's explanation may have reassured citizens of the United States. South of the border, however, Latin American officials had long since made up their minds to take a formal stand against policy based on the concept of great-power primacy. Two events brought matters to a head. One was the enormous increase in the financial and economic pre-eminence of the United States over the Latin American Republics. The other was its unilateral intervention in Nicaragua. The Sixth International Conference of American States, held at Havana, Cuba, during January and February 1928, was the forum of protest. Controversial political questions had heretofore been excluded from these meetings. This time the rights and duties of nations and the problem of intervention were on the agenda. In the discussion of these topics, the long-suppressed tension between the conflicting concepts was brought to the surface at an inter-American gathering.

THE DECLARATION OF RIGHTS AND DUTIES OF NATIONS

Elihu Root, speaking in 1915, saw in the analogy between the individual in domestic society and the nation-state in international society, the only method for avoiding international anarchy. He knew the comparison invited error, but he thought the risk worth taking. The development of international law along the same theoretical basis as domestic criminal jurisprudence, he suggested, provided the only means discovered by man of limiting the power of the strong over the weak.[3] As a step in this direction, the former secretary of state met with J.B. Scott, trustee and secretary of the Carnegie Endowment for International Peace, and Professor Alejandro Alvarez of Chile, lawyer, scholar, diplomat. Together they agreed on a proposed declaration of rights and duties of nations. In substance it was based on the political philosophy of the Declaration of Independence of the United States and the practice of the American republics.

A preamble perfected the analogy between individual human beings and nation-states. It asserted that the fundamental rights associated with real

3 'The Outlook for International Law,' *Second Pan American Scientific Congress*, Proceedings, Wash. D.C., 1915, vol IV, p. 123

persons could be applied to the relations between corporate persons. The declaration itself asserted the right of a state to 'the pursuit of happiness' in the sense of an equal right to be free from the control of other states as long as it did not violate their rights.[4]

A commentary accompanying the declaration suggested interpreting it in accordance with several authorities. Among them were two cases: *The Louis* (1817) and *The Antelope* (1825). The former contains the classic expression of the 'perfect equality' of states, and the latter, the well-known lines of Justice Marshall about Russia and Geneva enjoying equal rights. It results from this equality, according to Marshall, that no state can rightfully impose a rule on another.

In 1916 Root discussed the declaration in his inaugural address as president of the American Institute of International Law, an organization representing the various law associations of the American states. In his opinion, the declaration formed an integral part of a democratic community of nations. In such a community there was no room for paternalism. All American republics, then, were entitled to be treated as equals, and to be free from the oppressive power of others.[5]

Seven years later (1923) another secretary of state, Charles Evans Hughes, said there was no doubt about the declaration embodying the fundamental principles of the Latin American policy of the United States.

I have already suggested that the analogy between individual human beings and the state may serve to illuminate problems of international order. But it is imperative to keep in mind Shakespeare's line: 'They that dally nicely with words may quickly make them wanton.' Once the individual and the state are equated, wrote James Brierly, it is not an easy matter to keep the legal sense of corporate personality 'uncontaminated' by its non-legal associations. Brierly criticized the philosophical inadequacy of crediting states with natural rights. The state, he pointed out is the product of an historical process. Like all historical conceptions, the concept of the state is undergoing constant change. How, then, can there be anything fundamental or inherent in the nature of the state?[6] To assume otherwise, it is submitted, presupposes that corporate persons possess an inviolable essence in the same sense as individual human beings. Thus endowed, its claim to absolute political equality with all other corporate persons appears logically and philosophically irresistible.

4 Root, E. *Addresses on International Subjects*, Cambridge, Mass., 1916, pp. 415–16, n. 1
5 Ibid., pp. 417, 420–1, 425
6 *The Basis of Obligation in International Law*, Oxford, 1958, pp. 124–5

Returning to the declaration, its immediate use by Latin America will be to prod Washington for a non-intervention pledge – recognition, in part, of its absolute equality with the giant from the north.

INTERVENTION AND THE SIXTH INTERNATIONAL CONFERENCE OF AMERICAN STATES

The unilateral intervention by the US in Nicaragua and the sixth inter-American conference may be viewed as the beginning of a movement away from the paternalistic policy of the United States towards Latin America. The conference is particularly noteworthy for perpetuating the penchant for rhetoric that makes no distinction between nation-states and real human beings. First, though, a word on the Central American republic.

In 1926 Nicaragua, strategically located near the Panama Canal, was on the verge of civil war. The army was raised by the impressment of civilians; the country was full of armed bandits; and the economy appeared on its last legs. Aside from the heavy financial stake of American citizens in Nicaragua, the US had a special interest in the country because its peculiar geography made it an ideal site for an alternative canal route. Added to this was its concern over the Mexican government, believed to be shipping men and arms into the country in a bid to extend its influence over the Central American states.

Fearing the collapse of order in Nicaragua, the United States intervened, brought about the resignation of its president and the election of Adolfo Diaz, an old dependable friend. But the new government was weak and his rivals, Juan Sacasa and General Sandino, were growing stronger. With the danger of revolution appearing imminent, Diaz asked the United States to help maintain order and protect foreign lives and property.

As far as President Calvin Coolidge was concerned, sending in the Marines was in the best tradition of US responsibility for the welfare of the Central American states. In terms reminiscent of Theodore Roosevelt he said, 'We are not making war on Nicaragua anymore than a policeman on the street is making war on passers-by.' This coincided with Coolidge's inaugural address (24 March 1925) in which he accepted, on behalf of his country the 'obligation to bestow justice and liberty upon less favored peoples.'[7]

7 *Survey Of International Affairs*, Royal Institute of International Affairs, London, 1927, 419; *Inaugural Addresses of the Presidents of the United States*, 82nd Cong. 2nd Sess. House Document No. 540, Washington, D.C. 1952, 206

With the appointment of Stimson (1927) as his special representative to try to straighten out the Nicaraguan mess, United States Marines and non-military personnel began to concern themselves with the most intimate details of the administration of a foreign country. They trained a national guard to insure order and to supervise free elections. They studied sources of revenue, prepared tax schedules, computed interest rates. They watched over presidential and congressional elections, interpreted constitutional problems, fought bandits, and campaigned against the uncooperative revolutionary leader, General Sandino. Why? Because, said Stimson, to a certain extent the United States must take the position that the other American states fulfill their obligations to the outside world.

Against this background of great-power paternalism, and in sharp conflict with the Latin American republics insistence on non-intervention in their domestic affairs, the Sixth International Conference of American States opened in Cuba. For the first time in the history of inter-American conferences controversial matters were on the agenda. Dissatisfaction with the concept of great-power primacy would now come in for a public airing.

International reunions offer a tempting arena for impassioned oratory. Observers are often puzzled by the use of language incongruous to the real situation. Inter-American reunions are not exempt from this phenomenon. On the contrary, they offer a fertile breeding ground for exaggerated references to the personality of the state and the rights it is said to enjoy.

One may go so far as to point out national differences in the way men think. Not that there is a national or communal mind. Rather the quality of a nation's thoughts can be distinguished from that of other nations. Indians are said to find only beauty in the mind and do not get tangled up in the embarrassment of checking ideas against existential circumstances. Alexis de Tocqueville thought Americans were much more addicted to the use of general ideas than the English. Closer to our concern are the observations of Argentine scholar Professor Agustín Alvarez Suárez. He noted the tendency of Latin American politicians to live in a world of words, a world of pure fantasy where they remain completely cut off from reality.[8] In this respect, the remarks of Sanchez de Bustamante, permanent president of the conference are pertinent. He believed, in true Mazzini style, that nature

8 Crawford, W.R. *A Century of Latin American Thought*, Harvard University Press, 1962, p. 98; Smith, B. 'The Sometimes Baffling Mind of India,' *Harpers Magazine*, April 1962, 63; Tocqueville, Alexis de, *Democracy in America*, New York, 1954, vol. 2, 15, 18; Glenn, E.S. 'Semantic Difficulties in International Communication,' *A Review of General Semantics*, 1954, 163

had united the inter-American community. Then he drew the now typical analogy between individual human beings and the corporate persons called nation-states. 'Each individual, as also each nation,' he said, 'has in reserve two enormous forces which have moved humanity from the beginning of its existence – love and hate ... With love, everything that is great on this earth, has been obtained and, defeating hate, it heals the world's wounds and everywhere spreads good and happiness.' This profound religious message Bustamente found relevant to the world political scene. Harmony would be assured if all American states followed 'the principles of love' in their dealings with each other.[9]

Before the session ended the delegates heard speakers testify to the spirit of democracy which animated their dealings; to the principle of Pan Americanism as a 'biological law applicable to all organisms small or great'; to the absolute equality of the American states, where 'the smallest and the weakest among them speak with the same authority as the largest and most powerful'; and to the Declaration of Independence, 'the gospel of the rights of man and countries.'[10]

Doubts may be raised as to the causal relation of rhetoric to political action. But in the committee hearings, it is submitted, the effect of the constant repetition of the equation of individual and state was not lost: it was in the background of the crucial deliberations over intervention. To some extent it coloured the outlook of the delegates, distorted their perspective, exacerbated the conflict between the idea of equality and the concept of great-power responsibility.

The second Committee on Public International Law considered two projects of the International Commission of Jurists. On 4 February 1928 Dr Victor M. Maúrtua of Peru urged the delegates to accept as the fundamental bases of international law the Declaration of the Rights and Duties of Nations adopted by the American Institute of International Law. In brief, Maúrtua believed the individual in organized society and the state in the society of nations had eternal, inviolable rights. For the individual they originated in his conscience; for the state, from the conscience of nationality. Equality was the synthesis of all rights and included, among others, the same rights, duties, privileges, capacities, dignity, rank, and consideration; the same power to cause right to prevail; and the same limitation of all states by the just right of others. The Declaration of Rights and Duties, concluded Maúrtua, embodied these concepts and if adopted by the con-

9 *Delegates Report*, App. 2, 83
10 Ibid. pp. 61–84

ference would be hailed as the Magna Charta of the hemisphere.[11] On behalf of the United States, Charles Evans Hughes agreed fully.

The only trouble was that a majority of the delegates from Latin America found the declaration inadequate. Why? Because in condemning intervention the wording was not strong enough. A state was said to enjoy the pursuit of happiness only if it did not violate the rights of other states. Such an exception was too broad. All intervention was inadmissible. The United States, joined by Brazil, Colombia and Costa Rica, did not agree. They could conceive of situations where intervention should not be precluded.

To reconcile conflicting views, members of the Second Committee tried to draft an acceptable proposal. The language proved so illusive, however, that they decided to postpone all discussion until the next conference. At the final Plenary Session the other delegates greeted this recommendation with expressions of profound disappointment. The tension building up between those for whom the absolute equality of states admitted no exception and those for whom a right to intervene might be allowed without violating the principle, produced a highly charged atmosphere. So emotional did the discussion become that the president of the conference called for another try. Gustavo Guerrero of El Salvador introduced what seemed to many a clear-cut resolution: 'no state has the right to intervene in the internal affairs of another.'

The principal target was the United States, particularly for its most recent intervention in Nicaragua. Eduardo Alvarez, for example, called the right of intervention the right of might. He left no doubt about the country to which he was referring when he accused the powerful of intervening in the internal affairs of the weak. 'A country has no right to intervene,' he said, '... simply because it owns fleets, cannons and armies ...'[12]

After several speeches in this vein, the head of the United States delegation could remain silent no longer. Hughes arose to explain the policy of his government. First, he criticized the proposed non-intervention clause as a fragmentary statement of law. To do a proper drafting job would take time. Meanwhile, he wanted to assure his listeners about United States intentions. His country did not want the territory of any American state, did not wish to govern any American state, did not wish to intervene in the affairs of any American state. Frankly, he said, the real problem for the United States did not even involve external aggression.

11 Scott, J.B. 'The Sixth International Conference of American States,' *International Conciliation*, New York, June 1928, 295
12 FPA, vol. IV, 64

The he went directly to the source of the tension between the conflicting concepts. 'What are we to do,' asked Hughes, 'when government breaks down and American citizens are in danger of their lives? Are we to stand by and see them killed because a government in circumstances which it cannot control and for which it may not be responsible can no longer afford reasonable protection?' According to Hughes, it was a principle of international law that, under such circumstances, any government was justified in taking action. He refused to call such action intervention, and he offered the texts on international law to prove his point. The United States, he concluded, could not give up its right to protect its citizens. Nor could he sacrifice the rights of his country.[13] As proof that the United States was not really intervening in the domestic affairs of Nicaragua, Hughes decided to call on its foreign minister. This presented Carlos Cuadra Pazos with a delicate problem. How was he to reconcile the concept of equality and the inviolability of corporate personality with the presence of foreign troops on Nicaraguan soil?

First the foreign minister made it plain to the delegates that Nicaragua was on the side of its brother countries 'disposed to establish the right of equality of States ...' With obeisance duly made to the nominal world, he then acknowledged Nicaragua's debt to the United States. He told how both sides in the civil strife had asked the Americans to come to his country and end the conflict. 'They have assured us positively,' he said, 'that they will not impair our independence and that they will depart, leaving it intact just as they found it.'[14] (In like fashion, though with far less justification, the Kremlin would use a somewhat similar argument to defend its 1968 intervention in Czechoslovakia. Only Russian troops failed to depart and leave the country just as they found it.) After Pazos finished speaking, opposition to the United States collapsed. Guerrero withdrew his resolution, and the problem of intervention was deferred until the next reunion.

As the discussion continues we shall see that the United States succeeded only in delaying the inevitable. As for the mental habit of equating persons and things, it will serve to widen the scope of corporate personality until applying the principle of universal adult suffrage to states will become a commonplace of international experience.

Meanwhile, officials in Washington were seriously questioning the effectiveness of intervention based on the concept of great-power primacy. On its face, one is tempted to assert that when order broke down in the Caribbean area, policy based on the primary responsibility of the United

13 *Delegates Report*, pp. 13–14
14 *International Conciliation*, New York, June 1928, 303–4

States tended to be more relevant to the real situation than policy based on the absolute equality of the American republics. Whatever truth may lie in this statement, already there were those who recognized in the remarks of the chief of the Colombian delegation an expression that gave them pause. Olaya Herrera, who also served as his country's ambassador to Washington, called the Latin American policy of the United States *en la palabra*, fraternity. But when you got right down to it, its policy was fear and hate. Why, he wondered, should Latin Americans deceive themselves?[15]

Walter Lippmann gave a crushing description of the frustration building up for the United States by arrogating to itself the right to intervene unilaterally in the Latin American republics. Under the Monroe Doctrine, he wrote, 'we alone can intervene in this hemisphere; because the Central American countries are too immature to conduct elections they have chronic revolutions; because they have revolutions they have disorder; because they have disorder we are compelled to intervene; because we do not wish to intervene we have in effect forbidden revolution; to enforce our prohibition we have to intervene; because we intervene we are in the morally unpleasant position of always supporting the existing regime; because we think that some change of government must be allowed, because no change can take place peaceably, because we won't permit changes that are not peaceable, we have to intervene again to compel the natives to submit to peaceable elections.'[16] The acceptance of an absolute prohibition against all intervention was not necessarily the answer. But was it not clear, he asked, that when the United States made itself the sole judge of when to intervene it was asserting before the world a right which rested ultimately on its preponderant power?

In 1929 Stimson became secretary of state. Since his tour in Nicaragua he, too, had begun to have second thoughts about certain aspects of the concept of great-power responsibility. Whatever its relevance to the vital interests of the United States it posed bewildering contradictions. Clearly, Washington was devoting time and spending money in Nicaragua out of all proportion to what the situation merited, and with little to show for it but the most fragile type of stability.

As general criticism of United States policy reached a new pitch of intensity Stimson decided to take action. He pulled the Marines out of Nicaragua. In March 1930 the State Department published the J. Reuben Clark *Memorandum on the Monroe Doctrine*. (The Memorandum had

15 *Diario de la Sexta Conferencia Internacional Americana*, Habana, 1928, p. 399
16 Note 1, supra, pp. 549

been completed two years earlier but remained unpublished until Stimson became secretary of state.) It repudiated the idea Theodore Roosevelt had made into a corollary of the Monroe Doctrine: the role of the United States as the hemisphere policeman. The doctrine, according to the State Department, did not apply to inter-American relations. It stated a case against Europe, and not a case of the United States against Latin America.

Stimson did not abandon the concept of United States primacy in inter-American affairs. He did not propose to substitute any principle of joint action with the other American republics. While he was ready to defend intervention in Nicaragua as 'a long, patient and intelligent effort on the part of this country to do an unselfish service to a weak and sorely beset Central American state,'[17] he recognized the extent to which such interventions frustrated a critical approach to important problems. And when disorder broke out in Chile and Colombia he refused to send United States troops to protect American interests.

Finally, Stimson tackled the problem of recognition of revolutionary governments. The decisive element for their success in Latin America was US support. He stigmatized president Wilson's efforts to reform the internal policies of other nations in accordance with his own views. He refused to concern himself with the question: does a new Latin American government truly represent the will of the people? As soon as new governments in Bolivia, Peru, Argentina, Brazil, and Panama were in control of the administrative machinery of the state, with the apparent acquiescence of their people, and appeared willing and able to discharge their international obligations, they were recognized. In spite of his efforts to soften the spirit of US paternalism, he was disillusioned by the results.

On 11 November 1932, shortly before his term of office as secretary of state ended, Stimson confided to his diary his sense of frustration. 'I am getting quite blue' he wrote, 'over the bad way in which all Latin America is showing up. It seems as if there is nothing we could count on so far as their having any courage and independence ... and yet if we try to take the lead for them, at once there is a cry against American domination and imperialism.'[18]

Elihu Root with his emphasis on a declaration of rights and duties of states as a key to better inter-American relations, Charles Evans Hughes with his insistence on the legal right of the United States to intervene in Latin

17 Stimson, H.L. *American Policy in Nicaragua*, New York, 1927, pp. 111, 127
18 Stimson, H.L. and Bundy, McG. *On Active Service in Peace and War*, New York, 1948, pp. 185–6

America under certain circumstances, Henry Stimson with his oscillation between 'taking the lead' in Latin America and remaining aloof all lend themselves to criticism. George Kennan raises a timely warning. 'We are another generation, and we cannot be fully the judges either of the demands which faced our elders or of the adequacy of their responses ... we would do well to remember what Gibbon said of the great Byzantine general, Belisarius: "His imperfections flowed from the spirit of the times, his virtues were his own." '[19] Is it too far-fetched to suggest that the 'imperfections' of Root, Hughes, and Stimson flowed, at least in part, from the demands made upon them by the conflicting ideas of equality and great-power primacy, concepts more or less inadequate for the conduct of inter-American relations by the very complexity of existential circumstances?

FRANKLIN D. ROOSEVELT AND THE GOOD NEIGHBOUR

Eugene Rostow writes, 'The question always is, "Which Myth?" Is policy being formed in the image of a relevant and appropriate model?'[20] The fraility of order in the Caribbean, and widespread resentment against the United States, all revealed the unworkability of the myth of great-power primacy.

What, then, should the United States do when government breaks down in an area vital to its security? One way to make the use of force morally redemptive (Reinhold Niebuhr's term) is to place it in the hands of a community. Presumably such a community will transcend the conflicts between nations, and the moral responsibility of intervention can thereby be shared.

This insight was surely behind the letter Franklin D. Roosevelt, former assistant secretary of the navy (1913–29), wrote to Senator Carter Glass on 25 January 1928. In view of the latest United States intervention in Nicaragua, Roosevelt wrote, the time appeared ripe to act in unison with other American republics in solving such problems. Six months later, in an article in *Foreign Affairs*, Roosevelt called for the end of unilateral intervention in the affairs of other nations. A policy of co-operation, he was sure, was more likely to achieve order and dispel hatred.[21]

19 Kennan, G.F. *American Diplomacy*, 1900–1950 (A Mentor Book) New York, 1960, p. 80
20 Rostow, E. *Planning for Freedom*, New Haven, 1959, cited in *The Nature of Politics*, Curtis, M. (ed.) New York, 1962, p. 51
21 Wood, B. *The Making of the Good Neighbor Policy*, New York, 1961, p. 128; Roosevelt, F.D. 'Our Foreign Policy,' *Foreign Affairs*, July 1928, 585

In the same year, Sumner Welles, somtime chief of the Latin American Division of the Department of State, published *Naboth's Vineyard*. This two-volume study of the Dominican Republic was highly critical of United States interventions in the island. Welles, destined to work closely with Roosevelt as assistant secretary of state and later as under-secretary, set forth in his book principles that would one day underlie the Latin American policy of the United States. He, too, called on the government to share jointly with other American states responsibility for hemisphere order. As the proper basis of inter-American relations he advocated the principle of 'absolute equality.'[22]

Not long thereafter Roosevelt met Welles to discuss inter-American relations. Whenever questions threatening hemisphere peace arose, Welles argued, the American republics should first consult together on equal terms. In no event, he said, should the United States intervene unilaterally, not even to protect its own citizens, even those in imminent danger of their lives.

All this was in line with Roosevelt's own thinking and when he became President in 1932 he took the opportunity to reverse the conceptual approach to inter-American affairs. Before a special meeting of the governing board of the Pan American Union he drew on the analogy of people who live in the same residential area. Henceforth, in its relations with the other American states the United States would act in accordance with the principle of the good neighbour. At the core of such a relationship, the president added, lay the twin principles of equality and fraternity.[23]

How closely the myth corresponded with the facts of life in the Caribbean was soon put to the test. In 1933 Cuba was on the verge of anarchy as rival revolutionary leaders jockeyed for political power. The State Department sent Sumner Welles to Havana to try to mediate the differences. Under the pressure of events, the former advocate of non-intervention and consultation among equals soon found the United States had special responsibilities towards the Cuban people. (In fairness to Welles, under the Platt Amendment (1903) the US reserved a formal right to intervene in Cuba to maintain a government capable of protecting life, liberty, and property.) Welles recommended a limited intervention of United States troops and

22 *Naboth's Vineyard*, New York, 1928, vol. 2, 931, 937
23 *The Public Papers and Addresses of Franklin D. Roosevelt*, vol. 2, New York, 1938, pp. 129–31; *Inaugural Addresses of the Presidents of the United States*, 82nd Cong., 2nd Sess., House Doc. No. 540, Washington, D.C., 1952, p. 227. See also, Halle, L.J. *Dream and Reality*, New York, 1959, p. 168: 'What was this Good Neighbor policy? Basically, I suppose, it could be summed up by the term "equality."'

urged Washington not to recognize any government unless, shades of Woodrow Wilson, there was conclusive evidence that it represented the will of the Cuban people. Furthermore, he set about to pick a leader amenable to his own country.

This resurgence of paternalism infuriated the other American republics. In a crisis the United States had failed to behave like a good neighbour. Nor did it appear interested in sharing responsibility for Cuba with the other American states. In December 1933, when delegates to the Seventh International Conference of American States met at Montevideo, Roosevelt's pledge of equality and fraternity was roundly criticized as meaningless.

One aspect of the conference is noteworthy. To some extent it reveals how the ideas in men's minds about the nature of the state erect impediments to the quest for hemisphere order. Secretary of State Cordell Hull started the ball rolling by catering to Latin American sensibilities. He kept up the pretence of a conference among good neighbours. Notwithstanding the vast differences of power among them, and the overwhelming superiority in this respect of the United States, he assured his listeners of the 'perfect equality' of all.[24]

The image of twenty-one perfectly equal neighbours was followed by the accustomed analogies Latin American delegates make between the state and individual human beings. Consider these examples. José Camacho Carreno of Colombia said, 'State and Country are merely a human conscience which grows gigantic ... over them must prevail and gravitate the same principles which rule in the reduced scope of our own conscience.' Of the origins of the Republic of Bolivia he said: It was 'born of Theocali de Ayacauchi, who adopted her, made her, and formed her in his own image.' Bolivia was part of Colombia's 'very flesh and blood.'[25] Similarly, Angel Giraudy saw Cuba 'alive, viable, with human form,' while Puig Casauranc of Mexico described the American republics meeting 'not only in body, but in intellect and soul,' and then had high praise for the 'collective soul' of his own country.[26]

Surely the marriage of language appropriate to individuals to the nation-state only served to obscure the basic problem of hemisphere order. What appeared uppermost in the minds of the delegates was the perfect equality of the American republics. In the effort to protect the inviolability of corporate personality, the delegates concentrated uniquely on passing a resolution denying 'the right of any state to intervene in the internal or external affairs of another.' Intellectually unprepared to create any form of

24 *Minutes*, First Committee, p. 24
25 Ibid. Second Committee, p. 116
26 Ibid. p. 28; Plenary Session, p. 29

multilateral action on behalf of the inter-American community to maintain order in troubled areas, the delegates denounced intervention as the 'curse of America,' and the 'curse of curses.' They lauded non-intervention as one of the 'primordial moral postulates,' 'fundamental,' 'vital,' 'holy,' part of a 'decalogue,' and 'sacred to the conscience of America.'[27]

Secretary Hull tried to soothe the fears of the delegates, for the resolution was obviously aimed at the United States. No government need worry about any intervention under the Roosevelt administration, he said. What he regretted most was the lack of time to prepare a proper definition and interpretation of the term.

However, the weakness of the US economy, the collapse of inter-American trade, the rise of military dictatorships in Europe and the Far East, and the ill-will engendered by the Cuban adventure all played a subtle role in making closer ties with the Latin American states desirable. This time, when the resolution on non-intervention was submitted for approval, Hull cast his vote in the affirmative. He did append a reservation, though, designed to enable the United States to come to the aid of its citizens when their lives and property were in danger.

Latin American reaction to Hull's reservation was immediate and highly charged. As each delegate voted, he prefaced his unqualified approval of the convention with such remarks as, 'with no reservation whatsoever,' 'integrally word for word,' 'absolutely and categorically,' 'unconditionally.' One delegate even said, 'with all my heart.'[28] That the United States adhered to the convention at all was momentous. True, the reservation added a note of uncertainty, but for the first time in its history the United States had given a formal pledge not to intervene in the affairs of the Latin American republics.

Two days after the delegates dispersed (18 December 1933) President Roosevelt raised the issue of sharing responsibility for intervention when order in the hemisphere was threatened. 'The maintenance of constitutional government,' said the president, 'is not a sacred obligation devolving upon the United States alone.' Each nation bears the responsibility for maintaining law and order within its own borders. Only when domestic disturbances affect the other nations of the hemisphere, he said, were they concerned. And modifying Castlereagh's rule, he added, 'the point to stress is that in such event it becomes the joint concern of a whole continent in which we are all neighbors.'[29]

Here is the crux of the matter. For the alternative to the concept of

27 Ibid. Second Committee, pp. 103–7, 112, 117–18, 123–5
28 Ibid. p. 127
29 *The Public Papers and Addresses of Franklin D. Roosevelt*, n. 23, supra, pp. 545–6

great-power primacy is the existence of a close-knit community. When the orderly processes of government collapse, an unconditional pledge of non-intervention based on the equality of states is not necessarily the answer. Rather, the community, acting as a whole, has the responsibility to act. If they do so, intervention even by armed force takes on the colouring of legitimacy.

Roosevelt's speech was no incentive to the creation of an inter-American community capable of multilateral action in its name. Instead, the struggle was renewed to fashion policy among the republics without regard to power differences. At first the contrast was marked between declarations of faith in the equality of the American states and continued paternalistic involvements in their affairs. Gradually the attitude changed. By 1934 Sumner Welles was saying, 'The time has come when the United States realizes that in its American relationships it is an equal among equals, and no more and no less.' Not only did the United States abjure direct intervention, but indirect intervention, said Welles, would no longer be countenanced.[30]

Paradox is the stuff of history and one example is worth noting. In 1933 President Juan Sacasa of Nicaragua feared a coup d'etat. To prevent it he begged the United States to intervene, insisted, in fact, that it had an obligation to do so to protect his government. The United States refused. Large and small sovereign nations, explained American minister Arthur Bliss Lane, must be treated as perfect equals. That was the meaning of 'sovereignty.' In other words, said Lane, we can not treat Nicaragua differently from Great Britain. We do not advise Britain as to how its elections or political matters should be handled. Why should we so advise Nicaragua? At this point the paradox becomes complete. For if this was the meaning of perfect equality and its corollary, non-intervention, there was at least one president of a Latin American republic who wanted none of it. On the contrary, Sacasa immediately redoubled his efforts to get the United States to intervene in his country's internal affairs.

As for the United States, it found itself in the remarkable position of resisting his plea – because it would violate the concept of equality. When Sacasa's brother called on Welles for 'friendly moral assistance', Welles had none to give. Then, in 1936, riots broke out in Nicaragua, General Anastasio Somoza, head of the National Guard, refused to obey the president's orders to disperse the mob, and in the excitement, no doubt, Lane forgot official policy and swung back to the special responsibility of a

30 United States, Department of State, *Latin American Series*, No. 8, p. 10

good neighbour to calm passions. He insisted to both President Sacasa and General Somoza that order be maintained for the protection of the lives and property of Americans and other foreigners. Shortly thereafter Lane was replaced by a new minister who was advised by Hull that interference in Nicaraguan politics was out of the question even if such interference 'is requested or suggested by Nicaraguans.'[31] When the Nicaraguan chargé d'affaires, Henri de Bayle asked Hull to say anything possible to avoid a revolutionary outbreak, Hull answered, 'all of our twenty-one nations had been steadily preaching the doctrine of non-interference with the domestic affairs of each other and naught could be said or done that would lend color to the opposing view.'[32]

But suppose revolution actually did break out? Would the United States simply stand aside? Would it act in concert with the other American republics? Would it act unilaterally? In July 1934 W.R. Castle, under secretary of state during Hoover's administration, minimized the non-intervention pledge given by Hull. If it was accepted at face value, he said, the United States could no longer send a cruiser as a warning and could no longer land troops even to protect American citizens. He did not believe the pledge would be taken seriously. In his opinion it was designed merely to gain confidence in Latin America. But events proved him wrong. When civil war actually broke out in Nicaragua at the end of May 1936, the United States gave dramatic evidence of its resolve not to use its weight in that country's internal affairs. It sent no cruisers. No Marines landed. Washington simply refused to get involved. General Somoza, backed by the National Guard which he commanded, seized power and installed himself as president. True to its new policy the United States looked no further and recognized his government.

While these events were occurring in Nicaragua, Frank P. Corrigan, United states minister to El Salvador, was wondering if the United States did not, in fact, have a duty to use its power and influence when the future of democratic government was at stake. Corrigan had been in touch with bitter opponents of intervention, he wrote the State Department, yet they indicated that to prevent the establishment of autocratic rule they would welcome United States co-operation.

The problem, destined to plague the United States in Latin America and the far corners of the earth for years to come, soon moved out of the realm of theory. In July 1937, President Maximiliano Hernandez Martinez of El

31 *FR*, 1936, vol. v, 817
32 Ibid. 689–90

Salvador sought to amend a provision of the constitution which barred him as incumbent president from re-election. Corrigan wanted the United States to stop him on the basis of a moral responsibility implicit in the Good Neighbor policy. Failure to act, he argued, meant democratic institutions would soon be replaced by a totalitarian regime. Sumner Welles instructed Corrigan not to meddle in the internal affairs of El Salvador.[33]

The ever-recurring dilemma is this: let the United States oppose totalitarian rule and it is at once accused of violating the concept of equality and its corollaries: the principle of non-intervention and the right of each state to run its domestic affairs without external interference. Let it refrain from acting and it is accused of shirking its responsibility and of being soft on dictatorships. The necessity to choose between conflicting values is, of course, an inescapable part of human experience. But are there no absolute standards by which principle can be balanced against principle, interest against interest? Experience may offer some guide. Each attempt by the United States to ensure a particular form of government has had evil consequences far outweighing the intended good. No doubt the wisest maxim is to leave the choice of government to the people who must live under it. Far from being ideal, in the absence of extraordinary circumstances (where, for example, the actual security of the United States is directly threatened) it is probably the safest rule men have so far been able to devise.

THE INTER-AMERICAN CONFERENCE
FOR THE MAINTENANCE OF PEACE, 1936

By the winter of 1936 the world presented to Roosevelt a grim picture. In Fascist Italy Mussolini was close to the peak of his power. He had attacked and defeated Abyssinia, defied Great Britain and France, and further revealed the impotence of the League of Nations. Nazi Germany, under the fanatical leadership of Adolf Hitler, was rapidly creating the most powerful war machine in Europe. Already it had reoccupied the Rhineland. Already it had begun to intimidate Czechoslovakia and Austria. Revolution had broken out in Spain. Russian, German, and Italian 'volunteers' were making more precarious the uneasy peace in Europe. In the Far East Japan continued to act aggressively towards China – after having successfully invaded Manchuria – and to step up the expansion of its already imposing capacity to wage war.

33 FR, 1936 vol. v, 127; FR, 1937, vol. v, 524–5

A major goal of United States foreign policy was to remain neutral in the event of a European conflict. Ideally, this called for a uniform inter-American policy – a policy that would serve to strengthen political, economic, and military ties with the other American republics. President Roosevelt understood the peril to the Western Hemisphere inherent in the events shaping up in Europe. To alert the Latin American states was a paramount reason for calling the Inter-American Conference for the Maintenance of Peace.

Without exception all the American republics agreed that a meeting was necessary. President Alfonso Lopez of Colombia, in his reply to Roosevelt's invitation, reflected a way of thinking we have come to associate with Latin American statesmen of the period. The success of the conference, he wrote, depended upon a proper democratic idea. The delegates had to be certain not only of taking part in the discussions but of carrying weight in the decisions on the basis of absolute equality. For him Roosevelt's administration was a democratic guaranty. Nevertheless the time had come to free Pan Americanism from 'great and small hegemonies presuming to exercise more rights or exert more influence than the rest of nations ...'[34]

The president of Colombia, Antonio Bermudez, supplied the logic behind the demand for equal rights and equal influence of great and small powers. In what by now is an equation that elicits neither surprise nor protest he explained that nations are no more than individuals, both subordinated to the controlling norms of collective conduct, civil as well as political. Hull made his own contribution to this rationale. 'The conceptions of brotherhood and equality that underlie the relations between the citizens of a democracy,' he said, 'impart themselves to the shaping of relations between democracies.'[35]

With these remarks as a background we can better understand the primary accomplishment of the conference. On 12 December 1936, the Committee on the Organization of the Peace proposed two projects: a convention to consult and an additional protocol of non-intervention. Both instruments were predicated on the sanctity of the twenty-one corporate entities engaged in inter-American relations and the irrelevance of power in determining the weight to be given to their point of view.

According to the convention to consult, if a crisis occurred involving the American states alone, the object of consultation was limited to finding

34 *Documents on International Affairs, 1936*, Heald, S. (ed.), London, 1937, p. 555
35 *Report of the Delegation of the United States to the Inter-American Conference for the Maintenance of Peace*, Washington, D.C., 1937, p. 106; *Proceedings 1936*, p. 723

methods of peaceful co-operation. If the crisis involved an international war, the object of consultation was limited to finding those states prepared to co-operate in some action for the preservation of the peace of the hemisphere. However tenuous all this sounded, and indeed it was, consultation was not to be simply dismissed. It had never existed before. In the struggle to created an effective inter-American community capable of handling threats to its security it was a small step forward.

For the United States the convention to consult was a condition precedent to its signing the non-intervention protocol – a blanket declaration of the inadmissibility of intervention, directly or indirectly, and for whatever reason, in the internal or external affairs of any American state. Without reservation Hull accepted the twin projects. Cárlos Saavedra Lamas, the Argentine delegate, one of the most widely respected Latin American statesmen, praised the non-intervention protocol for reiterating 'the application of the principle of the sovereign equality of all the States on this Continent ...' Sovereign equality could be appraised, he said, 'through that juridical equality that levels up the weak ones and gravitates also upon the great States, the greatness of which will not be appreciated in times to come by the size of factories but by their moral radiation and the honesty of their conduct, the only things that makes peoples enduring.'[36]

Before a plenary session of the conference Hull gave one of the most striking statements on the future of United States policy. 'We recognize the right of all nations to handle their affairs in any way they choose ... [even though] their way may be different from our way, or even repugnant to our ideas.'[37]

The unanimous approval of the convention to consult and the protocol not to intervene, together with what today may appear as an extraordinary expression by an American secretary of state, raised emotions to fever pitch. Antonio Bermudez of Honduras embraced 'the brotherpeoples of the Continent in the joy of this conviction: No longer are there small nations in America.' Felip Barreda Laos of Peru found the Monroe Doctrine had disappeared, the policing of the hemisphere was far from every hegemony and all the American states now shared it upon terms of absolute equality.[38]

Few, however, could top the metaphorical confusion introduced by Francisco Castillo Najera of Mexico. On 12 December 1936 he said, 'Gentlemen, this is the day which anticipates the festival when Christianity

36 *Proceedings 1936*, pp. 793, 799
37 Ibid. p. 662
38 Ibid. pp. 90–1, 723

celebrates the coming of Jesus Christ; let us celebrate the divine festival of America.' Even Sumner Welles of the United States delegation was carried away: 'we are all equal,' he said, 'in every respect. Legally we have always been equal; but today there is not the slightest doubt that this equality has a solid foundation on this Continent and can never disappear from it.'[39]

Whatever the verbal satisfaction to orators and listeners, dangers abound in the cavalier use of language. Our thoughts do not necessarily select the words we use; rather words often determine the thoughts we have. Exaggerated repetition of the nominal idea of state equality may demonstrate the firmness of one's convictions. It may also degenerate into hypocritical jargon. According to George Steiner, Corneille, one of the great masters of French literature, 'was haunted by the destructive role of rhetoric in political affairs.' Corneille struck a central truth when he visualized politics as a translation of rhetoric into action. When this occurs, writes Steiner, 'Words carry us forward toward ideological confrontations from which there is no retreat. This is the root tragedy of politics. Slogans, clichés, rhetorical abstractions, false antitheses [and he could have added "false parallels"] come to possess the mind ... Political conduct is no longer spontaneous or responsive to reality. It freezes around a core of dead rhetoric.'[40]

The Inter-American Conference for the Maintenance of Peace was a landmark in the history of the concept of equality. In a Corneillian sense, we might say it was an attempt to translate a different rhetoric into action. The idea of equality had metamorphosed to embrace not only an absolute injunction against intervention, but a far wider notion. Hereafter, any threat to hemisphere security was a subject for mutual consultation. And when the parties took counsel together, the voice of the weakest was entitled to equal weight with the voice of the most powerful.

JOINT RESPONSIBILITY FOR HEMISPHERE SECURITY

By the end of 1938 the danger of war in Europe and the increasing menace of Nazi-Fascist activities in Latin America gave a new sense of urgency to the problem of hemisphere security. The United States would have liked the other American republics to join in a common policy of resistance to Axis threats to the hemisphere. The only question in Hull's mind was whether they would perceive the danger and be ready to act together decisively. Hull had touched the basic weakness of the idea of a community

39 Ibid. pp. 83, 268
40 Steiner, G. *The Death of Tragedy* (Faber ed.), London, 1963, pp. 56–7

of equal states capable of multilateral action; for the assumption of shared feelings about the future of the hemisphere and a common attachment to the same values were unsupported by any historical evidence.

How far the American states were from agreeing on a unified policy toward Germany, Italy, and Japan became apparent when war broke out in Europe in September 1939. Immediately the American ministers of foreign affairs arranged a first consultative meeting at Panama City. Axis influence in Latin America posed a potential threat to hemisphere security. The United States found itself in the position of having pledged not to intervene in Latin American affairs. But the Axis powers had given no such pledge. In fact, their agents were active and operating effectively. Already, pro-German and Italian sympathizers had infiltrated many Latin American political parties. The possibility of the government of an American republic being overthrown in favour of one loyal to a foreign power caused considerable concern among officials in Washington.

Here was a situation that demanded a community response. But the decisive element in making it impossible was fear of the United States. Notwithstanding the nominal world in which all American states were absolutely equal, Latin American ministers had not lost sight of a different reality. In any collective undertaking the overwhelming power of the United States would predominate. Was it not possible that, hiding behind the cloak of an inter-American action, the United States would seek to interfere in the domestic affairs of their country? In a choice between two evils, Axis infiltration and possible misuse of United States power, the latter loomed greater.

As a result, to meet the danger of subversion the Latin American states rejected collective action. Each one pledged to do its utmost to neutralize any foreign doctrines tending to jeopardize democratic government. For the future, the visceral attachment to the concept of non-intervention would prevent the American republics from acting decisively together against any politically disruptive movements in the hemisphere. In turn, the United States would be torn between respecting the equal right of its southern neighbours to run their affairs undisturbed and undertaking unilaterally to guard the tranquillity of the hemisphere.

More than any other leader in the New World, Roosevelt understood the threat to continental security if Nazi Germany dominated Europe. He had resolved to take the lead in securing help for Britain and its allies, even if it conflicted with Latin American ideas of equal concern for the hemisphere. On 4 November 1939 the United States repealed its embargo on the export of munitions to belligerents. In June 1940, after Italy had declared war on

France, the president extended the material resources of the United States to all those who opposed force as the basis of foreign policy, thus moving the country one step closer to war. Finally, the United States Navy received orders to shoot on sight all Axis vessels in its security zone.

No one can question that these decisions involved an international crisis affecting the peace of the hemisphere. Yet at no time did the United States even consider consulting with the Latin American republics. Unquestionably, in this twilight period before a formal declaration of war, Roosevelt considered the effort to arrive at a common policy with the other American republics useless.

Then, on 7 December 1941, the Japanese attacked Pearl Harbor. Two days later the United States moved back into the nominal world of equal states, of joint consultation and of equal concern for hemisphere security, and called a consultative meeting of American foreign ministers. Would the United States insist on all its Latin American neighbours declaring war? 'We do not function in that way in the American family of nations,' said Sumner Welles, head of the United States delegation to Rio de Janiero. The key to the safety of the hemisphere, he told the assembled foreign ministers, was to be found in full co-operation, 'equal and sovereign partners in times of aggression as in times of peace.'[41]

When the meeting ended Argentina and Chile proved to be the only republics that failed to terminate relations with the Axis immediately. Within a year Chile fell into line. Argentina held out the longest – until six weeks before Germany surrendered. By February 1943, a total of eleven Latin American states actually declared war. At least six others were ready to do so once the United States gave the word. Admittedly, they had come to recognize the danger to their very existence. Yet in assessing the part of Latin America in World War II one cannot overlook the conceptual change that blossomed under Roosevelt's administration. Policy based on the idea of equality, imperfectly realized to be sure, made the other American states feel as if they counted for something on the world scene. Hull called the contribution of Latin America during the war a 'striking justification of the Good Neighbor Policy.' In Welles's opinion, had it not been for the new conceptual approach to Latin America, the Panama Canal would have been the object of sabotage, the invasion of North Africa could not have been undertaken, and the United States would have been compelled to keep home a large percentage of its armed forces to meet airborne Axis armies landing south of its borders.

41 Welles, S. *The Time for Decision*, London, 1945, p. 177

During the war a new political slogan gained unexpected prominence. In 1936, Saavedra Lamas of Argentina had declared that the unqualified pledge of non-intervention by the United States reiterated the principle of the 'sovereign equality' of the American states. He may have picked up the expression from José Tible Machado when, in 1907 at The Hague, the Guatemalan delegate opposed an arbitral court for violating the principle of the 'sovereign equality' of states. Sumner Welles used a variation of the term on 16 February 1942 in an address before the Cuban Chamber of Commerce. The bedrock of inter-American relations, he said, was the recognition in fact as well as in word 'that every one of the twenty-one American republics is the sovereign equal of the others.'[42]

Finally, in the spring of the same year, when Welles had become active in the State Department's postwar policy planning preparations, he gave the principle international scope. 'If this war is in fact a war for the liberation of peoples,' he told an assembly at the Arlington National Amphitheatre (30 May 1942), 'it must assure the sovereign equality of peoples throughout the world, as well as in the world of the Americas.'[43]

We mention these historical origins because, a year later, when the Great Powers recognized the necessity of a postwar organization based on the principle of sovereign equality, it appeared to many as if an inter-American concept was finding its way into international politics. How the expression came to be included in Article 2(1) of the Charter will be discussed in chapter 6.

42 Welles, S. *The World of the Four Freedoms*, New York, 1945, p. 61
43 Ibid. p. 75

6
The idea of equality in regional and international organization

This chapter discusses the mounting tension between great and small states over their role in the postwar world. The Great Powers insisted on assuming primary authority. The small states, in general, wanted to share the burden equally. In trying to resolve the problem, we note how statesmen were torn between conflicting concepts, and how the idea of a world community of states, acting like a democratic representative assembly, eventually reached fruition.

POSTWAR PLANS AND OPPOSING CONCEPTS

In 1940 the State Department established a series of committees on postwar organization. Already the concept of great-power primacy played an important, though not decisive, role. In the spring of that year, members of a subcommittee of the Advisory Committee on Problems of Foreign Relations discussed the composition of a European security organization. The majority favoured a political body where practical power would remain in the hands of the strongest states. Nevertheless, they were not prepared to write off the alternative idea of a 'Federated Union,' along the same lines as the United States. Two years later another State Department subcommittee discussed an international as opposed to a European security organization. Those members who advocated a world executive council composed only of great powers were immediately challenged. But the debates were inconclusive. Sumner Welles, who was chairman, thought an authoritative body of any international security organization should certainly extend beyond the great powers in order to give smaller states the sense of participating.[1]

By 1943 high-ranking officials had rejected the relevance to world politics of the inter-American relationship based on the concept of sovereign equality. On 27 March Roosevelt, Hull, Welles, Harry Hopkins (special assistant to the president), British Foreign Minister Anthony Eden, and British Ambassador Lord Halifax met and discussed a postwar organization. The president and Sumner Welles, in Hopkins words, were determined that the 'real decisions' in any international organization should be made by the United States, Great Britain, Russia, and China, 'who would be the powers for many years to come that would have to police the world.' The British agreed in principle.[2]

Thereafter, at the Teheran Conference, in the last week of November in the same year, Roosevelt offered Joseph Stalin the concept of the Great Powers as the world's four policemen. The Russian premier also agreed in principle. In his opinion, great powers had special rights and were exempt from rules and restrictions binding others. As Winston Churchill said, 'The Kremlin had no intention of joining an international body on which they would be out-voted by a host of small Powers, who, though they could not influence the course of the war, would certainly claim equal status in victory.'[3]

During the period the concept of great-power primacy was crystallizing, the United States and Britain had become increasingly concerned over the attitude of their smaller allies. By the spring of 1943, they could no longer ignore the frequent expressions of uneasiness over the way the United States, Britain, and the Soviet Union tended to dominate international political developments. Roosevelt's idea of the Great Powers acting as the world's policemen was particularly disturbing. A general feeling prevailed among the small states that the Great Powers intended arbitrarily to decide their fate.

Even so, the Big Three were not at all disposed to weaken their claim to primary authority for preserving world peace. The concept of great-power primacy, they were convinced, reduced the complexity of international politics to its most manageable proportions. But for the United States and Britain to base their superior role only on elements of power, however closely this perception may have corresponded to political circumstances,

1 *PWFPP*, p. 458
2 Sherwood, R.E. *Roosevelt and Hopkins*, New York, 1958, p. 717
3 Ibid. p. 785; Churchill, W.S. *The Second World War*, 'Triumph and Tragedy,' London, 1954, p. 182

went against an Anglo-Saxon tradition. Historically, even the legitimate use of superior military force appeared to be tainted with immorality. The idea of forming a naked great-power alliance was something the peoples of the United States and the British Commonwealth, to quote Sir Charles Webster, 'instinctively rejected.' For this reason officials of the two countries never lost sight of an opposing idea. Above all others, men generally equated it with the concept of justice. Among small states, and especially among the Latin American republics, it was capable of arousing reverential tides of feeling. In a word, it was the idea of equality. A way had to be found, therefore, to link it with international relations in the postwar world.

Field Marshal Stalin may have given little thought to the connection between morality and the use of power, but he was fully aware of the tremendous emotional response evoked by the idea of equality. Nor did he abstain from catering to it. On 6 November 1942, for example, in the dark days when Nazi forces were moving toward Stalingrad, the Soviet leader spoke about the different goals of the Axis and Allied powers. He made a special point to emphasize the 'programme' of the Soviet Union, Britain, and the United States. Unlike that of Germany, Italy, and Japan, he said, it included the idea of 'equality of nations.' He did not elaborate. But he did say the Allies supported 'the right of every nation to arrange its affairs as it wishes.'[4] In short, the Big Three recognized the importance of keeping the idea of equality alive, imprecise as it might be, and of projecting it, in some form on international political reality.

On 11 August 1943, Roosevelt and Churchill were scheduled to meet in Quebec. The day before, the president conferred with Hull, Welles, Isaiah Bowman (president of Johns Hopkins University), Norman H. Davis (president of the Council of Foreign Relations), and Dr Leo Pasvolsky (special assistant to the secretary of state and chief of the State Department Division on Special Research). Incidentally, except for the president, these men formed the nucleus of the Political Agenda Group (chaired by Hull), the main State Department unit responsible for postwar organization. Among the problems discussed by this group of men were: the apprehension of small states over the future plans of the Great Powers, the importance of great-power co-operation after the war, and the need for a postwar security organization.

We do not know exactly what happened at the meeting, but all agreed on the importance of reassuring small states. The expectations of the Latin American republics were kept firmly in mind, for they constituted more

4 Stalin, Marshal Iosif, *On the Great Patriotic War of the Soviet Union*, London, undated, p. 41

than half of all the small states supporting the Allies. They had enjoyed the longest experience in dealing with a great power on a footing of equality. They were among the most vocal in decrying real or imagined infringements on their status. If the Latin American states formed a bloc opposed to the Great Powers, they could, in all probability, thwart their postwar plans.

At the meeting, the idea of the Great Powers announcing plans for a postwar security organization met with unanimous approval. Discussion centred on what its underlying principle should be. As a starting point, the participants discussed a draft of a four-power declaration drawn by the State Department Technical Committee. One of its paragraphs called for an international organization 'based upon the principles of equality of nations and of universal membership.' Evidently, this phraseology was considered inadequate, for immediately after the meeting ended, members of the Political Agenda Group reworked the language.

The next day, 11 August, Hull had a tentative draft of a Joint Four-Power Declaration. According to paragraph 4, the Great Powers declared their intention of establishing an international organization 'based on the principle of the sovereign equality of nations ...'[5] We can only speculate on who supplied the wording. Both Hull and Welles were present at the meeting on 10 August. Both were deeply involved in Latin American affairs. Both were sensitive to the jargon of inter-American conferences. So it could have been either one of them. But considering the speech by Welles the year before, when he called for 'the sovereign equality of peoples throughout the world, as well as in the world of the Americas,' we would not be far wrong in selecting him as the author. In any case, here is the origin of the principle that ultimately found its way into Article 2 (1) of the Charter of the United Nations.

Hull took the tentative draft with him to Quebec where he showed it to Eden. As soon as Eden read it he immediately said he liked it. Next, the tentative draft travelled with Hull to the Moscow Conference of Foreign Ministers, where Soviet Foreign Minister Vyacheslav Molotov, according to Hull, was also favourably disposed to its contents. From Moscow, on 30 October 1943, the Great Powers issued the Declaration of Four Nations on General Security. In paragraph 4, they proclaimed the necessity of establishing an international organization based on the principle of 'the sovereign equality of all peace-loving states.'[6]

5 PWFPP, p. 533
6 The Memoirs of Cordell Hull, New York, 1948, vol. 2, 1239, 1281; DAFR, vol. VI, 317–18

The Great Powers did not define 'sovereign equality.' Eden unquestionably spoke for all of them when, after his return from Moscow (17 November 1943), he said that the Moscow declaration made it clear 'that there was and there would be no attempt to impose a sort of great power dictatorship on other States.' The declaration, in his opinion, should quiet any apprehension felt by smaller powers of being 'subject to some kind of dragooning at the hands of the greater.'[7]

There was, of course, no general consensus about the meaning of the principle. Ambiguity, in fact, was probably an asset. Hull, for example, originally wanted all small states to adhere to paragraph 4. The British Foreign Office objected because it might raise questions 'which it would be awkward to dispose of.' To cite another illustration. Senator Tom Connally offered a resolution approving the creation of an international organization. The resolution quoted the language of paragraph 4 in its entirety. Thereupon, Senator John A. Danaher (Connecticut) proposed an amendment to the resolution in order to define all the key words. It was voted down by an overwhelming majority, and the original resolution was passed as it stood.[8]

Needless to say, the concept of sovereign equality had a perfectly well-defined meaning in the New World. It had become synonymous with equal concern and equal responsibility for the defence of the hemisphere. When peace was threatened, it meant all American states consulted together as partners and, in their deliberations, the voice of each republic, irrespective of power, carried the same weight.

After his return from the Soviet Union, Hull did nothing to dispel the notion that an inter-American concept was the basic principle of the proposed world organization. On the contrary he gave it further currency. On 18 November 1943 he addressed a joint meeting of both Houses of Congress on the results of the Moscow Conference. He equated sovereign equality with a partnership among all states regardless of size or power. With a special reassuring nod to the Latin American republics, he said, 'Nowhere has the conception of sovereign equality been applied more widely in recent years than in the American family of nations ...'[9]

Nonetheless, in the preparation of plans for the world security organization, Hull never deviated from the concept of great-power responsibility

7 Quoted in Corbett, P.E. *Moscow, Teheran, and International Organization*, Yale Insitute of International Studies, New Haven, 1944, p. 8

8 Russell, R.B. *A History of the United Nations Charter*, Washington, D.C., 1958, p. 166; *DAFR*, vol. VI, pp. 317–18

9 *DAFR*, supra, p. 13

for international peacekeeping. In May 1944 he met with a group of Democratic and Republican senators. Together they went over a United States draft for an international organization. Certain senators objected to a provision giving the Great Powers an exclusive veto in the Security Council. They maintained it discriminated against the equal rights of small states. Hull was not at all affected. In view of the world situation and public opinion in the United States, he said, 'our Government would not remain there [in the Security Council] for a day without retaining its veto power.' When pressed further he said it was the best that could be done as a start but as time went by he felt the veto could be placed on a 'milder basis.' For the present, time and patience were indispensable. The senators appeared satisfied.[10]

In his public statements, however, Hull continued to invoke the concept of equality. Two months before the Great Powers met at Dumbarton Oaks to draw up a proposed charter, he was quizzed on the role of the small states. The United States, he told the press on 1 June 1944, had always stressed the all-inclusive nature of world problems. It was the purpose of the United States government to see that all nations, large and small, but especially the small, 'are kept in a position of equality with all the others ...'[11]

What are we to make, then, of the principle of sovereign equality? Anyone familiar with the principles of 'Newspeak' might find an explanation under the 'B vocabulary.' The B vocabulary, wrote George Orwell in *1984*, 'consisted of words which had been deliberately constructed for political purposes: words, that is to say, which not only had in every case a political implication, but were intended to impose a desirable mental attitude upon the person using them.'[12] Existential circumstances, in the form of apprehensive and possibly rebellious small states, posed a threat to the establishment of an international security organization based on the concept of great-power primacy. This threat the Great Powers did not feel in a position to ignore. The wording of paragraph 4 of the Moscow Declaration can be described, in Orwellian terms, as verbal gloss designed to impose a desirable mental attitude on all those to whom it was addressed. We shall come back to this later.

THE DUMBARTON OAKS CONVERSATIONS

Official notice to the Latin American states of a great-power meeting at

10 *The Memoirs of Cordell Hull*, n. 6, pp. 1662–4
11 *DOSB*, p. 509
12 Orwell, G. *1984* (Signet Books), New York, 1950, p. 230

Dumbarton Oaks to draft a charter for a new world security organization appeared to make a mockery of the concept of sovereign equality and of the inter-American principle of joint consultations among equals. Once again, the Latin American states discovered how different a matter it is in human affairs to have the vision and to achieve the reality. They had hoped the United States would consult with them on broad principles. But what they experienced, in the words of a former State Department official, was a 'cavalier disregard' of their opinion.[13]

Secretary of State Hull said he had made every effort to keep the Latin American republics as fully informed as possible. A few statesmen, he wrote, thought there was not sufficient consultation, but it was impossible to have invited all of them to Dumbarton Oaks without at the same time bringing in the other small states. In words reminiscent of Castlereagh, he indicated that community of council was incompatible with the march of business. A full scale conference of large and small states, wrote Hull, might lead to 'innumerable difficulties and differences of opinion and to great delay.' The most effective way to prepare a charter was for the Great Powers to reach an agreement first among themselves. Such a tentative accord would be subject to modification after the smaller powers had been heard.[14]

With all the small states excluded, then, the Great Powers met at Dumbarton Oaks, Washington, D.C., during the summer of 1944, to exchange ideas on the maintenance of peace after the war and to agree on the main structure of an international organization. After their opening remarks had been published, no small state could fail to realize that the idea of sovereign equality held by the Great Powers was quite different from that held by most of them. At the first meeting on 21 August the representatives of the Big Three all played a variation on the same theme. Hull concentrated on the special burden of the Great Powers to maintain international order. In the opinion of Soviet Ambassador Andrei Gromyko, nations possessing the necessary power to keep the peace had the chief responsibility to preserve it. And British Under-Secretary Sir Alexander Cadogan said the new organization must be composed of great and small states, but the role each had to play depended upon its power.[15]

13 Duggan, L. *The Americas*, New York, 1949, p. 107. The author was a top official in the Latin American Division of the State Department.
14 *The Memoirs of Cordell Hull*, n. 6, p. 1709
15 *DOSB*, 27 August 1944, pp. 198–202; at the opening of the Chinese phase of the conversations, Chinese Ambassador Wellington Koo said responsibility for safeguarding peace may vary with a nations 'resources,' but the concept of sovereign equality should remain the guiding principle. The New York *Times*, 30 September 1944, p. 5

As we know, the proposed charter placed primary responsibility for all basic questions affecting the maintenance of peace in the hands of a security council of eleven members. Only the five Great Powers (France was included with China) enjoyed permanent status in the Council. Only they had the right to block the adoption of a decision of which they did not approve. The General Assembly, composed of all members of the organization, was strictly limited in the peacekeeping function to debating and recommending. If a dispute was already before the Security Council, the Assembly could be precluded even from expressing a collective opinion on the matter. There was a provision for regional organizations, but they were enjoined from taking enforcement action without prior authority of the Council.

The small states quickly made known their objections. Bolivia, Brazil, Colombia, Ecuador, Honduras, Panama, Paraguay, Uruguay, Turkey, and the Kingdom of the Netherlands were among those objecting to the failure of the proposals to respect the concept of sovereign equality as they understood it. Ecuador, to take an extreme example, sought to amend the proposals to make 'moral law' the supreme guide in international affairs. At the same time, according to the government's commentary, the charter should express the 'identical significance' of all states before the common law said to govern interstate relations. Recourse to these amendments, it was believed, would correct 'any practical or political inequality' between the great and small powers. Other small states wrestled with the dilemma: how reconcile greater responsibility for the Great Powers with the idea of juridical equality, according to which, wrote the government of Panama, all members were supposed to have the same rights and capacities. In this connection, the commentary submitted on behalf of the Kingdom of the Netherlands (author unknown) deserves special attention, for it provides an excellent example of what it means to be torn between contradictory ideas.[16]

The Netherlands government noted the paradox of a charter based on the concept of sovereign equality, and sanctioning, at the same time, a special and privileged position for the Great Powers. With this as a point of departure, the argument tended to swing back and forth, in turn supporting and denouncing both ideas. On the one hand, the superior role of the Great Powers was objectionable from the point of view of democracy, law, and theory. On the other hand, given the state of the world, it was necessary for the Great Powers to have a special place in the organization. Yet, while power might have to be invested with special rights, there was a question of how far it should be allowed. The government saw in the charter an invitation to small states to perpetuate and legalize their inferior position. But it appeared ready to accept the organization as long as the Great Powers did not seek 'exorbitant special rights' that placed them above the law.

But what about the veto? The government opposed this special privilege when a Great Power was a party to a dispute. Otherwise, the organization would be useful for settling disputes between small states only, and even here on a small scale. Nonetheless, it recognized what a delicate subject would be presented if it became necessary to enforce a decision against a Great Power. According to the official Dutch position, as long as the Great Powers could veto enforcement actions against themselves there was no advantage for the Netherlands in belonging to the organization. This position was weakened by the contrary assertion that any organization not 'too imperfect' was better than no organization at all. Taking everything into consideration, the government was ready to approve the veto for Great Powers, reserving only the hope that they would not insist upon it.

Another major concern of the Netherlands turned out to be the absence of any standard of justice in the proposed charter. The superior role of the Great Powers could, perhaps, be justified if the small states knew upon what principles they would act. Here, too, there were no easy answers. The government admitted its puzzlement not only over how to formulate guiding principles for the Great Powers, but over how to devise measures to ensure their observance once they were formulated. As to the former problem, the government wondered if 'those moral principles which live in every normal human heart would not be enough.' (That membership in the international organization was limited to states, reflecting something less than what is presumably possessed by every normal human heart, was not considered.) As to how to ensure the observance of principles of justice once they were revealed, the government had no solution, but it insisted that an answer would have to be found. Meanwhile, there was little the Netherlands or any of the other small states could do except wait for the general United Nations conference. Perhaps in full assembly their objections to the Dumbarton Oaks proposals would carry greater weight.

THE YALTA CONFERENCE, 4–11 FEBRUARY 1945

Among the issues left unsettled at Dumbarton Oaks were the scope of the veto enjoyed by the Great Powers, and the role of the Soviet Republics in the world organization. The former involved the outer limits of the concept of great-power primacy, and the latter involved the application of the concept of equality. Both were a source of tension among the Big Three. At Yalta, Roosevelt, Churchill, and Stalin reached an understanding.

Originally, the Soviet Union favoured the broadest possible interpretation of the veto power. In the Russian view, if a Great Power was opposed, a small state should not have the right to bring a matter before the Security Council even for discussion. Otherwise, small states would enjoy a mischievous device permitting them to arouse public opinion against a Great Power. The United States was troubled about the reaction of the small states, particularly the Latin American republics, if the Soviet view prevailed. Roosevelt could foresee their support for the proposed world organization diminishing to the vanishing point. He was determined, therefore, to have the role of the Great powers made 'more acceptable to all nations.' Churchill had similar fears about small-state support. By not giving them the absolute assurance of being able to bring their disputes before the Security Council, Stalin was carrying the concept of great-power primacy too far. He was, in fact, laying the basis for a valid charge against the Great Powers of trying to rule the world.[17]

At Yalta, the Anglo-Saxon leaders joined forces to avoid this stigma. All the Great Powers really needed, they argued, was the right to veto enforcement actions by the Security Council. The Soviet Union, the United States, and Great Britain were, in Churchill's metaphor, eagles. Surely, the prime minister told Stalin, eagles could not object to small birds singing.[18]

Stalin's hegemonic pretensions for the Great Powers forced Roosevelt and Churchill to review their moral responsibilities. Roosevelt had previously called on Stalin to join with him and Churchill in exercising moral leadership and in demonstrating their 'fidelity to principles of justice.' The concept of great-power primacy was based not only on a nation's superior resources and military strength. In the view presented to Stalin, it was based on 'those enduring qualities of moral leadership which can raise the whole level of international relations the world over.' Churchill personally told Stalin how important it was for them to exercise their power 'with moderation and great respect for the rights of smaller nations.'[19] Incidentally, at no time did the Great Powers consider giving up their right to prevent the Security Council from redressing the grievance of a small state.

17 *Malta Yalta*, pp. 59, 664
18 Ibid. p. 590. Stalin's answer was, in effect, that some countries would not be content with singing but would demand a decision. Ibid. p. 665
19 Ibid. pp. 58–50, 590

None of them thought the retention of the veto for this purpose was a violation of any principle of justice.

Be that as it may, the appeal by Roosevelt to what was just and moral was hardly likely to move the Russian dictator. As Lenin had long ago explained, Communist morality was 'entirely subordinated to the class struggle of the proletariat.'[20] What appeared, therefore, as just and moral to Britain and the United States would probably appear to the Soviets as false bourgeois norms. Nevertheless, Stalin knew that if he pushed too hard he might doom an organization potentially useful to the Soviet Union. As it stood, each Great Power had the right to veto any request to the Security Council involving: enforcement actions, the investigation of disputes, and the recommendation of settlements. Clearly, the USSR was adequately protected. Stalin finally agreed: the birds would be capable of singing before the eagles. Now, presumably, the concept of great-power primacy no longer implied a cabal of Great Powers with designs on ruling the world.

The second matter to be settled at Yalta concerned the sixteen Soviet republics. The summer before, at Dumbarton Oaks, a problem had arisen over conflicting ways of regarding the corporate persons eligible for initial membership in the organization. On 28 August 1944 Ambassador Andrei Gromyko revealed two different conceptions of the Soviet Union. There was the Soviet Union as a single Great Power. And there was the Soviet Union as sixteen equally sovereign republics. The Soviet Union was ready to take its place as a Great Power on the Security Council. And the sixteen Soviet republics were each ready to take their place as initial members of the General Assembly.[21]

When Gromyko broke the news at Dumbarton Oaks, Hull said it left him disturbed and Eden and Cadogan 'breathless.' But the more the British thought about their claim to a total of six equal places in the General Assembly (representing the United Kingdom, the Dominions, and India), the more they came to appreciate the logic of the Russian position. On its face, the independent status of the Dominions was more plausible than the

20 Lenin also said, 'When people talk to us about morality we say: For the Communist, morality consists entirely of compact united discipline and conscious mass struggle against exploiters.' Quoted in United States, Department of State, *Soviet World Outlook*, Publication 6836, Washington, D.C., 1959, pp. 68–9. According to O.J. Lissitzyn, in the West the observance of law may very well be a matter of expediency, but the idea that keeping the law is morally good exists side by side. There is a tradition of respect for the law that at least in 1945 did not exist in the Soviet Union. 'Western and Soviet Perspectives on International Law,' *Amer. Soc. Int'l. Law*, Proceedings, Washington, D.C., 1959, 29

21 *PWFPP*, p. 317

independent status of the sixteen republics. They were free and equal members of the Commonwealth. To some extent they did engage in the conduct of foreign relations. None of them could be committed to the acceptance of active obligations without the consent of their respective governments. And all this had been formally attested to by the Statute of Westminister of 1931, and before that, by the Imperial Conference of 1926.

The role of India as a sovereign equal member of the organization was harder to justify. It was not a partner in the Commonwealth. In fact, dominion status was still two years away, but Alger Hiss (deputy director, Office of Special Political Affairs of the State Department, and a member of the United States delegation to Yalta) was, presumably, the author of one argument in favour of its initial membership. Even if India was not really independent, he wrote, it had been 'gradually developing international relations, and is generally considered as having more of the attributes of separate nationhood than the Soviet Republics.'[22] What these were he did not set forth.

The historical evidence of the independence of the Union republics was less impressive. In theory, the Soviet Union was 'a voluntary association of equal Soviet Republics.' This is the way it was defined in the 1936 constitution. Article 17 guaranteed the right of each republic to secede from the Soviet Union, and Article 18 guaranteed each one's territorial integrity. But there was a catch. Article 6 vested in the USSR exclusive title to *all* Soviet land. Over the years, as power became concentrated in the central government, few observers took seriously the right of the republics to secede. Nominally, however, they had the right.[23]

Maybe because the claim was far-fetched, Gromyko did no more than send out feelers at Dumbarton Oaks. But he could have backed up his claim with additional documentary evidence, for on 1 February 1944, less than six months before the Dumbarton Oaks Conference opened, the Soviet government had amended its constitution. By the changes, each of the sixteen constituent republics of the USSR obtained both the right to enter into direct relations with foreign states, and the right to maintain armed forces.[24] There is a certain magic in written evidence. To write that something exists is often accepted as a substitute for its existence. Surely, the independence of the Soviet republics was not going to be an easy one to refute.

22 *Malta Yalta*, pp. 746–7
23 Peaslee, A.J. *Constitutions of Nations*, The Hague, 1956, 2nd ed., vol. 3, pp. 485–7
24 'Report of Vyacheslav M. Molotov to the Supreme Soviet of the USSR, *International Conciliation*, March 1944, pp. 234, 246–7. See also, *Malta Yalta*, p. 72.

As the Yalta Conference got under way, Foreign Minister Molotov demanded multiple membership in the international organization for the USSR. It is remarkable that, armed with the amended constitution to 'prove' the existence of sixteen equal states, Molotov sought admission for only the Ukraine, Byelorussia, and Lithuania. And he immediately reduced the demand to 'at least two' of them. Theoretically, either the Soviet Union was entitled to sixteen members or to one. All we can do is note the paradox and say that it served the Kremlin's purpose to propose two republics.

Roosevelt did not go along with the concept of sixteen Soviet states. He saw the issue as a straight demand by Russia to obtain more than one vote in the General Assembly. When he had first learned of Gromyko's request at Dumbarton Oaks to admit all sixteen republics as initial members, he contemplated demanding representation for the then forty-eight states of the American Union. Perhaps it was regrettable that the US was unable to amend its constitution as speedily as the USSR had done, in order to back up such a claim. In the opinion of James Byrnes, director, Office of War Mobilization and Reconversion, and a member of the delegation to Yalta, the Soviet republics were no more independent than the American states. If, therefore, Stalin should insist on three votes in the General Assembly, he told Roosevelt, the least the United States should do is to demand exactly the same number. Among Great Powers, it would appear, there could be no inequality.[25]

Senator Arthur Vandenberg worried about public opinion in the United States, asking 'why we stopped at "three" [votes] instead of "six" to match the British.' While Byrnes was ready to justify initial membership for the Dominions because they frequently differed from the United Kingdom, Vandenberg did not agree. It was not enough to argue abstractly about the independence of the British Dominions. He wanted tangible proof. When and where did they differ from Great Britain?[26]

But whether the Dominions or the Soviet republics were or were not sovereign independent entities ceased to be the problem. The general consensus among the world leaders was this: In view of the support Britain could, in general, count on from the Dominions and India, and the United States from the Philippines and some Latin American states, the Soviet Union's request for additional seats in the General Assembly was not entirely unreasonable. Roosevelt, however, anticipated a storm of disap-

25 *The Memoirs of Cordell Hull*, n. 6, pp. 1679–80; Byrnes, J. *Speaking Frankly*, New York, 1947, p. 40
26 *The Private Papers of Senator Vandenberg*, ed. A.H. Vandenberg, Jr., Boston, 1952, pp. 159, 163

proval at home. For as it now stood, the United States with one vote was not the equal of the Soviet Union with three votes. He therefore took the precaution of agreeing to the Soviet request only if Stalin and Churchill would support three votes for the United States. Naturally, both agreed. No one, wrote Churchill to Roosevelt, disputed the equality of the United States with the other members of the proposed organization. All the United States needed to do was to propose 'the form' in which their equality should be expressed.[27]

In the real world each small state and some Great Powers would have only one vote in the General Assembly. The United States and the Soviet Union would enjoy three. But in the conceptual world all states remained sovereign equals. It was all a matter of the form in which their equality was expressed.

According to Senator Vandenberg, when Roosevelt met with members of the United States delegation to the United Nations Conference on International Organization, he told them how he had talked Stalin out of six votes for himself and got him to agree to three votes for each of them. The more Senator Vandenberg thought about it the more he realized that talk about the sovereign equality of all states had become, in his words, 'a travesty.' In a real sense it was. On 29 March 1945 the State Department publicly announced that, if the Soviet Union obtained three votes in the General Assembly, the United States intended to ask for three votes too. A week later, when members of the press asked the new secretary of state, Edward Stettinius, how extra votes for the two Great Powers could be squared with the concept of sovereign equality, United States policy had already changed. Under no circumstances, Stettinius now said, would the United States ask for any extra seats in the world organization. But what about the Soviet request? Was it not a violation of the concept to give some members more seats in the Assembly than others? Stettinius avoided the question. All matters pertaining to voting proposals and their effect on the concept of sovereign equality, he said, were for the conference to decide.[28] In other words, sovereign equality meant whatever the members of the United Nations agreed that it meant.

As a result of the Yalta agreement, the Ukraine and Byelorussia were admitted to the international organization as initial members. Incidentally, their admission also played tricks with the concept of sixteen equal Soviet republics. For under the Soviet constitution all the republics were sup-

27 Malta Yalta, pp. 966–7
28 Vandenberg, n. 26, p. 162; DOSB, 8 April, 1945, p. 601

posed to enjoy equal rights. Yet as members of the United Nations the two favoured republics clearly enjoyed superior rights. A semantic explanation is suggested by reading Soviet jurist V. Vadimov. Before the question of membership in an international organization arose, Vadimov discussed the advantages to the republics of their constitutional guaranty of equality. Since all the republics were equal, he reasoned, each had an equal opportunity to assume great-power status in international affairs.[29] On the basis of his logic, we can say the Soviet republics have a new advantage. Thanks to membership of the Ukraine and Byelorussia in the United Nations, all the Soviet republics have an equal opportunity to assume the position of a small power as well.

The Yalta agreement also provided for the admission of India, and the Philippines, whose defence, foreign relations, and major finances remained under the control of the United States. No small state, by any stretch of the imagination, could be said to be entitled to more then one vote. Few doubted that the USSR had three votes. The Kremlin was convinced that Britain had six votes and, thanks to its influence in Latin America, the United States had even more. One can hardly say that the procrustean efforts of the Great Powers to make the conceptual world of equal states fit the existential world of unequal states left membership in the organization free from ambiguity.

THE UNITED NATIONS CONFERENCE ON INTERNATIONAL ORGANIZATION

On 25 April 1945 the United Nations Conference on International Organization opened at San Francisco as World War II was nearing its end. Fifty states attended: five Great Powers (the United States, Britain, the Soviet Union, China, and France) and forty-five small ones. Among the latter, the largest group with any degree of affinity was composed of twenty Latin American republics. The population of about half the small states invited was below five million, and for at least ten of them was a million or less. The states excluded from the conference, twenty or so, comprised the enemy powers and the neutrals.

The United States, Britain, and the Soviet Union dominated the proceedings. They were resolved to keep in the hands of the Great Powers primary responsibility for preserving peace. But the political atmosphere was charged with egalitarian ideas. To a large extent it was the creation of the Great Powers. Catering to their estimate of world public opinion and

29 Cited in Aspaturian, V.A. *The Union Republics in Soviet Diplomacy*, Geneva, 1960, p. 19

the demands of small states, the Big Three had filled their pronouncements with such undefinable political abstractions as equal rights, a democratic world order, and the subordination of states to principles of justice. Actually, the United States bears the major responsibility. Virtually all declarations on the nature of the postwar world originated with its officials. They, in turn, were caught up in century-old mental habits that had nourished ambivalent approaches to international relations.

As a result, there was the image of the United States as one of several policemen – the one adopted for world affairs. Existing side by side with it, was the opposite image – the one adopted for Latin American affairs. The core of inter-American rhetoric, characterized by the identification of the state and the individual, and by the perennial acknowledgment of the perfect equality of each state, large and small, and its right to speak with an equal voice, was too ingrained to be lightly tossed aside. High-ranking members of the United States government, and to a lesser extent, of the British government, believed that to ignore this jargon was to risk an open breach not only with the small states but with their own constituencies as well. Consequently, the world they tried to deal with had to make room for another environment. Even if the most workable concept was to charge the Great Powers with responsibility for keeping the peace, a place had to be found for the idea of a world community of equal states. By and large, in this quest they were not opposed by the Soviet Union.

The Charter of the United Nations, then, reflects a contradiction between opposing concepts. Taken as a whole, it expresses incompatible judgments about the nature of international society and about the entities engaged in international relations. One of these judgments is in the Mazzini-Barbosa tradition. It emphasizes the transcendental worth of the corporate personality of the state, accentuates principles of justice as the primary political force, and advocates the application of egalitarian ideas to international affairs as the best means of ensuring world peace and security. The opposing judgment is in the tradition of Lord Castlereagh. Its proponents view the state as an artifical creation designed to serve man's social and political goals. They concentrate on the role of power as the exclusive starting point for trying to bring order into world affairs, and place ultimate responsibility for preserving peace on the great powers. Within the framework of these conflicting ideas, we shall seek to understand the tension between the great and small powers at San Francisco.

Let us consider for a moment the first point of view. When President Roosevelt said the United Nations represented an association of peoples and not an association of governments, he helped to perpetuate a confusion over the identity of the corporate persons comprising the world and over their status in international politics. Roosevelt's expression is straight out of Mazzini. But it is not necessary to go back so far. At the Twelfth Plenary Session of the League of Nations (6 December 1920), Lord Robert Cecil, one of the staunchest advocates of the concept of great-power primacy as the underlying basis of the League, did a complete about-face. He declared the old methods of diplomacy to be dead, and he described the new diplomacy as one between people and people and not one between governments. Some years later, Cecil was prepared to say that the state was an individual. It was a moral individual. And because it was a moral individual it was subject to moral law. Cecil went on to speak of a mysterious element in human nature which permitted individuals to make themselves into a corporate whole. The new entity thus created by their joining together was more than the sum of its parts. It represented the creation of a new character, subject to its own moral laws and moral duties. Cecil admitted the abstract nature of his view of the state, but for him it was more in accordance with political reality.[30]

In the years between the creation of the League of Nations and World War II, as we have already noted, this conception of the nation-state was proving particularly agreeable to Latin Americans. Thus, with the publication of plans for a world security organization, it was not entirely unexpected to find the former minister of foreign affairs of Brazil, José Carlos Macedo Soares, making the following comment. The framers of the new organization, he said, had fallen into serious error. They had failed to recognize the true source of international peace and security. Had they been able to do so they would have created not a league of governments but a world organization composed of 'peoples.'[31]

Finally, at San Francisco, Peruvian Ambassador Victor Andres Belaunde, member of the Peruvian delegation, picked up the analogy between state and individual. His address on corporate personality touched a theme to which most of the delegates of the small states were responsive. On 15 June 1945, before Committee III, charged with problems associated with

30 *DOSB*, 7 January 1945, p. 25; League of Nations, Official J. *Records of the First Assembly*, Plenary Meetings, 6 December 1920, p. 279; Cecil, Viscount Robert, 'The Moral Basis of the League of Nations,' *The Essex Hall Lecture*, London, 1923, pp. 12–13. Compare an extreme hypostatization of the state in an official Hungarian decree requiring all school children, after World War I, to repeat twice a day, as part of the national creed, 'I believe in the resurrection of Hungary from the dead. Amen!' Cited by Page, K. *National Defense*, New York, 1931, p. 256

31 *Inter-American Affairs*, 1944, Whitaker, A.P. (ed.), New York, 1945, p. 68

the Security Council, Belaunde recalled how international order was based on the personality of the state just as the legal order was based on the personality of man. But for the Peruvian ambasador the concept of corporate personality was something more than just an abstraction, more than just a philosophical notion. It was also a reality. Thereupon, he called on the delegates to show proper respect for the state as 'a living synthesis of moral values.' The United States, he insisted, not only represented the love of freedom and justice. It represented 'human love.' In the concept of state personality Belaunde found the basic element of Christian culture.[32]

The Great Powers showed their respect for the corporate personality of the states meeting at San Francisco in several ways. They organized the conference along the lines of a democratic legislative assembly. It seemed extraordinary to J.B. Scott, United States delegate to the Second Hague Peace Conference in 1907, to find governments answering a roll call as if they were ordinary individuals. In 1945 few observers found similar arrangements at all singular. The atmosphere of the conference could be compared to a gathering of individual voters, each with an equal right to select the policy of the community. Irrespective of military power, industrial capacity, or political maturity, the delegation of each state had one vote. According to the rules, procedural questions were to be decided by a majority of the delegations present and voting. All other questions required a two-thirds majority.

Of great significance was the repeated reference to the Dumbarton Oaks proposals as something tentative, serving no more than a basis for discussion among all the delegates. The intimation was clear: it would be left entirely to the conferees to accept or reject by their votes what the Great Powers had proposed. Eden confirmed this at the First Plenary Session. The Dumbarton Oaks proposals, he told the delegates on 26 April 1945, were suggestions only. The Great Powers were presenting ideas to the delegates for their consideration. In no event should they be interpreted as an attempt at dictation.[33]

In drafting the Preamble to the Charter, the Great Powers also tried to give maximum verbal satisfaction to those who conceived the state as a moral person with a single will. The United Nations nominally represents peoples. The opening words: 'We the Peoples of the United Nations' was another tribute to the conceptual level of existence inhabited by separate and distinct corporate persons. From the analogy with individual persons

32 *UNCIO*, vol. 6, 66–9
33 Ibid. vol. I, 138

flowed the principle of all peoples being equal. The concordance was perfected in the sentence of the Charter: the Peoples of the United Nations reaffirm faith 'in the equal rights of men and women and of nations large and small ...' To put it another way, like every man, every people counts for one; and no man and no people counts for more than one. The provision of Article 2 (1), basing membership on the principle of sovereign equality, is a logical reflection of what the relationship among peoples must be. Here again, the fiction of the indivisible character and absolute value of all peoples is preserved.[34]

The Great Powers were willing to yield even further to the image of international reality conceived by the small states. The General Assembly became the nucleus of a democratic community of equal states. In this organ all members were on an equal footing. Each had one vote – its power no longer weighing in the balance. Each stood prepared to follow the will of the majority.

This brings us back to the statement about the charter reflecting a contradiction between opposing concepts. For, in spite of all that has been said, the principal actors in the world organization are not peoples or nations but states and their governments. Some of the governments of these states are representative of nations. Others are not. Even when they are a question remains, because it is within the power of governments to make up the minds of the nations they represent. Next, far from being governed by the concept of equality, the standing of the members of the organization was determined by their power, real or potential. Only those considered Great Powers obtained permanent status in the Security Council. The Military Staff Committee, created to direct the use of armed force in the event of a threat to the peace, represented the Great Powers. They alone enjoyed the right to block its use against either themselves or their allies. They alone could prevent the Security Council from investigating disputes and recommending settlement. Their veto could prevent the appointment of the secretary-general, the admission of new members, the amendment of the Charter. What symbolized the small states' share in the organization was their right in the General Assembly to debate, to advise, to discuss, to recommend. No one took seriously the right to pass resolu-

34 Compare Mazzini and Secretary of State Stettinius. Mazzini said, 'The Pact of Humanity cannot be signed by individuals, but only by free and equal peoples ...' *Life and Writings*, London, 1864, vol. 3, 15. Stettinius said, 'We have first to write the Charter of the world Organization. It must then be accepted by the peoples of the world.' *DOSB*, 11 March 1945, p. 393.

tions. As originally conceived, resolutions were expected to be a rare occurrence.

In order to point up the conceptual split at San Francisco when the higher rank of the Great Powers was established, I have culled the views of the delegates presented at various meetings and sessions. For greater impact, and without in any way distorting the context, I present them in the form of an argument that took place at a single sitting.

Guillermo Belt Ramirez, chairman of the Cuban delegation, opposed the superior status afforded the Great Powers in terms fashioned during the development of the inter-American system. Permanent membership in the Security Council for Great Powers only was completely undemocratic. According to him, the United Nations had been fighting a war to make democratic ideas prevail. Among the most important were the principles of equality and majority rule. His delegation would, therefore, continue to strive for a truly democratic world organization based on the equal rights of all members, where the minority submitted to the will of the majority.[35]

The delegate for the United Kingdom, while not addressing himself directly to the Cuban delegate's remarks, provided one reply. Great and small powers, he said, had to be differentiated. Historically, it had never been possible for small states, by their votes, to require great powers to take action for peace. He admitted the role of the Great Powers was subject to criticism for violating democratic principles. But inequalities existed. There was no easy way to alter them. While the privileged status of the Great Powers could be considered unequal treatment, even undesirable, it was only a consequence of the realities of international existence.[36]

The Netherlands delegate, Alexander Loudon, could understand that it might be necessary to give the Great Powers special rights in the organization. But to recognize it and to sanction it officially would be regrettable. For what was at stake was giving legal sanction to the overwhelming might of the Great Powers. Once again, from the British came the counter argument. Theoretically, it was possible to draft a better charter, one devoted to legal and democratic principles, but the task was not to design a perfect instrument which was theoretically satisfying. The job was to draft something that would work within the limits of a world composed of great and small powers.[37]

The small states felt pushed to the wall. Their inability to influence the

---

35 *UNCIO*, vol. I, 500, vol. II, 351
36 Ibid. vol. II, 320–22
37 Ibid. 163–4, 322. The Mexicans saw a world order where 'the mice could be stamped out but in which the lions would not be restrained.' Ibid. p. 474.

Great Powers became strikingly evident when the delegate from Australia refused to resign himself to British estimates of the limits of reality. Like many of the representatives of small states, he would grant the Great Powers permanent seats in the Security Council. He would also support their right to veto enforcement actions. Beyond that he would not go. He introduced a resolution to foreclose use of the veto when a simple majority of the eleven members of the Council either favoured investigating disputes or sought to recommend procedures for pacific settlement. According to the rules of the conference, the resolution would have to be put to a vote. The small states commanded an easy two-thirds majority. It looked as if a great-power defeat was imminent. But the Great Powers had no intention of bowing to democratic principles of majority rule any more than President Wilson had at the Paris Peace Conference in 1919. Disturb the scope of the great-power veto, came the blunt warning, and there would be no international security organization. How could the delegates face public opinion at home, asked Senator Connally, if by killing the veto they killed the Charter? Reluctantly the small states surrendered. The parties went through the formality of a vote and the Australian resolution was soundly defeated.[38]

Clearly, the small states needed reassurance. The Big Three gave it, pointing out one of the elements in the concept of great-power primacy vital to its successful operation, that is, the good faith of those who demand primary responsibility for world peace. A spokesman for the Soviet Union was reported to have told members of the press that the Great Powers would rarely exercise the veto. According to the British delegate, the United Kingdom would not abandon its traditional policy of upholding the rights of small nations. And Senator Connally revealed the Great Powers in a new role: as members of the United Nations, no longer would they perform their duties as representatives of their respective governments, but as representatives of the international organization as a whole.[39]

Miguel Angel Carcano, chairman of the Argentine delegation provided an insight for all those who had hoped to create a democratic community of nations based on the principle of absolute equality. At the root of the frustration experienced by the delegates, he said, was a tragedy of the human mind, torn between its capacity to conceive perfect plans for world order and the harsh realities tending to embarrass their execution.[40]

38 Ibid. pp. 492–3, 319
39 Ibid. pp. 434, 475, 131
40 Ibid. vol. 1, 101

For those who sought to create international stability on the opposing concept of great-power primacy, a tragedy of the human mind was no less in evidence. For the unanimity of the Big Three in blocking any change in their veto power concealed the essential disunity among them. It would not take long before the workability of an international organization based on this concept would raise serious doubts even among its most faithful adherents. To get a better grasp of the weakness inherent in the concept of maintaining peace and security on the basis of the Great Powers acting together unanimously, let us recall the growing discord among the Big Three in 1944 and 1945. This was the period when Russian military forces gained control of Poland, Rumania, Bulgaria, and Hungary, and set in motion the changes needed to monopolize power in Czechoslovakia. At the time, the critical issue for the United States and Britain was whether those states would fully regain their former independence or whether they would wind up as Soviet satellites. In February 1945 Russia had joined with the United States and Britain in subscribing to a Declaration on Liberated Europe. They pledged to observe the right of all peoples, without qualification, to choose their own form of government. Nevertheless, King Michael of Rumania was forced to bow to Soviet pressure and to install a Communist-dominated government in his country. The United States and Britain protested this violation of their joint declaration and urged tripartite consultations. Russia categorically refused. The mythical aspects of great-power harmony were not difficult to see.

Nothing had changed with regard to Russian control of Poland. After its occupation, the USSR continued to recognize the Committee of National Liberation which it had unilaterally set up as the provisional Polish government. Again the United States and Britain protested. Again to no avail. Unprepared to contest the Soviet presence by force of arms, the other two Great Powers were reduced to appealing to the Russians to apply the principle of self-determination embodied in other great-power declarations. The Kremlin, however, considered the Polish government it had created representative of the Polish people, and the presence of the Red Army loomed as indisputable evidence of the government's legitimacy.

Captain Peter Thorneycroft, member of the House of Commons for Stafford, analysed the disagreement among the Big Three as a conflict between policy based solely on the conceptual level of existence and policy based on the military power necessary to carry it out. Thorneycroft took a slap at the United States and Britain. The rights of small states, he said, were not safeguarded simply by signing documents like the Atlantic Charter. But he had equally strong reservations about the ruthless power politics practised by the Russians in Eastern Europe. His recommendation was for the Big Three 'to marry' the opposing schools of thought.[41] Unfortunately, the parties were too far apart in their thinking for connubial bliss.

The conflict over Soviet predominance in the countries it liberated continued all during the months preceding the opening of the general United Nations conference. The possibility of the Big Three arriving at a common policy in international affairs had become increasingly remote. Yet at no time during this period did they seriously consider any other idea to ensure order than a security system based on the primacy of the Great Powers acting unanimously. At San Francisco the flaw in the concept was brought sharply into focus. It happened when the question of the relationship of regional systems to the world organization came up for discussion. Thoughtful members of the United States delegation now considered a striking paradox. The concept of great-power primacy and its corollary, the veto, might actually jeopardize the security of the Western Hemisphere. Suppose, for example the USSR or Communist-inspired forces disturbed the peace in Latin America. Would the United States and the Latin American republics be obligated to appeal to the United Nations where the Soviet Union could block effective action?

Latin American delegates were said to be up in arms over the possibility of a non-American power exercising a veto over inter-American affairs. Two months previously, at the Inter-American Conference on Problems of War and Peace, the twenty-one American states had moved another step towards the perfection of a collective security system. Resolution VIII, known as the Act of Chapultepec, provided for multilateral action in case of aggression against an American state. Coercive measures ranged from severing diplomatic relations to the use of armed force. The Act of Chapultepec was limited to the duration of the war, but it provided the framework for a regional organization based on the concept of shared responsibility for hemisphere security. As Alberto Lleras Camargo of Columbia reminded the delegates at San Francisco, the inter-American system was far superior to the world organization. In the former, he said, sanctions were applied according to democratic principles of majority rule. No one possessed a privileged status. No one enjoyed the right of veto.[42]

At this point the United States delegation split over the conflicting concepts. The secretary of state and Leo Pasvolsky, his formidable special

41 *Hansard*, vol. 408, London, 1945, 1454–61
42 *UNCIO*, vol. I, p. 363. As to breaking diplomatic and economic relations, in 1947 the Inter-American Treaty of Reciprocal Assistance provided for decisions to be taken by majority rule.

assistant, the man considered by Senator Vandenberg as having the greatest influence on the development of the United Nations, led the fight for the primacy of the world organization based on the concept of great-power primacy. Opposed to them, among others, were Senator Vandenberg and Nelson Rockefeller, assistant secretary of state for American Republic Affairs. In Vandenberg's opinion, the authority vested in the Security Council over regional organizations violated a cardinal principle of United States foreign policy; that is to say, primary responsibility for an attack against an American state was the joint obligation of the inter-American community. According to the opposing members of the United States delegation, the international organization had to come first. Unless it had the right to prevent the use of force everywhere, including the Western Hemisphere, it would be doomed to failure. Pasvolsky fought off all attempts to compromise the international organization. He and his supporters at first refused even to consider the possibility of the United States and the Soviet Union being unable to work together harmoniously regardless of the conflicting interests at stake.

The story of Article 51 is well known. By recognizing a collective right of self-defence it paved the way for regional peace-keeping organizations – a victory for the inter-American system and the future Organization of American States. What is particularly pertinent to our theme is this contradiction. For the United States, the idea of an international security organization based on the concept of great-power primacy had, at first, transcended every other type of organization for maintaining order. Slowly, the defect in the concept came to the surface. The United States might not, after all, be able to count on working harmoniously with the Soviet Union. For those with eyes to see, the two potential superpowers had different ideas of right and wrong and, to paraphrase President John F. Kennedy, different ideas of where the world was and where it was going. At length, to safeguard its own security and that of the hemisphere, the United States found itself trying to cope with intractable reality by supporting, on the one hand, a world organization based on the concept of great-power primacy, and on the other, a regional system based on the alternative concept of equality.

As we review the contrary beliefs of members of the United States delegation, we are struck by how vigorously Leo Pasvolsky fought against introducing into the Charter of the United Nations any provision likely to weaken the overall responsibility of the organization – even when it was intended for the protection of an area vital to American security. One explanation lies in the rigidity of his conceptual thinking. The special assistant of the secretary of state had drawn an ideal model from the orderly conceptual world. Notwithstanding its remoteness from reality, he refused to consider any other system. Unwieldy, chaotic circumstances would have to be forced to conform to the image in his mind. He refused even to consider that it could not be done.

Senator Vandenberg, on the contrary, reacted differently. He also favoured the idea of an organization run by the unanimous decision of the Great Powers. But the give-and-take of domestic politics, the need to compromise and horse-trade in order to reduce the gap between ideals and political necessity, and the experience of discharging responsibility in the world as it is, were all part of his daily routine. Given the cast of his mind he was able to free himself, as Pasvolsky was not, from an absolute commitment to a single scheme for ordering international affairs.

On 4 June 1945, as the conference neared its end, Article 2(1) of the Charter, basing membership on the principle of sovereign equality, came in for final criticism. The Belgian delegate took exception to an instrument granting superior status to the Great Powers and relegating the small ones to a minor uninfluential role. Yet it boldly declared the principle of sovereign equality as the basis of membership in the organization. In view of the 'striking inequalities' in the Charter, he felt compelled to register his dissent, and that of other small states, over the use of words in Article 2(1) conveying a meaning opposite to their literal sense.[43]

What is the explanation of the paradox? One response seems to emerge. If the organization was to achieve worldwide legitimacy, the Great Powers believed it had to be based on the idea of equality. So they suited the *words* to the action. They took the term sovereign equality and they *named* it the basic principle of membership in the organization. Is the nominal pretence in Article 2(1) to be attributed simply to scheming men? Perhaps a better way to understand those who bore the burden for winning the war, for planning the peace, and for retaining, at the same time, the loyalty of forty-five small states, is to see them caught in a dilemma as they struggled with problems far beyond their capacity to solve. From this standpoint, Article 2(1) is a reminder of what happened when statesmen were groping for a way to harmonize incompatible ideas that, alone or combined, fitted existential circumstances only approximately.

One may also approach the principle from another direction. Article 2(1)

43 Ibid. vol. 6, 332. Because of the emotional content the concept of sovereign equality had acquired, the Peruvian delegate wanted the words to appear only in the Preamble to the Charter. Ibid. 331–2

may be said to represent a standard constantly to be laboured for, even though it may never be perfectly attained. Before we consider how the ideal interacted with political circumstances to reform them, a word on Latin America and the United States is essential.

DISREPUTABLE GOVERNMENT AND THE IDEA OF EQUALITY

In the immediate postwar period the United States was again torn, as it had been constantly, between conflicting concepts. This time it had serious consequences for the perfection of the inter-American system. Did the United States recognize the equal right of each Latin American republic to organize its internal affairs under whatever form of government it chose? Or was it something in the nature of a sacred duty devolving upon the United States to eliminate from the hemisphere all governments of which it disapproved; namely, those that were not constitutional democracies?

In reviewing the conceptual split, in essence no more than another aspect of the tension between the idea of absolute equality and the idea of great-power primacy, our attention is focused on the period when Spruille Braden was ambassador to Argentina and, subsequently, assistant secretary of state for American Republic Affairs.

In early April 1945 the United States entered into diplomatic relations with the same Argentine government it had previously refused to recognize because of its alleged 'Nazi-Fascist' character. Among certain members of the State Department, however, a government that limited free speech and press, that was not above jailing political opponents, and that continued to retain Axis sympathizers in high office, was seen as a direct challenge to the ideals for which the United States had been fighting. Their concern extended beyond the Farrell-Perón military dictatorship that governed Argentina. Once and for all the United States had to determine its policy towards any Latin American government with fascist trappings.

Spruille Braden, newly appointed ambassador to Argentina (May 1945), represented one point of view. A new world had come into being. No longer was man to be humiliated by governments based on violence. He called on the victorious democracies to establish the only legitimate governments: representative democracies based on the will of the people. Braden was prepared to rid every aspect of the political life of every American republic of Axis influence. The difficulty involved, the cost of such a venture, left him undeterred. As a start, at least, he concentrated his fire on the country to which he was accredited. Mercilessly, he denounced the Argentine government in terms rarely heard by a man of his rank acting in his official capacity.[44]

What may have started out as Braden's personal attempt to eliminate a 'totalitarian' régime was soon picked up by Assistant Secretary of State Rockefeller. He had previously favoured a policy of conciliation and co-operation with Argentina, regardless of how repugnant some of its domestic policies might be. Now, with Braden showing the way, he did not want to appear to be dragging his feet on the subject of fascism. He, too, openly condemned the Argentine government for failing to fix a date for free elections and for tolerating activities inimical to a free society.

In August 1945 Braden was nominated assistant secretary of state for American Republic Affairs. The influential *New York Times* praised his promotion and described Braden as a symbol throughout Latin America. To the editors he represented the militant forces of democracy ever alert to the Fascist menace. The United States would find all its efforts to destroy Facism overseas to have been in vain, predicted the *Times*, if it allowed this alien philosophy to remain in power unchallenged 'anywhere.'[45]

From his new position of authority Braden soon presented Argentine Foreign Minister Juan Isaac Cooke with two conditions under which friendly relations with the United States were possible: fulfilment by the government of its inter-American commitments, and the establishment of a constitutional representative democracy. Nevertheless, many officials did not agree with what Braden was trying to do. On 22 October 1945, when his nomination came before the Senate for approval, his increasing paternalistic concern with the form of government of certain Latin American republics was sharply criticized. Senator Robert LaFollette considered Braden's interference a threat to the principles of equality and non-intervention at the heart of inter-American relations. If he voted to approve his appointment, he said, he could not visualize how the cause of joint co-operation and mutual consultation could be advanced.[46]

Senator Vandenberg went a step further. Responsibility for encouraging freedom and liberal ideas was too great for the United States to undertake unilaterally. Dangerous situations involving the violation of essential democratic beliefs called for multilateral action by all the American states and not independent action on the part of the United States alone. Some-

44 The *New York Times*, 18 August 1945, p. 6, 29 August 1945, p. 1, 2 September 1945, sec. 4,
    p. 4; *DOSB*, 5 August 1945, p. 190; *Inter-American Affairs*, n. 31, pp. 41–6
45 The *New York Times*, 28 August 1945, p. 18
46 Ibid. 8 September 1945, p. 6; United States, *Congressional Record*, Senate, 79th Cong. 1st
    Sess., vol. 91, 22 October 1945, p. 9904

how, Braden was able to overcome the senators misgivings and his appointment was confirmed. As the session ended, Senator Connally wanted to make sure no one got the wrong inpression. The vote for Braden, he said, did not mean the United States had swung back to the old policy of strong-arm diplomacy.[47]

On 26 October 1945 the United States chargé d'affaires in Argentina, John Moors Cabot, issued a statement to the press. It did little to clarify future policy. According to the press report, the government would adhere to its pledge not to interfere in the internal concerns of other countries. But at the same time it would not compromise with any dictatorial régime. There were no details on how it was possible to have it both ways. Finally, Secretary of State James Byrnes stepped into the breach. He said the principle of non-intervention remained at the heart of United States policy. While this did not mean approval of what he called 'local tyranny,' any development threatening the peace of the hemisphere would be handled by joint consultations with the other American states.[48]

A month later the foreign minister of Uruguay, Alberto Rodriguez Larreta, gave formal effect to the secretary of state's remarks. With Argentina firmly in mind, he branded as a menace any American state repeatedly depriving its citizens of the 'elementary rights of man.' Then he made an official proposal. If the American states, after consultation, found such a menace to exist, they had the right to intervene collectively to restore constitutional government.[49]

Within a matter of days the United States announced its unqualified support of Larreta's idea. Other states moved more slowly. Argentina was not the only country with something less than constitutional government. Understandably, military rulers in Latin America like Vargas in Brazil, Villaroel in Bolivia, Marinigo in Paraguay, Batista in Cuba, Somoza in Nicaragua, and Trujillo in the Dominican Republic did not welcome the proposal. Nor was their opposition the only stumbling block. Even such anti-fascist countries as Mexico, Cuba, and Venezuela feared the consequences of Larreta's plan. The vagueness of what constituted repeated violations of the elementary rights of man was a serious defect. Did it not offer the United States an excuse to interfere in the domestic affairs of any Latin American republic whose government it did not like? Braden's presence in the State Department was hardly reassuring on that score. The United States might picture the Argentine government as the archetype of to-

47 Ibid. pp. 9901–2
48 The New York Times, 27 October 1945, p. 5; DAFR, vol. VIII, 763
49 DOSB, 25 November 1945, 864–6

talitarianism in the hemisphere, but there was more personal freedom in Argentina then in many other Latin American states. Who could say which rulers, representing perhaps a totally different ideology, might next incur United States disapproval? For all these reasons an overwhelming majority of states rejected the Larreta proposal.

The failure of the inter-American community to assume collective responsibility for the form of government of its members did not stop Braden. He was determined to remain vigilant. If an armed gang seized power in Latin America, he said, trampled on the civil liberties of the people, denied them their essential rights, the United States was immediately concerned. He accused exponents of non-intervention in such a case as standing 'on the book of diplomatic etiquette.' United States policy remained that of the Good Neighbor. But this did not prevent it from 'pointing the finger of accusation' at all governments following fascist ideology. Accusation was not intervention. It was something a good neighbour owed as a matter of integrity to itself.[50]

Braden got his chance to act as a good neighbour when Argentina finally decided to hold a presidential election. Colonel Juan Perón was the Nationalist candidate. Dr José Tamborini, representing a coalition of Radical, Socialist, Progressive, Democratic, and Communist parties, was permitted to run as his principal opponent. Braden might have interpreted the election in two ways. Either his denunciations of the government had been unjustified or his finger of accusation had pointed to the democratic light. Instead, in an extreme reversion from the principle of non-intervention he decided to help the Argentinians unseat a régime which he considered disreputable.

His reasoning appears to have been as follows. Why not make the public aware of the true character of their rulers? The great mass of people are democratic, freedom-loving. Let them have the facts about their dictatorial officials and they will surely banish them from office. On 14 February 1946, two weeks before election day, without consulting the other American republics, the State Department published its files on Nazi influence in official circles. Now the people would know. The 'Blue Book,' the work of Braden and his staff, showed Perón's involvement with Nazi agents and native collaborators. It also brought home the impossibility of good relations with the United States until Argentina was represented by a govern-

---

50 The *New York Times*, 20 January 1946, pp. 1, 16. It should be noted that during this same period both President Roosevelt and President Harry S Truman denounced General Francisco Franco for his government founded on Fascist principles. Ibid. 27 September 1945, p. 1, 24 August 1945, p. 1

ment that inspired confidence at home as well as abroad. By this Wilsonian attempt to teach Latin Americans how to elect good men, the State Department grossly underestimated national feelings. Perón's campaign slogan became, 'O Perón, O Bradon' ('Either Perón or Braden'). When the final returns were counted, in what was generally considered a fair election, Perón had swamped his opponent. The paternalistic policy of the United States had produced the opposite effect of what was intended.

Two contradictory views are worth considering. Sumner Welles equated the policy fashioned by Braden with Russian policy in the Balkans, where solely because of its military power the strong asserted a right to dictate the form of government of the weak. J.M. Jones, an editor of the highly reputed magazine *Fortune*, disagreed. In an article written for *Harper's Magazine* in April 1946, he described the principle of non-intervention as a useful concept. It was capable, however, of becoming a dangerous fiction when acted upon as if it were true. As he saw it, the policy associated with Braden's name was justified as an effort to promote democratic government. He backed representatives of the United States in Latin America who were not afraid to speak up for democratic principles, even when confronted by cries of American intervention.[51]

Jones was wrong: not about the danger of acting on fictions as if they were true, but on the other recommendation. The continued concern shown by the United States over the type of government of its Latin American neighbours was arousing old suspicions. Worse, inter-American relations were deteriorating at a time when the Communists were increasing their drive for world power. Not only was Soviet pressure apparently being applied in Greece and Turkey, but renewed Communist activity in the Western Hemisphere raised the spectre of a Soviet foothold in Latin America.

The United States had intended to negotiate a mutual defence treaty with all the Latin American republics. Patterned after the Act of Chapultepec it would create a regional organization in which the American states, as sovereign equals, would assume the responsibility for policing the hemisphere. In fact, an inter-American conference, scheduled four months previously, had been postponed by the State Department on Braden's initiative. The official reason: the United States could not properly enter into an inter-American treaty of military assistance if the Argentine government was one of the parties.

51 Manross, L.M. *United States Policy Towards Argentina*, Library of Congress, Washington, D.C., 1947, pp. 49, 51

With the danger of Communist aggression taking on menacing proportions, the United States faced a dilemma. It could not strengthen hemisphere defences effectively without Argentina. It could not consent to a conference with Argentina. By the spring of 1947 the lack of correspondence between the conceptual basis of Braden's policy and the reality perceived as aggressive Russian designs on the New World forced a change. Regardless of its form of government, the equal status of Argentina with the other American states could no longer be denied. No less than the safety of the United States was believed to be at stake.

On 15 April 1947 President Harry Truman met with Argentine Ambassador Oscar Ivanissevich. The misunderstanding between the two countries, the president said, could be ended if Perón cracked down on former Nazi sympathizers. No mention was made of restoring individual political liberty under a constitutional democracy. The ambassador agreed. Braden had no alternative but to resign. Almost immediately after he did so, a date was set for the Inter-American Conference for the Maintenance of Continental Peace and Security. The twenty Latin American states, regardless of their form of government, were invited to perfect their war-time pact for meeting aggression by establishing an inter-American regional organization. The paternalism designed by the State Department to catch Fascists gave way to an equal partnership with the United States – to stop Communists.

One may see in Braden's policy evidence of a crusading spirit wellknown in the history of the United States. But, because inter-American affairs are involved, another dimension must not be overlooked. In the New World the concept of the American states as sovereign equals implies an equal devotion to the same political principles. This notion has long been fostered at inter-American conferences. Over the years delegates have adhered to innumerable declarations proclaiming the ideological solidarity of the inter-American community. The picture has been drawn of twenty-one equal republics, all moved by common ideals, all dedicated to representative government as the one best calculated to satisfy man's aspirations. Many officials of the United States had come to see in the presence of Latin American dictators (or even in the existence of a lesser degree of democracy than they themselves enjoyed) a stain on the concept of the Good Neighbor. If all American republics were not in fact representative republics, then, according to their thinking, they had to be made representative – a paternalistic obligation the United States willingly undertook and for which it felt itself unusually well qualified.

But how do you combine a policy of equality and non-intervention with a policy of cleaning up disreputable governments? One might think the dilemma posed by the conflicting concepts had become an historical oddity. As the reader well knows, the Latin American policy of the United States continues to find officials divided between contradictory ideas.

THE FLOWERING OF THE IDEA OF EQUALITY

When the delegates first assembled at the Inter-American Conference for the Maintenance of Continental Peace and Security (Rio de Janeiro, August-September 1947) Secretary of State George B. Marshall, chairman of the United States delegation, greeted them with a well-known inter-American tune. He recalled their devotion to the principle of nation-states bound by the same norms of moral conduct applicable to individual human beings. On the basis of this equation, said Marshall rests 'our fundamental belief in the equality of individuals [and] of the equality of states.' With the ritual performed, Marshall next lent colour to Shakespeare's line, 'a sentence is but a cheveril glove to a good wit.' He first described the state as existing for man and not the other way around, but in the very same breath he rejected any infringement on the fundamental rights of the state.[52]

These preliminaries over, the conferees drafted and signed the Inter-American Treaty of Reciprocal Assistance. The Rio Treaty, as it is popularly called, applied the democratic principle of majority rule to nation-states. In domestic politics, no matter how rich, how eminent, how experienced the individual may be, he agrees to abide by the will of the majority of his fellow citizens, even though the majority may include the poor, the ignorant, and the inexperienced. The Rio Treaty applied the same principle to states. Thus, with one exception, the United States agreed that, notwithstanding its vast military power, its industrial might, and its political maturity, in the key issues affecting hemisphere security, it would abide by the will of a two-thirds majority of the American republics.

Briefly, the treaty provided for collective action in case of armed attack or in case the independence of an American state was threatened by any situation endangering the peace of the hemisphere. Collective measures included breaking off diplomatic relations, interrupting all links of communication and transportation, and employing armed force. However, neither the United States nor any Latin American republic could be obligated to use armed force without its consent. In all other cases, agreement by any fourteen countries bound the United States to sever diplomatic ties, break off economic relations, or otherwise conform to the will of the

52 *DAFR*, vol. IX, 534

majority even when opposed to the decision. As Senator Vandenberg noted after his return from Rio de Janeiro (he and Senator Connally were members of the United States delegation), the Rio Treaty, unlike other international instruments, contained no 'paralyzing veto' on any peaceful sanction, and no nation, whatever its size or power, could stop the others from using collective force. He hailed the accomplishment for placing active responsibility for hemisphere order in the hands of the inter-American community, forming a '*true* partnership.'[53]

The Rio Treaty was a high point in the efforts of the Latin American republics to have the United States base its policy on the concept of sovereign equality. For the United States it represented the furthest departure from the opposing concept of great-power primacy.

The inter-American experience appears to have had worldwide repercussions on the relationship between great and small states. For in November 1950, three years after the Rio Treaty was signed, similar democratic principles of equality and majority rule were adopted by the United Nations General Assembly in its Uniting for Peace Resolution.

Ever since the Charter had gone into effect, the gap between the concept of great-power primacy and international political reality had widened. By 1950 great-power disunity had rendered the Security Council impotent in the face of threats to world peace. A way had to be found to deal with such disturbances in the name of the international community. While the Charter placed primary responsibility for the maintenance of international peace and security in the Security Council, a subtle distinction came to prevail. Primary responsibility did not mean exclusive responsibility. Based on that premise the United States proposed calling on all members of the United Nations to share the peacekeeping function as sovereign equal partners, just as the twenty-one American republics had done in the New World.

The Uniting for Peace Resolution was the result. Hereafter, when the Security Council is unable to act because of lack of unanimity among the Great Powers, in any case where peace is threatened, the General Assembly may recommend collective measures to preserve or restore international order, including the use of armed force. General Assembly resolutions are recommendations only. But members of the United Nations act on these recommendations as if they were legally binding decisions – even to the extent of providing the emergency military power necessary to enforce them.

By the middle of the twentieth century, thanks to the resolution,

53 Ibid. 541–2

nation-states were able to employ armed force to maintain peace in the name of the international community. They arrived at their decisions according to democratic principles normally identified with electorates in domestic politics. Each state, regardless of size or power is entitled to one vote, and the decision of the majority prevails with or, in theory at least, without the approval of the Great Powers.

What at first may have been no more than a nominal tribute to an ideal of equality cherished by small states, conceded by the Great Powers under the pressure of creating the United Nations, had evolved far beyond its original intention. In this way the conceptual level of existence had come to mould the real world of international relations as it had done in inter-American affairs.

From all this one thing stands out. Workable solutions to current problems affecting the peace of the world are not going to be found outside the realm where the human mind forms its basic concepts.[54]

54 The idea of finding 'solutions' to international problems brings to mind the view of a former professional diplomatist who sees the task of diplomacy 'as essentially a menial one, consisting of a process one is powerless to control, tidying up the messes other people have made, attempting to keep small disasters from turning into big ones, moderating the passions of governments and of opinionated individuals, and attempting to transmit to one's own government the unwelcome image of the outside world ... bearing in mind that the truth about external reality will never be wholly compatible with those internal ideological fictions which the national state engenders and by which it lives.' George F. Kennan, 'History and Diplomacy by a Diplomatist,' *Review of Politics*, 1956, 176.

7
Equality in a world of superpowers

The international scene is marked by several stunning facts. The political system is overloaded with sovereign states. A large majority of them, incapable of playing an independent role in foreign affairs, are able to and often do manipulate the world organization to their own ends. The United States and the Soviet Union, armed with thermonuclear weapons and sophisticated delivery systems, tower above their relatively puny neighbours. This chapter discusses the continuing confusion in international affairs, as statesmen strive to achieve a measure of congruity between the world as it actually is and the contradictory concepts of sovereign equality and great-power primacy.

EQUAL STATES AND THE UNITED NATIONS

When the Charter of the United Nations was drafted, statesmen were bedeviled by the gap between chaotic circumstances and conceptual thinking. No critical voice was raised against lumping together 'the equal rights of men and women and of nations large and small.' In the light of this idea, according to Dag Hammarskjöld, the Charter established not only a system of equal votes to express the sovereign equality of the membership. It also committed the organization to the furtherance of self-determination.

In an encyclical letter (12 April 1963) Pope John XXIII provided an authoritative version of the rationale. 'All men are equal in their natural dignity,' wrote the Pope. 'Consequently there are no political communities which are superior by nature and none which are inferior ... since they are bodies whose membership is made up of these same human beings.' Because all states are by nature equal in dignity, continued His Holiness, each has the right to exist and to be primarily responsible for its own future. Here, then, is the underlying philosophical premise of the concept of sovereign equality.

For the identical reason this logic is applied to peoples as well. To develop friendly relations among nations based on the equal rights of peoples is an express purpose of the Charter. General Assembly Resolution 1514 (xv) confirms the equal right of all peoples to self-determination. Subjecting them to alien rule constitutes, in the words of the resolution, a denial of 'fundamental human rights.' By 1971, Resolution 2787 (xxvi) affirmed the creation of a new basic human right: to fight for the self-determination of one's people.

All this raises the immense question: who are a people? Who, indeed, are entitled to self-determination? On 18 December 1918, after the American Commission to Negotiate Peace landed in France, Secretary of State Lansing, one of the commissioners, searched in vain for an answer. Puzzled over the meaning of self-determination, he wondered what unit the president had in mind when he used the term. Was the right to be enjoyed by every race, every territorial area, every community? Perplexed as to how a nation comes into being, unable to find any standard for determining the groups entitled to independence, Lansing saw at once that the principle was loaded with dynamite. He ventured a prediction – the Wilsonian principle was a calamitous utterance, bound to raise unrealisable hopes, and sure to cause misery and death to thousands of people.[1] One need only recall the Congo, Biafra, Bangladesh, and Vietnam (where the goal of the United States was to safeguard the right of the peoples of Southeast Asia to select their form of government according to principles of self-determination) to realize the accuracy of Lansing's prediction.

Today, the principle of self-determination, not one whit closer to definition than in Lansing's time, has resulted in a striking phenomenon: the indiscriminate creation of a multiplicity of sovereign states. Indiscriminate, I say, for several reasons. The national boundaries of some of the recent participants in world affairs are a caprice. Rarely are they pertinent to natural geography. Rarely do they encompass all persons with a common culture, religion, race or even, in the case of Africa, tribal affiliation.

Most serious is the problem of survival. A majority of the new countries simply do not have the resources to achieve viability. Niger, Chad,

1 Lansing, R. *The Peace Negotiations*, Boston, 1921, p. 97

Lesotho, Laos, Mali, Burundi, to take random examples, have only the flimsiest pretensions to modern statehood. As independent sovereign entities they have practically no future.

According to Lansing, even those who in Wilson's day subscribed to self-determination as a great fundamental truth recognized its limitations. They did not suggest it for those people beyond the European continent that civilization had passed by. Yet in most of the new countries governments are primitive and ill-equipped. Because illiteracy is so high they suffer from a desperate lack of professionally trained officials to run their own countries, let alone to staff consulates, missions and delegations to international organizations. It is not altogether surprising to read about an African representative to the United Nations, a member of the main committee concerned with the Korean question, who first became aware of the division of the country into North and South Korea during a luncheon conversation in the delegate's dining room.[2]

That no criteria exist for statehood was first confirmed in 1960 by the General Assembly Declaration on the Granting of Independence to Colonial Countries and Peoples. There are no conditions, no reservations. To nail home the point the declaration contained an extraordinary provision. Neither political, social, nor economic preparedness was to serve as a pretext for delaying independence. If any doubts still existed, they were removed in 1971. General Assembly Resolution 2869 (xxvi) expressly eliminated size, limited resources, or geographical isolation as valid objections to attaining sovereign statehood.

Consider the implications for the 280 inhabitants of the South Atlantic island of Tristan da Cunha. For almost a century and a half the island has been cut off from the main stream of civilization. The population, temporarily evacuated to England in 1961 after a volcanic eruption endangered their lives, speak a nineteenth-century cockney English typical of the language spoken by soldiers of Wellington's army. The habitable area of the island is twelve square miles and a total of thirty acres of land are under cultivation. Before coming to England, potatoes and fish were the principal items of their diet. And rare were the individuals who had seen a sidewalk, a bridge, a river, a tree, or had even heard a bird sing, so desolate is their island. Yet today neither the size of Tristan da Cunha, nor its handful of people, nor the simplicity of their way of life would stand in the way of this British dependency acquiring independence and eventually taking its place as a sovereign equal member of the United Nations.

2 Hovet, J. Jr. *Africa in the United Nations*, Northwestern University Press, 1963, p. 219

To carry the argument to a preposterous but not altogether illogical conclusion, let us recall the story of Mrs Irene Pearl Smith Cliett. Claiming to have been wrongly deprived of 350 acres of good farm land in Waller County, Texas, as a result of a Federal Court order, Mrs Cliett resolved to defend her property by force of arms. As a first step she founded the one-woman nation of 'Eneri' – Irene spelled backward. Next, she designated 'Lraep' – Pearl spelled backward – as the seat of government. Finally, her sister presented reporters with a proclamation declaring the property to be a separate nation seeking admission to membership in the United Nations.[3]

Relatively speaking, and at least from the standpoint of literacy, ability to pay its own way, and military preparedness, this 'nation' is on no lower level than many members of the world organization. Does it, too, qualify for independence and UN membership? The question sounds ridiculous. Only in this democratic age, the concept that all men are created equal is firmly entrenched in the mind as a principle applicable without qualification to abstract collective persons: to 'peoples,' to 'nations,' to 'nation-states.' Self-determination has become a sacred maxim of international politics, a right to be enjoyed by the inhabitants of practically any scrap of real estate or archipelagic oddity. And to judge any of these sovereign entities, however meagre its qualifications, as unworthy of admission to the UN, is considered a blasphemy against the spirit of the times.

As early as 1960, Secretary-General Hammarskjöld recognized the bitter fruit of the Wilsonian principle: the swollen membership of the UN. The admission of the former African colonies, he thought, was likely to impair the efficiency and executive capacity of the organization. The implicit warning went unheeded. His successor did not question the principle of independence – even for Pitcairn Island, with less than 100 inhabitants living in an area two miles square. But U Thant did worry about the automatic admission to the UN of micro states – automatic because the membership simply refused to question whether an applicant was able and willing to carry out its Charter obligations. He therefore recommended establishing criteria for joining, and for those not meeting these criteria, alternative forms of association. Nothing definite could be agreed upon. By 1973 UN membership had increased over 160 per cent since the world body was formed. At the lowest end of the poverty scale at least 20 per cent of the members have a per capita gross domestic product of less than $100 a year, and count fewer than one fifth of their people as literate. With over

3 The New York *Herald Tribune*, International ed. 20 March 1953, p. 3

seventy-odd dependent territories looming as potential sovereign equal members (the population of more than half of them is less than 100,000), it is the turn of Secretary-General Kurt Waldheim to wrestle with the problem.

Some idea of Mr Waldheim's conceptual thinking about the matter may be gleaned from his 1972 report to the General Assembly.[4] Along with technological advances, he said, 'democratization' is producing a new form of world society, and the UN has to keep in step. He conjured up Mazzini's abstraction, 'the peoples of the world,' and claiming intimate knowledge of their thinking, announced that the concept of great-power primacy cannot, in the long run, be acceptable to them. According to Mr Waldheim, the UN provides, or should provide, the means by which all nations, great and small, take part in 'the political process' of keeping the peace. The only conceptual basis for such participation, he concluded, is the principle of sovereign equality.

Following this, the Secretary-General drew an analogy between the behaviour of men and women and of nations large and small. In this way he was able to explain the failure of members to implement UN decisions. There is a period in the development of most states, he said, when individual citizens, not feeling duty bound to the central government, have failed to give effect to its commands. The UN, he declared, was simply going through a similar stage. In effect, what Mr Waldheim was saying was this: if individual citizens have developed a sense of obligation towards state authority, then the political collectivities belonging to the UN will also develop a sense of obligation towards UN authority. By using the same logic we can arrive at this conclusion regarding the membership. Criteria for the corporate persons permitted to take part in the international political process must not differ in any consequential way from those existing for the real persons permitted to take part in the domestic political process.

All of the foregoing factors taken together explain how the innovation Metternich assured the king of Würtemberg no wise man would think twice about before protesting has become the order of the day. In the General Assembly, members meet under the spell of a conceptual affinity between the equal rights of men and women and of nations large and small. By political magic they are transmuted into an international electorate enjoying universal statehood suffrage. No political distinction is made between the strong and the weak, the rich and the poor. James Bryce's dictum is changed to read: Each state, like each adult, is more likely to be right than

4 United Nations, General Assembly, *Official Records*: Twenty-Seventh Sess.,
   'Introduction to the Report of the Secretary-General on the Work of the Organization,' 9
   August 1972, Supp. No. 1A (A/8701/Add.1), New York, 1972, p. 2

wrong; and each state's vote, like each adult's, must be treated as equally good with another's. As in domestic politics, a majority decision is binding.

In democratic societies, the popular will, however imperfectly expressed through the electoral process, is accepted as the ultimate basis for determining political authority. In Soviet-type régimes, the Communist Party, by making known the interest of the masses in accordance with a metaphysical appreciation of the laws of history, is also said to express the will of the people. In doing so the Party claims a legitimacy comparable to what Western governments find through free elections. Whatever the myth, legitimate authority depends upon a notion of right, of approval, of consent in the consciousness of the subject.

The resolutions of the United Nations are theoretically capable of expressing the general will of its members. The claim to legitimacy, however, is wide open to question. There is a gross disproportion between voting power and real power. The smallest and financially weakest states, representing a minority of the total population in the organization, possess a majority of the votes. Paying a fractional share of the assessments of the organization, they are able to outvote those paying the highest rates. At budget time, when the expenditures for the coming year come up for approval, the major powers, paying two-thirds of all UN costs, feel the full impact of majority rule. They find themselves chosen to foot the bill for projects which they voted against and which the majority, by themselves, could never afford.

All this is manifestly unjust: to the states involved and to the real human beings making up the population represented in the organization. Because members are not bound by a single code of behaviour, because they are not devoted to common basic values and aspirations, because they are not committed to accepting the will of the majority, what emerges from the UN and proceeds to speak for the international community is a particularly corrupted voice. In playing out the myth of democracy and sovereign equality, irresponsibility is reflected in a stream of resolutions on a wide variety of matters based on emotion and without regard to the consequences for the organization or for world order.

Attempts to apply the concept of sovereign equality to the raw facts of international existence have left a path marked by ambiguity, contradiction, and frustration. Ponder, for example, the reasoning of the General Assembly with regard to the inhabitants of the colony of Gibraltar who, by a massive vote, elected to remain under British rule. In 1713 Spain transferred the rock to Britain under the terms of the Treaty of Utrecht. In recent years Spain has contested before the appropriate organs of the

United Nations the ancient cession of its territory. A 1966 resolution of the General Assembly invited the two parties to start negotiations and both accepted.

In 1967 the minister of state for Commonwealth Affairs, Mrs Judith Hart, explained that Britain could not simply transfer one population to the rule of another country without regard to the opinions and desires of the people concerned. To do so clearly violated the Charter based on the equal rights and self-determination of peoples. It also violated Britain's sacred trust under the same instrument to promote the well-being of the inhabitants (Article 73). In accordance with the spirit of these provisions, the British government decided to let the people of Gibraltar choose: either to retain their association with Britain or to elect to live under Spanish sovereignty. Both the United Nations and the Spanish government received invitations to send observers. Each refused. According to their reasoning the matter did not involve a colonial situation but the territorial integrity of Spain. The fate of Gibraltarians was a matter to be determined solely by bilateral negotiations between the British and Spanish governments.

Britain, nevertheless, held the referendum. Forty-four voters chose to be affiliated with Spain; over 12,000 elected to remain under British rule. In spite of this overwhelming expression the General Assembly sought to nullify the result. Resolution 2429 XXIII declared the continuation of the colonial situation in Gibraltar incompatible with the purposes of the Charter and previous Assembly resolutions. Britain was given a deadline: to end its rule by 1 October 1969.

That day has long since come and gone. Neither Spain nor Britain has changed its position. The UN is powerless to enforce its resolution. Spain and Britain have resumed bilateral talks. But the contradictory levels of meaning embodied in the idea of equality and its corollary, the principle of self-determination, stand exposed. In the General Assembly the territorial integrity of the corporate person known as Spain takes precedence over the clearly expressed wishes of the vast majority of real men and women who live in Gibraltar. Evidently, as long as a colonial people do not wish their freedom from British rule, they are not the equal of other peoples, and they do not possess the fundamental human right to determine their own future.[5] Such a conclusion hardly speaks for the sense of responsibility of the organization.

5 United Nations, General Assembly, Resolution 2429 (XXIII), 1747th Plenary Meeting 18 December 1968, A/Res 2429 (XXIII), 31 December 1968

An equally specious conceptual approach marked the General Assembly's response to Rhodesia. When that self-governing colony declared its independence from Britain, logic might have told us it was exercising its fundamental right to be free. Instead of receiving the blessing of the UN, it stood condemned. London insisted on a date being fixed for the principle of majority rule to go into effect. Salisbury, ready to grant its people of African origin a progressive extension of the right to vote, refused for reasons of internal stability to set a specific time when their voice would command a majority. The General Assembly insisted on a rigid formula: no independence without universal adult suffrage and majority rule. In the ensuing deadlock, the Assembly called on Britain to use force if necessary to establish full democratic freedom and equal political rights.[6] Upon its failure to take such stringent measures, and Rhodesia's insistence on independence, the Security Council declared the Rhodesian government a threat to the peace and made sanctions obligatory on all members.

Trying to act on the basis of the concept of sovereign equality produced these ironic results. The UN, opposed to intervention (a violation of a corollary of the concept of sovereign equality), recommended its use against a government whose domestic legislation on suffrage it repugned. The UN, opposed to colonialism (a violation of a corollary of the concept of sovereign equality), ordered Rhodesia punished for not behaving like a good colony and submitting to its nominal master's will. The UN, declaring Rhodesia a threat to the peace because it refused to fix a definite date for majority rule, made the threat believable by calling on Britain to intervene by armed force to set matters right. One final point. The authority and credibility of the UN has been weakened by the response to its call for economic sanctions. To be successful in unseating the Rhodesian government, if trade embargoes can be, would require a blockade of South Africa and the Portuguese colonies of Angola and Mozambique, a step no member with the power to do so is prepared to undertake for the UN. Actually, sanctions are being openly evaded by such powers as the United States, West Germany, and Japan, among others, and are being totally ignored by South Africa and Portugal.

Juxtaposing the equal rights of men and women and of nations large and small raises a perplexing question of priorities. The concept of a state's

6 United Nations, General Assembly, *Official Records*: Nineteenth Sess., 'Resolutions Adopted by the General Assembly During its Nineteenth Session,' 1 December 1964–1 September 1965, Resolution 2022 (XX), Supp. No. 15 (A/5815), p. 54

inviolable personality and its sovereign equality with all other states serves to condemn outside meddling on behalf of the personality and equal rights of individual human beings. Yet, where domestic policy systematically degrades the essential dignity of large numbers of the population, it often touches a sensitive nerve among members of the international community. Life being the way it is, however, choosing between the individual and the state often defies our limited powers of accommodation. Inevitably the General Assembly has been caught in the confusion. Thus, it has been a forum for calling world attention to the evil of racial prejudice against blacks. It has repeatedly condemned South Africa's policy of apartheid as a crime against humanity, giving precedence to human rights over sovereign rights. At the same time, it has applied different standards of behaviour, depending on race, towards two other African states. In 1973 the UN took no action with regard to the tragic events in Uganda, when General Idi Amin deported almost the entire Asian population, around 30,000 Indians and Pakistanis, and confiscated their assets. Those remaining were reduced to second-class citizens. Similarly, no resolutions were passed regarding the black minority Tutsi régime in the central African nation of Burundi. The government of Colonel Michel Micombero is allegedly responsible for the slaughter of at least 100,000 members of the black population belonging to the rebellious Hutu tribe. (According to Swedish Pentecostal missionaries in Tanzania, refugees estimate the total number of Hutus killed by 1973 at 250–300,000.)[7]

Is the racist policy of South Africa more detestable than that of Uganda? than the acts of tribal vengeance against the Hutus of Burundi? It does not strike me as fanciful to suggest that if the Tutsi leader and General Idi Amin were white, an outraged majority in the General Assembly would have condemned such acts as a crime against humanity. Not being so, the UN subordinates the essential worth of human personality to corporate personality. To concern itself with what takes place in Uganda and Burundi would violate a corollary of the concept of sovereign equality: each member's right to be free from UN intrusion in its domestic affairs.

In the field of peacekeeping the idea of equality comes into major conflict with the concept of great-power primacy. To appreciate the present impotence of the United Nations it may be worthwhile to review certain events. In the 1960's the Soviet Union and its allies, together with France, were the most vigorous supporters of the original concept of great-power primacy

7 *Keesing's Contemporary Archives*, London, 28 May–3 June 1973, p. 25910

underlying the creation of the United Nations; that is, peacekeeping was to be the exclusive concern of the Great Powers acting together in the Security Council. Differing from them in one major respect was the United States and a majority of the other members. When the Security Council was immobilized by the use of the veto, as it was then, the burden of maintaining peace shifted to the General Assembly under the Uniting for Peace Resolution. At this point, the initiation and financing of security operations was based on the democratic principles of sovereign equality, one-state one-vote and majority rule.

The organization almost broke apart over the costs of the United Nations operations in the Middle East and the Congo (1964–5). Briefly, a good part of the membership, led by the Soviet Union and France, had failed to pay their share of the assessments voted by the General Assembly. Financing peacekeeping operations, said N.T. Federenko, Soviet representative, fell within the sole competence of the Security Council. The United States and the International Court of Justice backed the authority of the Assembly.

Under Article 19 of the Charter, a nation more than two years in arrears on its assessments could lose its vote in the General Assembly. As time went by the United States prepared to invoke this sanction. But first Arthur Goldberg, us Ambassador to the UN, tried to bring the alternative concepts into closer harmony with the facts of international life. No member, he said, neither the Soviet Union nor the United States, had a right to frustrate the General Assembly's residual authority in peacekeeping matters. Nevertheless, to preserve a better balance between the exercise of power and the responsibility for its use, members bearing the main burden of the operation should have a more appropriate vote. To prevent unacceptable resolutions from being passed, he would create a special finance committee composed of large contributors. All financial arrangements for maintaining order would then have to be approved by a two-thirds vote of this committee.[8]

Ambassador Goldberg got nowhere. Federenko opposed any residual peacekeeping authority in the General Assembly. He opposed the creation of a special finance committee. And he was unmoved by the loss-of-vote sanction under Article 19. The us received no comfort from small states. For most of them the creation of a special finance committee contributed to

8 United Nations, General Assembly, Twentieth Sess., Special Political Committee, *Summary Record of Meetings*, 22 September–17 December 1965, 465th Meeting, 24 November 1965

a further derogation of their power. Pushing the matter of unpaid assessments to the point where a state would lose its vote was even more intolerable. Here is the way one delegate from a small state expressed the longing of the weak to make reality conform to the conceptual world. Countries such as Tanzania, Saudi Arabia, or Upper Volta, he said, are 'placed on the map' by the vote they can cast at the UN. Small states reason as follows: 'My vote makes me equal in one way to the United States.' To disenfranchise a state under the Charter, he concluded, supports a rule that threatens small countries by taking away their only weapon – the vote that makes them equal to the giants.[9]

In the face of such opposition the US backed down. Members then agreed to a system of voluntary contributions to permit the organization to resume its functions. A Special Committee on the Financial Situation of the United Nations, created in 1971, still searches for acceptable financing procedures. The disparity between existential reality and the conflicting nominal ideas for securing international order have left peacekeeping operations on a completely improvised basis.

The need to manage the world's oceans – a treasure chest of food and mineral wealth – has revealed a new awareness of the inadequacy of the concept of sovereign equality. In 1967 Ambassador Arvid Pardo of Malta, realizing that there was nothing to prevent technologically and militarily powerful countries from grabbing the greater part of such riches, declared the high seas and its resources to be the common heritage of mankind. At the United Nations he advocated the creation of an international régime, an agency acting in the nature of a global trustee to regulate the exploitation of the seabed beyond the limits of national jurisdiction.

But in a world of nation-states, once you speak of an international régime the question of who participates in the decision-making immediately comes to the fore. Mr Pardo did not consider it wise to make the United Nations itself responsible for administering such an international authority. What bothered him in such a case was the fundamental principle of the world organization: the idea of one-state one-vote embodied in the concept of sovereign equality. As a practical matter, he told UN members with startling clarity, 'it is hardly likely that those countries which have already developed a technological capability to exploit the ocean floor, would agree to an international régime if it were administered by a body

9 Keohane, R.O. 'Political Influence in the General Assembly,' *International Conciliation*, March 1966, p. 60

where small countries, such as mine, had the same voting power as the United States or the Soviet Union.'[10]

Shortly thereafter, with the establishment of the UN Seabed Committee, members quickly became enveloped in confusion as they searched for a way to institutionalize Pardo's proposal. Frequent and intensive debates have been marked by the Soviet Union's opposition to any supranational organization with jurisdiction to exploit the seabed, by United States plans for the distribution of mankind's legacy which allegedly favour industrial nations, and by great and small coastal states extending their jurisdiction over increasingly wider areas of water and seabed lying off their shores. Meanwhile, among those states capable of exploiting seabed resources, a dog-eat-dog competition is in the making. Essentially the problem is philosophical: how to bring into more harmonious relation Ambassador Pardo's egalitarian image of mankind's common heritage and what the Secretary-General of the United Nations calls 'matters as they are.'

In 1966 a Russian delegate to the United Nations, juggling the idea of 'the state' and 'the people,' unwittingly revealed how easily the concept of sovereign equality can be misshapen. His argument has continued to plague men's thinking ever since. At the time, the Soviet Union was seeking to implement a General Assembly declaration on the inadmissibility of intervention in the domestic affairs of states. At the Twenty-First Session, V.V. Kusnetsov denounced the United States. Not only did it engage in armed intervention in Latin America and elsewhere, he said, it also practised indirect forms of intervention, bending small states to its will by economic pressure, political blackmail, and *Diktat*.

The United States countered by referring to the Tri-Continental Conference, held in Cuba earlier that year, as an example of a pernicious form of indirect intervention practised by the international Communist movement. The Soviet Union was represented at the meeting by a top Communist party official, a member of the Supreme Soviet. There, together with other high-ranking Communist party leaders, the conferees openly advocated interference in the internal affairs of Latin America and certain Asian and African countries. Steps were taken to form a permanent organization to promote the overthrow of non-Communist governments. What, asked the

10 United Nations, General Assembly, First Committee, *Provisional Verbatim Records*, 1516th Meeting, 1 November 1967, A/C.1/PV 1516, p. 3. For some of the best-known efforts to create an international agency to control activities on the seabed, see Hayashi, M., 'An International Machinery for the Management of the Seabed: Birth and Growth of the Idea,' *Annals of International Studies*, vol. 4, Genève, 1973, p. 251

American delegate, could be a more flagrant defiance by the Soviet Union of the very principle of non-intervention it was seeking to implement?

The representative of the Byelorussian Socialist Soviet Republic, G.G. Tchernouchtchenko, dismissed the rejoinder as irrelevant. He found nothing extraordinary about the Tri-Continental Conference. Nor did it violate in any way accepted principles of international behaviour. On the contrary, it conformed directly to countless resolutions of the United Nations by supporting the equal right of all peoples in their struggle for freedom.[11]

Not averse to having it both ways, Tchernouchtchenko's argument makes this singular contribution to the crumbling of precision and good sense. All states are equal. Therefore, intervention by one state in the domestic affairs of another is inadmissible – a violation of the concept of sovereign equality. But all peoples are also equal. Therefore, intervention to support their right to be free is admissible – no violation of the concept of sovereign equality.

As we shall see in the discussion of Czechoslovakia that follows, the contradiction between the Brezhnev doctrine, which came to light two years later, and continued official statements from Moscow on the absolute inadmissability of intervention in the domestic affairs of another state, reflects the same sadly confused logic.

Looking back on the attempts to act on the concept of sovereign equality and to apply it to the world as it is, brings to mind two comments by senior diplomats. George Bush, United States Ambassador to the United Nations in 1972, urged members not to pass resolutions pertaining to the Arab-Israeli crisis lest they *impede* peaceful settlement and further endanger the area's shaky truce. A year later, Secretary-General Waldheim publicly deplored the way members use the organization for their own narrow interests rather than for the sake of the world community. The link between the concept of sovereign equality and responsibility is tenuous, if it exists at all.

SUPERPOWERS AND INTERVENTION

American and Soviet decision-makers live in two worlds simultaneously: the hypothetical world in which they oscillate between conflicting con-

11 United Nations, General Assembly, Twenty-First Sess. First Committee, *Prov. Summary Record*, 1473 Meet., 5 December 1966, A/C./I/SR 1473, p. 10; Ibid. 1479 Meet., 9 December 1966, A/C/I/SR 1479, p. 12; Ibid. 1482 Meet., 12 December 1966, A/C.I/SR 1482, p. 6

cepts, and the infinitely diverse world of concrete existence. Nowhere is this better illustrated than by the United States military intervention in the Dominican Republic (1965) and the Soviet military intervention in Czechoslovakia (1968). Both Washington and Moscow have the strongest interest in not allowing themselves to get involved again in such situations. The essential dilemma, though, will not go away. It arises out of collective security arrangements among nominally equal states where, in fact, one of them overwhelmingly dominates the others. From this perspective the unworkability of the concept of sovereign equality in the previous decade is worth recalling.

In 1964, Thomas C. Mann, assistant secretary of state for Inter-American Affairs, is reported to have announced a shift in the Latin American policy of the United States. The previous administration had returned to wielding a type of big stick. Hardest hit were military juntas which had overthrown democratic régimes. Under the old policy, unless the United States government received assurance of the speedy return to democratic rule, such juntas were threatened with the loss of economic and military aid, the key to their survival. Now this policy was over and done with. The United States had developed no particular affection for military juntas, said the assistant secretary. The new approach was an expression of the American desire to avoid becoming involved in the domestic affairs of its Latin American neighbours. A great power, Mann explained, could not impose its beliefs on weaker allies.

While military juntas overturning constitutional Latin American governments would not incur overt United States displeasure, the same was not true in the 1960s of Communist dictatorships. By the provisions of the Declaration of Caracas, passed in 1954 when the cold war was reaching its peak, Communist control of an American state endangered the peace of the hemisphere. The threat of its coming into existence warranted a joint consultative meeting of all foreign ministers to consider appropriate collective action. On paper, at least, the problem was now a shared responsibility. Only for the United States it was posed in different terms. What does Washington do if it believes the inter-American community is shirking its responsibility?

After the success of Fidel Castro in Cuba, the United States had become increasingly jittery about another Communist takeover in the Caribbean. So much so, that many government officials became insensitive to a new development in Latin America: the rise of articulate groups in the population who were not Communists and who sought drastic changes in political, economic, and social relationships. With the election of Juan Bosch as president, the relevance of the idea of equality and great-power primacy were soon put to a crucial test.

Once in office Bosch, who had polled 64 per cent of the votes cast, started a reform program which appeared to threaten the very structure of Dominican society. Opposition began to mount among those groups most likely to suffer from the proposed changes. As has so often happened in Latin America, a military junta took the lead in deposing Bosch and itself seizing the reins of government. As long as the United States refused to interfere, its policy was hailed as heralding the end of great-power paternalism.

A dilemma for the United States arose after the military fell out among themselves and a group of young officers, opposing reactionary elements of the junta, sought to reinstate Bosch as head of the government. The immediate reaction of President Lyndon Johnson of the United States was to favour this democratic resurgence. But when the dreaded word was spread that Bosch was 'soft on Communism' the United States felt compelled to act fast. On 28 April 1965 it unilaterally intervened in the Dominican Republic by sending in the Marines to support the military junta.

The entire structure of the inter-American community is founded on the concept of sovereign equality. The renunciation of unilateral intervention, joint consultation, and collective action among equal partners are the supporting pillars. How could the United States have broken its pledge? One answer is clear. In the fell clutch of circumstance the conceptual world of sovereign equal states had veered too far out of the orbit of reality. To lessen the gap between the dual worlds, action was called for based on the alternative concept of great-power primacy. As President Johnson explained, in the strategic Caribbean a band of Communist conspirators was threatening to take control of what had begun as a popular democratic revolution. The American nations, he told a nationwide TV audience on 2 May, 'cannot, must not and will not' permit it to happen.[12]

In the event, there was no time to consult with the foreign ministers of the other American republics. The president did not think the American people wanted him to vacillate just because the decision was hard. Moreover, there was strong doubt as to whether the other Latin American

---

12 *Keesing's Contemporary Archives*, London, 1965–6, p. 20814; the *New York Times*, 9 May 1965, sec. 4, pp. 1, 3; Draper, T. 'The Dominican Crisis,' *Commentary*, December 1965, pp. 33–68

republics would approve the decision. Mexico, Chile, Uruguay, and Venezuela were known to distrust the judgment of the United States on the threat of Communist influence. To them, collective intervention was no more than a term of art used by the United States to support governments it approved of.

Only after the United States intervened did it feel compelled to pay homage to the idea of equality. If the Organization of American States would co-operate, United States troops could easily be transformed into an inter-American peace force. Had not the United States, a decade before, turned its unilateral defence of South Korea into a legitimate collective undertaking by the United Nations?

At a meeting of American foreign ministers, Latin American representatives were divided on whether to support the intervention. They had ambivalent feelings about the extent of the threat to hemisphere security posed by the events in Santo Domingo. They cherished the language embodied in the Charter of the OAS attesting to the sovereign equality of the members, and its corollary, subscribed to by the United States, the principle of non-intervention. Eventually the United States viewpoint prevailed. Ten days after the unilateral intervention, the OAS agreed to assume collective responsibility for the return of orderly government in the Dominican Republic. By the end of May 1965, 250 infantry men from Honduras and 20 policemen from Costa Rica complemented US troops. Ultimately, 1500 soldiers from three Caribbean countries and Brazil and an army of 35,000 men from the United States made up the inter-American peace force.

A year later, after free elections had been held and all foreign troops had quit the Dominican Republic, demands for a change in the OAS became insistent. To most Latin American members of the organization the so-called 'copper rivetted' non-intervention clause, based on the concept of a community of sovereign equal states, had clearly rusted through. Yet the problem of subversion and internal disorder remained. To avoid a repetition of unilateral intervention by the United States, and to meet dangers to hemisphere security, a permanent inter-American peace force was proposed. Fear of United States domination outweighed all other considerations. It was overwhelmingly rejected.

Averell Harriman, President Johnson's ambassador at large, publicly stated his disagreement with the principle of non-intervention lying at the heart of the Latin American policy of the United States. Valid when formulated, he said, because it was created to guard against external aggression, it no longer answered the needs of the twentieth century when internal aggression posed the real, pressing danger to hemisphere security.[13] That danger has not abated. And to this day, when the vital interest of the United States is at stake, no effective alternative exists to unilateral action based on the concept of great-power primacy.

Under President Richard Nixon the United States acquired more sophistication in handling some of its ideological enemies south of the border. Latin American states have also developed a greater understanding of the essential flaw in the OAS. Members are not all bound by the same rules of conduct, do not feel the same moral obligations, or share the same ultimate goals. So incomplete is their identity of interest that, except under rare circumstances, they cannot be counted on to agree spontaneously on what constitutes a threat to hemisphere security.

Some statesmen have tried to reduce the tension between the contradictory concepts of equality and great-power primacy by approaching hemisphere instability on a different level. The origin of massive dissatisfaction in many Latin American countries is tied to antiquated political, economic, and social structures. The threat of a breakdown of orderly government, it is said, must be met by reform programs originated and instituted by Latin Americans. As early as 1967 a meeting of American chiefs of state in Punte del Este, Uruguay, projected plans for what one day may become a Latin American free trade area. Meanwhile, the Central American republics are developing the framework for their own common market. These may be steps in the right direction. Fundamental changes, however, are not expected overnight. For the foreseeable future the United States is likely to continue to deal with disorder and subversion in the hemisphere in its ambiguous dual role: Latin America's guardian-partner.

To veer between the antithetical concepts of sovereign equality and great-power primacy is not indigenous to the inter-American community. Only a cursory glance at the Soviet Union and the relationship with its East-bloc allies reveals, on the surface at least, a similar swing.

Thus, in February 1955 the Supreme Soviet of the USSR found the concept of equality to be the essence of relations among Socialist states. The Treaty of Friendship, Cooperation and Mutual Assistance (the Warsaw Pact) is based on the concept of the sovereign equality of all participants. Over the years the principle has been confirmed by numerous statements of meetings of Communist and Workers' parties.

Our concern is with a Consultative Meeting of Representatives of Com-

13 The *New York Times*, 7 May 1965, p. 14; *Yearbook of the United Nations*, New York, 1966, p. 211

munist and Workers' Parties held in Budapest (February 1968). The delegates had met to determine whether to convoke an international conference. By doing so they hoped to strengthen the solidarity of the Communist movement. The Central Committee of the Communist Party of the USSR ascribed great importance to the atmosphere of full equality pervading the conference.[14]

In his welcoming address to the delegates, Hungarian leader Janos Kadar referred approvingly to the absolute principle of independence of all Communist parties. And M.A. Suslov, head of the delegation of the Soviet Union, after noting dangerous national tendencies in certain socialist countries, said his country supported the strict observance of the principles of independence and equality.[15]

Flowing directly from the concept of equality is the principle of non-intervention. Russian affection for this pretentious generality goes all the way back to Lenin. On 17 June 1920 he told the All-Russian Central Executive Committee: 'We do not use bayonets to impose our system or our rule.' Since then, to read Soviet authorities, the policy of the USSR has never deviated from Lenin's precept.[16]

On 18 July 1968, however, the Central Committee of the Communist parties of Bulgaria, Hungary, the German Democratic Republic, and the Soviet Union sent the Central Committee of the Czechoslovakia CP a letter. They were disturbed, according to the text, by hostile forces pushing their ally off the path of socialism. Of course, they had no intention of interfering in its internal affairs or of violating the principles of autonomy and equality. But revisionist forces had gained control of the press, radio, and television, thus endangering the peace of the other socialist countries.[17] As we can clearly see, Czechoslovakia was passing the limit beyond which the idea of equality could not be pushed.

On 3 August, after Czechoslovakia met with its equals from the five concerned countries, they issued a joint communiqué. All resolved to intensify co-operation 'on the basis of the principles of equality, respect for sovereignty, and national independence.' But the Czechs kept pressing

14 *The Current Digest of the Soviet Press*, pub. by the Joint Committee on Slavic Studies, New York, 21 March 1968, 10, 16
15 Ibid. 17, 19
16 Piradov, A. 'The Principle of Non-Interference in the Modern World,' *International Affairs* (Moscow), January 1966, 53, quoting Lenin; Levin, D. 'The Non-Intervention Principle Today,' ibid. November 1966, 21; Korovin, Y. 'International Law Today,' ibid. July 1961, 20; Durdenevsky, V. 'The Five Principles,' ibid. March 1956, quoting the Declaration of the Supreme Soviet, 7
17 *Current Digest*, n. 5, August 7, 1968, 4, 7

principle to its logical conclusion and soon reality began to take its revenge. Members of the Soviet Politburo decided that the security of the Soviet Union and its allies was at stake. The formal trappings for collective action existed, just as it had for the United States. But the Kremlin was more skilful. According to first reports from Tass, the Soviet news agency, leading Czech officials authorized armed intervention by Warsaw Pact troops to assist the people in their struggle against counter-revolutionary elements.[18]

The deed ruthlessly accomplished, non-Russian divisions departed, and Soviet occupation forces took over the job of policing the wayward country. Immediately the discord of equality began to vibrate again. A joint Soviet-Czech communiqué marked the studied inconsistency between word and deed. It confirmed the desire for co-operation, among other things, 'on the basis of mutual respect and equality.' Furthermore, according to the statement, Russian troops would 'not interfere in the internal affairs' of the country. On 2 September 1968 *Pravda* assured its readers that the Soviet Union and Czechoslovakia were 'sovereign, equal partners.'[19]

The basic principle on which relations among signatories of the Warsaw Pact is based is the concept of sovereign equality. How could the Soviet Union have broken its pledge? Like their counterparts in the United States, leaders of the Soviet Union are faced by their own estimate of when and where their vital interests are at stake. The former president of the Czechoslovak National Assembly, Joseph Smrkovsky, described his country as the heart of Europe, beating where history placed it. Unfortunately, together with its uranium mines, history placed it in an area deemed indispensable to Russian security. The Kremlin was not prepared, any more than Washington was in the Dominican Republic, to tolerate policies judged dangerous to its future existence.

On 12 November 1968 Leonid Brezhnev, general secretary of the Soviet Communist Party, made manifest the basic contradiction between the idea of equality and the preponderant role of the Soviet Union. His speech to the Polish United Workers' Party was a form of double-talk commonly associated with the Kremlin. Endorsing the doctrine which bears his name, the Soviet leader said, 'We emphatically oppose interference into the affairs of any states, violations of their sovereignty.' He defended the right of each socialist country to 'determine the specific forms of its develop-

18 Ibid. 21 August 1968, p. 4, 11 September 1968, p. 3.
19 *Current Digest*, 18 September 1968, 3, 15–16

ment along the road to socialism with consideration for its specific national conditions.' Then he called attention to 'common laws governing socialist construction.' Any deviation from these laws might lead to a deviation from socialism itself. If that happened, military aid to cut short the threat to the cause of socialism was permissible.[20]

The Brezhnev doctrine of limited sovereignty continued to exist side by side with the Soviet Union's unalterable opposition to interference in the internal affairs of another state. In 1973 Vsevolod Sofinsky, chief spokesman for the Soviet Foreign Ministry, said, 'Intervention is completely excluded in the field of international relations.' According to him, there was no interference in the domestic affairs of Czechoslovakia. The Soviet Union and its allies simply met the government's request to give it aid.[21]

We are now back to Mr Tchernouchtchenko at the Twenty-First Session of the General Assembly. His reasoning, however, has taken on an added twist. All states are equal. Therefore, intervention by one state in the domestic affairs of another is inadmissible – a violation of the concept of sovereign equality. All peoples are also equal. Therefore, intervention to support their right to be free is admissible – no violation of the concept of sovereign equality. But where a people seeks to deviate from the path of socialism they do not possess the right to be free. Therefore, the use of military force to cut short the threat is not intervention – no violation of the concept of sovereign equality.

The United States intervention in the Dominican Republic and the Soviet intervention in Czechoslovakia were similar in kind, however different in style and aftermath. Determined to act when their vital interests were believed to be in jeopardy, both superpowers proferred an egalitarian embrace to a group of states in order to have them serve as partners. With this as a legitimating device they improved reality for themselves and the corporate persons they dominated so overwhelmingly.

NUCLEAR EQUALITY

The idea of nuclear equality has meaning insofar as it describes the capacity of the United States and the USSR to deter each other from starting a nuclear war out of fear of mutual annihilation. On any lesser scale than the superpowers: China, Britain, France, it is debatable if their possession of a

20 *Czechoslovakia and the Brezhnev Doctrine*, United States Government Printing Office, Washington, D.C., 1969, 91st Cong. 1st Sess., Subcommittee on National Security and International Operations, pp. 4, 22, 23
21 *International Herald Tribune*, 5 July 1973, p. 2

second-rate nuclear armament serves as a deterrent or adds to their pres-
tige on the international scene. Perhaps sooner than we expect, one of
them, or one of the near-nuclear countries, will have a credible thermonuclear capability of worldwide range. When this occurs, equal status with
the nuclear giants will be assured – unless by then some technological
breakthrough has again left all others far behind. In the meantime, the
United States and the Soviet Union are so far ahead of other states in terms
of the development and possession of sophisticated conventional military
hardware that nuclear weapons do little more than increase their already
overwhelming superiority.

At present, nuclear weapons may be unusable, but the strategic balance
known as mutual deterrence would be threatened by the continuous development of nuclear systems and their spread to other countries. If, in
addition to the five nuclear powers, a sixth, seventh, or eighth should
emerge, it would intensify the danger of nuclear war. Here, the interplay
between the concepts of equality and great-power primacy arose in connection with the treaty on the Non-Proliferation of Nuclear Weapons.
Among many near- and non-nuclear countries the non-proliferation treaty
was viewed as instituting a permanent discrimination among states, by
perpetuating the existing nuclear monopoly of a privileged few. Superpowers argued differently. Other states, by denying themselves nuclear
weapons, might be foregoing some right based on the principle of sovereign
equality. But the proliferation of nuclear powers involved so great a danger
to world peace and security that nothing should be allowed to stand in the
way of ratifying the treaty.[22]

As early as 1968, at a United Nations conference of non-nuclear
weapons states, participants expressed concern over their growing inequality with the nuclear powers. For them the treaty needed to be sup-
plemented by security guarantees. The superpowers were also urged to get
on with the problem of disarmament. The conferees discovered that the
'inalienable right' to use nuclear energy for their technological and
economic benefit included full access to equipment and scientific information for its peaceful use. Because of the shortage of resources at their

---

22 United Nations, General Assembly, *Official Records*, 1965, Twentieth Sess., First
   Comm., 1355–1361 Meet; ibid. 1966, Twenty-First Sess., First Comm., 1431–2 Meet. See
   also, Documents A/C.1/SR 1431, 25 October 1966; A/C.1/SR 1432, 28 October 1966; A/C.1/SR
   1448, 14 November 1966. *Conference of the Eighteen Nation Committee on
   Disarmament*, ENDC/PV 286, 25 August 1966; ENDC/PV 294, 16 March 1967; ENDC/PV, 297,
   18 May 1967. Willrich, M. 'The Treaty on Non-Proliferation of Nuclear Weapons: Nuclear
   Technology Confronts World Politics,' *Yale Law J.*, July 1968, 1447

disposal, non-nuclear states looked to the superpowers for financing such arrangements.[23] Most interesting for our purpose was Switzerland's attempt to apply the concept of sovereign equality in its widest, though not necessarily its clearest, sense. The NPT provided for the signatories to accept safeguards to prevent nuclear energy, fissionable material or equipment for processing it from being diverted from peaceful uses to nuclear weapons. To this effect they were required to conclude agreements with the International Atomic Energy Agency. But the agreements were not intended to hamper the economic and technological developments of the parties or to restrict the exchange of nuclear processing for peaceful uses. In its puzzling proposal, Switzerland recommended that safeguard agreements be drawn with 'due regard for the principle of the sovereign equality of States, so as to impose equivalent political or economic responsibilities on all ...'[24]

In 1970 the NPT came into effect. It recognized the 'inalienable right' of all parties to the treaty to develop, produce, and use nuclear energy for peaceful purposes. Little progress has been made on the problem of financing such projects or on the non-nuclear states other concern – disarmament. The agreement of 22 June 1973 may, to some extent, satisfy their demand for supplemental security guarantees. The United States and the Soviet Union pledged themselves to act in such a manner as to exclude the outbreak of nuclear war between them and between either of them and other countries.

Increasingly, Washington and Moscow have become ill at ease with the concept of nuclear equality. The only way to deal with a potential enemy, the argument goes, is from a position of strength. Both superpowers have come to dread the idea of their own nuclear missiles being knocked out before they can be fired in retaliation. Discussion persists on who has the strategic edge. Highly placed officials urge their governments to press ahead with scientific research to acquire superior offensive systems. One mitigating factor is a mutual interest in diverting the vast spiralling sums spent on nuclear arms to pressing domestic problems. This finds the superpowers disposed since 1969 to engage seriously in bilateral talks on the limitations of defensive and offensive weapons (SALT I and II). Notwithstanding agreements regulating defensive systems, the sophistication and destructive capacity of nuclear devices continues to increase. In view

23 *United Nations Conference of Non-Nuclear-Weapon States*, A/Conf. 35/10, Geneva, 1 October 1968, pp. 13, 17
24 Ibid. Annex IV, p. 5

of the extraordinary complexity of the SALT conversations, hardly miti-
gated by China's perfecting of hydrogen bombs and delivery systems, the
continued development and deployment of nuclear arms remain a cause for
concern. This situation also brutally confirms the obvious basic inequality
between the two superpowers and the other participants in international
affairs, and keeps alive the question of which one of the Big Two is more
equal than the other.

THE PERSISTENT EGALITARIAN DRIVE

Throughout this study we have considered the concepts of sovereign
equality and great-power primacy as contradictory responses to the quest
for international order. Designed to help us cope with a complex reality
only dimly perceived, both ideas have proved to be more or less out of
correspondence with an intractable existence. The inability of the Security
Council to take effective action without the unanimous consent of the
United States, the Soviet Union, China, Britain, and France remains a
formula for chronic paralysis. A similar prescription applies to the General
Assembly, where what a majority wants done rarely includes those with
the power and the will to act.

   Yet the tension between the conflicting concepts has become unsprung.
An extraordinary change has occurred since the days when a concert of
Great Powers enjoyed superintending authority in world affairs – an authority recognized by the tacit consent of the other states. The change
derives from the grip with which the concept of sovereign equality has
fastened itself to the inner recesses of the human mind. Few question the
'natural' right of each people to be free, to assume sovereign statehood,
and to participate both in the process of keeping the peace and in creating a
viable world community – all, of course, as sovereign equals.

   In 1973 the concept of sovereign equality lay at the heart of the Conference on Security and Co-operation in Europe – a reunion attended by the
United States, Canada, and thirty-three nations from every European
country (Albania excepted), ranging in size from San Marino to the Soviet
Union. The concept is reflected in a communiqué of the Political Consultative Committee of the Warsaw Treaty member-states (1972), furnishing the
vision of Europe transformed into an area of 'fruitful co-operation among
Sovereign equal states ...'[25] The concept is the fundamental principle of the
world organization and of the inter-American community. It is the basis on

25 *Nato Review*, Documentation, March/April 1972, p. 31

which forty-one members of the Organization of African Unity meet to manage the problems affecting the dark continent. Even in COMECON, the Communist trading group, according to Article I of the Charter of the Council on Mutual Economic Aid, membership is 'based on the principle of the sovereign equality of all member countries.'[26] In short, our thinking is dominated by the concept of sovereign equality. It is on this concept that the structure of the international system has come to rest.

Historically, the idea of a world community of equal states has had great uses. Appealing as it does to man's innate sense of justice, it has served as a device for poor, weak states to maintain their independence. It has proved an important countervailing moral force against the hegemonic pretensions of the strong. Pressed to its ultimate conclusion, however, it has introduced a new spirit of discord in the world.

The concept of sovereign equality lies at the core of man's failure to devise a more trustworthy political system. It reflects a distorted view of the sovereign entities engaged in international relations. Like you and me, whatever entities call themselves 'nation-states' are projected as persons possessing a unified will capable of being expressed and acted upon. From this fiction flows the anthropomorphic tendency to regard them as persons of flesh and bone, and to transfer to national conduct political and moral principles associated with the conduct of individual liberal democrats. Enticing in its simplicity, seductive in its sense of what is right and fair, the analogy obscures the problem of instability in world affairs, making sound judgment unlikely.

But is there no fiction by which the vote of sovereign entities, great and small, can be deemed to enjoy equal weight? I think there is, but only by advancing an extraordinary hypothesis: the existence in each state making up the international community of a people so closely bound by common ties and single-minded purpose that, on any issue, their voice unfailingly represents the unified will of the entire population.

On this absurd assumption it is possible to defend the vision of one collective will of human beings being neither greater nor less than any other such collective will. To attach a disproportionate consequence to the number of inhabitants, geographical size, or power making up one of the wills in order to deny it sovereign equality with the others, would be arbitrary and difficult to condone.

Such speculation, though, is idle. Nation-states are not, like human beings, endowed with a single will. Nation-states do not, like human

26 Note 20, supra, p. 32

beings, possess an infinite worth, sharing an inviolable essence as part of their common humanity – even if their populations are composed of these same human beings. In fact, it is virtually impossible to say what nation-states are – other than mythical beings capable of existing, coalescing, dividing, and even disappearing by the exercise of men's imagination. As the poet Robert Lowell wrote somewhere:

> The state, if we could see
> behind the wall
> is woven of perishable vegetation.

To insist in the name of morality and justice on nation-states sharing equally in the exercise of power, when so vast a majority possess so insignificant an amount and are thus able to avoid responsibility for its use – what Stanley Baldwin in another context described as the prerogative of the harlot through the ages – is no way to manage world affairs. On the contrary, it is an invitation to disaster.

None of this means that the voice of less powerful states should be stifled. They should have the equal right to take care of their interests by participating in the decisions affecting them. The Secretary-General is right when he says, 'The interests, the wisdom and the importance of the vast majority of medium and smaller Powers cannot, at this point in history, be ignored in any durable system of world order.'[27] But nation-states cannot handle international problems efficiently as if they were individual voters of a representative democracy tackling local problems in the town hall.

In sum, no mythical concept of sovereign equality can charm away the brutal character of group behaviour, the wide variations of power existing among nation-states, and the reality that it is to the facts of power that they invariably make responses of a more or less respectful nature. Compared, then, to the metamorphosed idea of equality, the concept of great-power primacy, with all its faults and with all its shortcomings, and there are many, offers a more plausible interim artifice for reducing matters concerning international order to more manageable proportions. Perhaps this is the most we can hope for until men recognize the confusion inherent in living in two inter-related worlds that do not correspond – the nominal and the existential – and devise an operational concept capable of keeping them from diverging too far.

---

27 Note 4, supra, p. 2

Aristophanes, no professional political philosopher, would undoubtedly have considered with interest the development of the concept of sovereign equality. The ancient Greek dramatist was fascinated by ideas that move men, especially when they are misunderstood and move them to foolishness.

Bibliography

I SOURCES

A Documents

Codification of American International Law, Pan American union, Washington, D.C. 1926
Conference of the Eighteen Nation Committee on Disarmament, ENDC/PV 286, 25 August 1966; ENDC/PV 294, 16 March 1967; ENDC/PV 297, 18 May 1967
Current Digest of the Soviet Press, the Joint Committee on Slavic Studies, New York, 1968
Diario de la Sexta Conferencia Internacional Americana, Habana, 1928
Documents on American Foreign Relations, World Peace Foundation, Boston, 1940–1947, vols. II–IX
Documents on International Affairs, Royal Institute of International Affairs, 1936, London, 1937
Encyclical Letter (Pacem in Terris) of His Holiness John XXIII, Catholic Truth Society, London, 1963
Great Britain, Foreign Office
– *British and Foreign State Papers*, 1814–1815, London, 1839
– *Cmd. 8264*: 'A Report on the Proceedings of the Fifth Session of the General Assembly of the United Nations, New York, 19 September–15 December 1950,' London, 1951
– *Peace Handbooks*, No. 153, 'The Congress of Vienna,' London, 1920

Great Britain, Parliament, *Parliamentary Debates*, House of Commons, Fifth Ser. London, 1945, vol. 408; 1963, vol. 670

Hertslet, E. *The Map of Europe by Treaty*, London, 1875, vol. I

Inter-American Conference for the Maintenance of Peace, 'Proceedings,' 1936, Buenos Aires, 1936

International American Conference, Washington, D.C., 1890

International Commission of Jurists, Pan American Union, Washington, D.C., 1927

International Conciliation, 'Report of Vyacheslav M. Molotov to the Supreme Soviet of the U.S.S.R.,' New York, March 1944

Keesing's Contemporary Archives, London, 1965–6; 1973

League of Nations, *Official Journal*
– Records of the First Assembly, Plenary Meetings, 6 December 1920
– Records of the Third Assembly, Plenary Meetings, 7 September 1922
– Records of the Fourth Assembly, Plenary Meetings, 29 September 1923

Martens, F., *Recueil des Traités et Conventions conclus par la Russie avec les Puissances Etrangères*, St Petersbourg, 1875, vols. II, IV

Meeting of American Chiefs of State, Punta del Este, April 1967, Pan American Union, Washington, D.C., 1967

Peaslee, A.J., *Constitutions of Nations*, The Hague, 1956, 2nd ed., vol. III

Proceedings of the Second Pan American Scientific Congress, 27 December 1915–28 January 1916, Washington, D.C., 1916, vol. VII

Recommendations on International Law and Official Commentary Thereon, of the Second Pan American Scientific Congress, ed. J.B. Scott, Carnegie Endowment for International Peace, Division on International Law, New York, 1916

Report of the Delegate [sic] of the United States of America to the Meeting of the Foreign Ministers of the American Republics, 23 September–3 October 1939, Washington, D.C., 1940

Report of the Delegates of the United States of America to the Sixth International Conference of American States, Habana, 16 January to 20 February 1928, Washington, D.C., 1928

Report of the Delegates of the United States of America to the Seventh International Conference of American States, Washington, D.C., 1933

Report of the Delegation of the United States of America to the Eighth International Conference of American States, Lima, Peru, 1938, Washington, D.C., 1941

Report of the Delegation of the United States of America to the Inter-American Conference for the Maintenance of Peace, Washington, D.C., 1937

Report of the Delegation of the United States of America to the Inter-American Conference on Problems of War and Peace, Mexico City, 1945, Washington, D.C., 1946

Second Pan American Scientific Congress, 'The Report of the Secretary-General,' Washington, D.C., 1917

Seventh International Conference of American States, 'Minutes and Antecedents,' Montevideo, 1933

The Hague Conventions and Declarations of 1899 and 1907, New York, 1915

The Proceedings of the Hague Peace Conferences, 'The Conference of 1907,' New York, 1920, 1921, 2 vols.

The Reports of the Hague Conferences of 1899 and 1907, edited, with an introduction, by J.B. Scott, Oxford, 1917

United Nations Conference on International Organization, United Nations Information Organization, New York, 1945, vols. 1, 3, 6, 11

United Nations, General Assembly

- Introduction to the Annual Report of the Secretary-General on the Work of the Organization, 1959–60, 1960–1, 1964–5, 1965–6, 1966–7, 1967–8, 1971–2

- *Fifth Sess.*, Supp. No. 20, 'Resolutions Adopted by the General Assembly during the Period 19 September–15 December 1950,' 377 (V) Uniting for Peace, pp. 10–12

- *Fifteenth Sess.*, Supp. No. 16, 'Resolutions Adopted by the General Assembly during its Fifteenth Session,' vol. 1, 20 September–20 December 1960, 1514 (XV) Declaration on the Granting of Independence to Colonial Countries and Peoples, 66–7

- *Seventeenth Sess.*, Special Political Committee, Summary Record of Meetings, 19 September–19 December 1962

- *Eighteenth Sess.*, Special Political Committee, Summary Record of Meetings, 27 October–3 December 1963

- *Nineteenth Sess.*, Summary Record of the Third Meeting, 28 April 1964, Sub-Committee 1, 'Special Committee on the Situation with regard to the Implementation of the Declaration on the Granting of Independence to Colonial Countries and Territories,' A/AC. 109/SC2/SR.3, 28 May 1964; Summary Record of the Fourth Meeting, 29 April 1964, ibid.

- *Twentieth Sess.*, Special Political Committee Summary Record of Meetings, 22 September–17 December 1965

- *Twenty-First Sess.*, First Committee, Provisional Summary Record, 5 December 1966, A/C.1/SR 1473; ibid. 9 December 1966, A/C/1 SR 1479; 12 December 1966, A/C.1/SR 1482

– *Twenty-Third Sess.*, Provisional Verbatim Record, 1752 Meet., 21 December 1968, A/PV 1752; 1747th Plenary Meet., 18 December 1968, A/Res/2429 (XXIII); Special Political Committee, Provisional A/SPC/SR 609, 11 November 1968; A/SPC/PV 615, 15 November 1968
United States, *Congressional Record*, Senate, 79th Cong., 1st Sess., vol. 91, pt. 2, 8, March, October, 1945
United States, *Inaugural Addresses of the Presidents of the United States*, 82nd Cong., 2nd Sess., House Document No. 540, Washington, D.C., 1952
United States, Department of State, *Conference Series*
– No. 26, Welles, S. 'The Accomplishments of the Inter-American Conference for the Maintenance of Peace,' 4 February 1937, Washington, D.C., 1937
– No. 27, Hull, C. 'The Results and Significance of the Buenos Aires Conference,' 25 February 1937, Washington, D.C., 1937
– No. 29, Welles, S. 'The Practical Accomplishments of the Buenos Aires Conference,' 7 April 1937, Washington, D.C., 1937
United States, Department of State, *Latin American Series*
– No. 8, Welles, S. 'Inter-American Relations,' 10 December 1934, Washington, D.C., 1935
– No. 12, Welles, S. "'Good Neighbor" Policy in the Caribbean,' 2 July 1935, Washington, D.C., 1935
– No. 14, Sayre, F.B. 'Our Relations with Latin America,' 11 March 1937, Washington, D.C., 1937
United States, Department of State
– *Memorandum on the Monroe Doctrine*, prepared by J. Reuben Clark, Senate, 71st Cong., 2nd Sess., Senate Document No. 114, Washington, D.C., 1930
– *Foreign Relations of the United States*, Diplomatic Papers, 1895; 1902; 1903; 1904; 1906; 1912; 'The Lansing Papers 1914–1920;' 'The Paris Peace Conference 1919;' 1927; 1933, vols. IV, V; 1934, vols. IV, V; 1935, vol. IV; 1936, vol. V; 1937, vol. V
– *Postwar Foreign Policy Preparation*, 1939–1945, Washington, D.C., 1949
– *Press Releases*, Washington, D.C., 1934
– *Soviet World Outlook*, Department of State Publication 6836, European and British Commonwealth Series 5b, Washington, D.C., 1959
– *The Conference at Malta and Yalta*, 1945, Washington, D.C., 1955
– *The Department of State Bulletin*, 1944–1945, Washington, D.C.
– *Treaty Information Bulletin*, No. 56, 31 May 1934, Washington, D.C.
Yearbook of the United Nations, 1946–1947, New York, 1947

B   Memoirs, Correspondence, Surveys, Etc.

Byrnes, J.F. *Speaking Frankly*, New York, 1947
Chodzko, L.J.B. *Le Congrès de Vienne et les traités de 1815*, Paris, 1863, vols. 2, 4
Churchill, W.S. *The Second World War*, 'Triumph and Tragedy,' London 1954
Correspondance Inédite du prince de Talleyrand et du Roi Louis XVIII pendant le Congrès de Vienne, préface par M.G. Pallain, Paris 1881
Correspondence, Despatches and other Papers of Viscount Castlereagh, ed. Charles W. Lane, Marquess of Londonderry, London, 1952, vols. IX–XII
Czartoryski, A. *Mémoirs et correspondance avec l'Empereur Alexandre Ier*, Paris, 1887, vol. II
Daniels, J. *Shirt-Sleeve Diplomat*, University of North Carolina Press, 1947
Dictionnaire Géographique de la Suisse, Attingeur, V., éditeur, Neuchâtel, 1902, 6 tomes
Federalist, The, ed. Henry Cabot Lodge, New York, 1888
House, Col. E.M. *The Intimate Papers of Colonel House*, arranged by Charles Seymour, London, 1926
Hull, Cordell *The Memoirs of Cordell Hull*, New York, 1938, 2 vols
Living Lincoln, The, ed. P.M. Angel and E.S. Miers, New Brunswick, 1955
Macmillan's Historical Atlas of Modern Europe, ed. F.C. Hearnshaw, London, 1920
Mazzini, J., *Life and Writings*, London, 1870, vol. VI
– *The Duties of Man and Other Essays*, London, 1907
Mémoires, Documents et Ecrits Divers, laissés par le Prince de Metternich, publié par son fils, le Prince Richard de Metternich, Paris, 1880, vols. 2, 4
Mémoires du Prince Talleyrand, publiés avec une préface et des notes par le Duc de Broglie, Paris, 1891, vol. 2
Memoirs by Harry S Truman, 'Year of Decisions,' New York, 1955
Miller, D.H. *My Diary at the Conference of Paris*, set No. 23, printed by the author, New York, 1928, 20 vols.
– *The Drafting of the Covenant*, New York, 1928, 2 vols.
Poole, R.L. *Historical Atlas of Modern Europe*, Oxford, 1902
Robertson, C.G. and Bartholomew, J.G. *An Historical Atlas of Modern Europe*, London, 1924
Roosevelt, F.D. *The Public Papers and Addresses of Franklin D. Roosevelt*, 'The Year of Crisis,' New York, 1938

– *The Roosevelt Letters,* ed. Elliott Roosevelt, London, 1951, vol. 3
Sherwood, R.E. *Roosevelt and Hopkins,* New York, 1948
Shotwell, J.T., *At the Paris Peace Conference,* New York, 1937
Social Contract, with an introduction by Sir Ernest Barker (World's Classics), London, 1957
Stalin, Marshal Iosif *On the Great Patriotic War of the Soviet Union,* London, n.d.
Statesman's Year-Book, The, 1964–5, ed. S.H. Steinberg, London, 1964
Stettinius, E.R. Jr. *Roosevelt and the Russians,* New York, 1949
Stimson, H.L. and Bundy, McG. *On Active Service in Peace and War,* New York, 1948
Toynbee, A.J. *Survey of International Affairs,* Royal Institute of International Affairs, 1927, 1928, 1933, 1936, 1938, 1939–1946, London
Vandenberg, A.H. *The Private Papers of Senator Vandenberg,* ed. A.H. Vandenberg, Jr., Boston, 1952
Wellington, Supplementary Despatches, Correspondence and Memoranda of Arthur Duke of, London, 1862, vol. IX
Woodrow Wilson: Life and Letters, ed. R.S. Baker, Garden City, New York, 1931, vol. 4
– *The Public Papers of Woodrow Wilson,* 'The New Democracy,' 1913–17, ed. R.S. Baker and W. Dodd, New York, 1926, 2 vols; 'War and Peace,' 1917–24, ed. R.S. Baker and W. Dodd, New York, 1927, 2 vols

II STUDIES

A   *General Studies*

Agar, H. *The United States,* London, 1950
Aspaturian, V.A. *The Union Republics in Soviet Diplomacy,* Genève, 1960
Baker, R.S., *Woodrow Wilson and World Settlement,* New York, 1922, vol. II
Barker, Sir E. *Principles of Social and Political Theory,* Oxford, 1951
– *The Ideas and Ideals of the British Empire,* Cambridge, 1951, 2nd ed.
Bemis, S.F. *The Latin American Policy of the United States,* New York, 1943
Berle, A.A. *Latin American Diplomacy and Reality,* New York, 1962
Bertier de Sauvigny, G. de, *Metternich and His Times,* London, 1962
Blum, J.M. *The Republican Roosevelt* (Atheneum), New York, 1962
Borgese, E.M. *Pacem in Maribus,* New York, 1972
Bourquin, M. *Histoire de la Sainte Alliance,* Genève, 1954

Bowle, J. *Politics and Opinion in the 19th Century*, London, 1954
Boyd, A. *United Nations: Piety Myth and Truth*, London, 1962
Brierly, J.L. *The Basis of Obligation in International Law*, Oxford, 1958
Brinton, C. *The Shaping of the Modern Mind* (Mentor Books), New York, 1959
Bryce, J. *The American Commonwealth*, New York, 1937, vol. II
Brzezinski, Z.K. and Huntington, S.P. *Political Power USA/USSR*, London, 1964; *The Soviet Bloc* (Praeger Paperbacks), New York, 1961
Buchan, A. *Crisis Management*, the Atlantic Institute, France, 1966
Cahn, E. *Common Sense About Democracy*, London, 1962
Cambridge History of British Foreign Policy, ed. A.W. Ward and G.P. Gooch, London, 1923, vol. 2
Carr, E.H. *The Twenty Year Crisis*, 1919–39, London, 1939
Claude, I.L., Jr. *Power and International Relations*, New York, 1962
Cobban, A. *In Search of Humanity*, New York, 1960
– Rousseau and the Modern State, London, 1934
Corbett, P.E. *Moscow, Teheran, and International Organization*, Yale Institute of International Studies, New Haven, 1944
Crawford, W.R. *A Century of Latin American Thought*, Cambridge, Mass., 1915
Crocker, L.G. *An Age of Crises*, Baltimore, 1959
Crozier, B. *The Morning After: A Study of Independence*, London, 1963
Dallin, A. *The Soviet Union at the United Nations* (Praeger Paperbacks), New York, 1962
D'Arenberg, Prince Jean-Englebert, *Les Princes du St. Empire*, Louvain, 1951
De Pradt, Abbé Dominique, *Du Congrès de Vienne*, Paris, 1815
Derry, T.K. and Jarman, T.L. *The European World*, London, 1950
Dickinson, E.E. *The Equality of States in International Law*, Cambridge, Mass., 1920
Duggan, L. *The Americas*, New York, 1949
Dunning, W.A. *History of Political Theories*, 'From Luther to Montesquieu,' New York, 1905
Dupuis, C. *Le Ministère de Talleyrand en 1814*, Paris, 1920, vol. II
Fenwick, C.G. *International Law*, New York, 1948
First, R. *Power in Africa* (Pantheon Books), New York, 1970
Flassan, J.B. de, *Histoire du Congrès de Vienne*, Paris, 1829, vol. II
Goebel, J. *The Equality of States*, New York, 1923
Gierke, O. *Political Theories of the Middle Ages*, introduction by F.W. Maitland, Cambridge, 1927
Guggenheim, P. 'Emer de Vattel et l'étude des relations internationales en

Suisse,' *Mémoires publiés par la Faculté de droit de Genève*, No. 10, Genève, 1956
Halle, L.J. *Dream and Reality*, New York, 1959
– *Men and Nations*, Princeton, 1962
Hallowell, J.H. *The Decline of Liberalism as an Ideology*, London, 1946
Hazzard, S. *Defeat of an Ideal: A Study of the Self-Destruction of the United Nations*, Boston, 1973
Hill, H.C. *Roosevelt and the Caribbean*, Chicago, 1927
History of the Peace Conference of Paris, ed. H.W.V. Temperley, Institute of International Affairs, London, 1920, vol. II
Holland, T.E. *Studies in International Law*, Oxford, 1898
Hook, S. *Marx and the Marxists*, New York, 1955
Howland, C.P. *American Relations in the Caribbean*, New Haven, 1929
Inter-American Affairs, 1945, 'Annual Survey: No. 5,' ed. A.P. Whitaker, New York, 1946
Inter-American Affairs, 1944, 'Annual Survey: No. 4,' ed. A.P. Whitaker, New York, 1945
Jones, C.L. *The Caribbean Since 1900*, New York, 1936
Kennan, G.F. *American Diplomacy*, 1900–50 (A Mentor Book), New York, 1960
Kissinger, H.A. *American Foreign Policy*, London, 1969
– *The Troubled Partnership*, New York, 1965
– *A World Restored*, Boston, 1957
Kleiman, R. *Atlantic Crisis*, New York, 1964
Knorr, K. *Power and Wealth: The Political Economy of International Power*, New York, 1972
Koo, W., Jr. *Voting Procedures in International Political Organization*, New York, 1947
Kooijmans, P.H. *The Doctrine of the Legal Equality of States*, Leiden, 1964
Langer, W.L. and Gleason, S.E. *The Challenge to Isolation*, New York, 1952
Lansing, R. *The Peace Negotiations*, Boston, 1921
Lawrence, T.J. *International Problems and Hague Conferences*, London, 1908
Link, A.S. *Wilson: The Struggle for Neutrality*, Princeton, 1960
– *Wilson: The New Freedom*, Princeton, 1956
Lippmann, W. *A Preface to Politics* (Ann Arbor Paperbacks), Ann Arbor, 1962
– *U.S. Foreign Policy* (Pocket Book Edition) New York, 1943

Manross, L.M. *United States Policy Towards Argentina*, Library of Congress, Washington, D.C., 1947

Marriott, Sir J.A.R. *A History of Europe from 1815–1923*, London, 1931

Mende, T. *De l'aide à la recolonisation* (editions du Seuil) Paris, 1972

Moon, P.T. *Imperialism and World Politics*, New York, 1926

Moore, D.R. *A History of Latin America*, New York, 1916

Morison, S.E. and Commager, H.S. *The Growth of the American Republic*, New York, 1937

Mowat, R.B. *A History of European Diplomacy 1815–1914*, London, 1927

Myers, A.H. *Are Men Equal?* (Great Seal Books), Ithaca, 1955

The Near Nuclear Countries and the NPT, Stockholm International Peace Research Institute, New York, 1972

Nicolson, H. *Peacemaking 1919*, London, 1933

Niebuhr, R. *Moral Man and Immoral Society*, New York, 1932

Niemeyer, G. *Law Without Force*, Princeton, 1941

Orwell, G. *1984* (Signet Books), New York, 1950

Osgood, R.E. *Nato, The Entangling Alliance*, Chicago, 1962

Padover, S.K. *The Living U.S. Constitution* (Mentor Books), New York, 1958

Page, K. *National Defense*, New York, 1931

Perkins, D. *Hands Off*, Boston, 1941

Phillips, W.A. *The Confederation of Europe*, London, 1920

Pufendorf, S. 'De Jure Naturae et Gentium Libri Octo,' 1688, *Classics of International Law*, London, 1934, vol. II, translation

Quintanilla, L. *A Latin American Speaks*, New York, 1934

Reitzel, W., Kaplan, M.A., and Coblenz, C.G. *United States Foreign Policy*, 1945–55, Washington, D.C., 1956

Report of the Commission to Study the Organization of Peace, 'New Dimensions for the United Nations: The Problems of the Next Decade,' New York, 1966

Robertson, W.S. *History of Latin American Nations*, New York, 1925

Root, E. *Latin America and the United States*, Cambridge, Mass., 1917

– *Addresses on International Law Subjects*, Cambridge, Mass., 1916

Russell, R.B. *A History of the United Nations Charter*, Washington, D.C., 1958

Scott, J.B. *The Hague Peace Conference of 1899 and 1907*, Baltimore, 1909

Seaman, L.C. B. *From Vienna To Versailles*, London, 1955

Singer, M.R. *Weak States in a World of Powers*, New York, 1972

Snyder, L. *The World in the Twentieth Century*, Princeton, 1955

Spiegel, S.L. *Dominance and Diversity: The International Hierarchy*, Boston, 1972
Sprout, H. and M. *The Rise of American Naval Power*, Princeton, 1939
Stead, W.T. *La Chronique de la Conférence de La Haye*, La Haye, 1899
Steiner, G. *The Death of Tragedy* (Faber Editions), London, 1963
Stimson, H.L. *American Policy in Nicaragua*, New York, 1927
Temperley, H. *The Foreign Policy of Canning*, London, 1925
The United Nations in International Politics, ed. L. Gordenker, Princeton, 1971
The United States and Latin America, ed. H.L. Matthews, Princeton, 1963
The World's Great Thinkers, ed. S. Commins, and Linscott, New York, 1947
Thomson, D. *Europe Since Napoleon*, London, 1957
– *Equality*, Cambridge, 1949
Tocqueville, Alexis de, *Democracy in America*, New York, 1954
To Turn the Tide, 'A selection from President John F. Kennedy's public statements,' ed. J.W. Gardner, New York, 1962
Treitschke, H. von, *History of Germany in the 19th Century*, London, 1916, vol. II
Van Doren, C. *The Great Rehearsal*, New York, 1948
Vattel, E. de, 'The Law of Nations,' 1758, *Classics of International Law*, Washington, D.C., 1916, vol. III
Vital, D. *The Inequality of States*, Oxford, 1967
Webster, C.K. *British Diplomacy*, 1813–15, London, 1921
– *The Art and Practice of Diplomacy*, London, 1961
– *The Congress of Vienna*, London, 1934
– *The Foreign Policy of Castlereagh*, London, 1931, 2 vols.
– *The League of Nations in Theory and Practice*, London, 1933
Welles, S. *Naboth's Vineyard*, New York, 1928, vol. II
– *The Time for Decision*, London, 1945
– *The World of Four Freedoms*, New York, 1945
– *Where Are We Heading?*, New York, 1946
Whitaker, A.P. *The Western Hemisphere Idea: Its Rise and Decline*, Ithaca, 1954
Williams, M.W. *The People and Politics of Latin America*, Boston, 1930
Wilson, E. *To The Finland Station* (Fontana Library), London, 1960
Wood, B. *The Making of the Good Neighbor Policy*, New York, 1961
Woolf, L.S. *After the Deluge*, London, 1937, vol. I
Zimmern, A. *The League of Nations and the Rule of Law*, 1918–35, London, 1939

B Articles

Alfaro, R.J. 'The Rights and Duties of States,' *Receuil des Cours, Académie de droit international de La Haye*

Alvarez, A. 'Latin America and International Law,' *AJIL*, 1909, vol. 3, 269

Aron, R. 'The Anarchical Order of Power,' *Daedalus*, Spring 1966, 479

Aspaturian, V.A. 'The Theory and Practice of Soviet Federalism,' *Journal of Politics*, 1950, 20

Baker, P.J. 'The Doctrine of Legal Equality of States,' *British Yearbook of International Law*, 1923–4, p. 1

Barrea, J. 'The Counter-Core Role of Middle Powers in Processes of External Political Integration,' *World Politics*, January 1973, 274

Bastert, R.H. 'A New Approach to the Origins of Blaine's Pan American Policy,' *Hispanic American Historical Review*, 1959, 375

Berlin, I. 'Equality,' *Proceedings of the Aristotelian Society*, 1955–6, New Series, vol. LVI, London, 1956, 301

Blair, P.W. 'The Ministate Dilemma,' *Carnegie Endowment for International Peace*, October 1967

Bloomfield, L.P. 'Foreign Policy for Disillusioned Liberals,' *Foreign Policy*, Winter 1972–3, 55

Bowie, R.R. 'Strategy and the Atlantic Alliance,' *International Organization*, 1963, p. 775

Brown, S. 'The Changing Essence of Power,' *Foreign Affairs*, January 1973, 286

Brzezinski, Z. 'Peace and Power,' *Encounter*, November 1968, 3; 'Moscow and the MLF: Hostility and Ambivalence,' *Foreign Affairs*, 1964, 126

Buchan, A. 'The Multilateral Force: An Historical Perspective,' *Adelphi Papers*, No. 13, The Institute for Strategic Studies, London, October 1964; 'A World Restored?' *Foreign Affairs*, July 1972, 644

Bundy, McG. 'An Alliance of Equals,' *The Observer*, 17 December 1961, 8

Burr, R.N. 'The Balance of Power in Nineteenth Century South America: An Exploratory Essay,' *Hispanic American Historical Review*, vol. 35, 1955, 970

Burton, D.H. 'Theodore Roosevelt: Confident Imperialist,' *Review of Politics*, July 1961, 356

Campbell, J. 'Historical Development of Mythology,' *Daedalus*, Spring 1959, 232

Cate, C. 'Charles De Gaulle, The Last Romantic,' *The Atlantic*, November 1960, 56

Cecil, Viscount Robert, 'The Moral Basis of the League of Nations,' *The Essex Hall Lecture*, 1923, London, 1928

Claude, I.L., Jr. 'Collective Legitimization as a Political Function of the U.N.,' *International Organization*, Summer 1966, 367

− 'United Nations Use of Military Force,' *Journal of Conflict Resolution*, 1963, 117

Cohen, M. 'Communal Ghosts and Other Perils in Social Philosophy,' *Journal of Philosophy*, 1919, 673

Cohen, S., 'Equality,' *The Universal Jewish Encyclopedia*, New York, 1948, vol. 4, p. 147

Cronon, E.D. 'Interpreting the Good Neighbor Policy: The Cuban Crisis of 1933,' *Hispanic American Historical Review*, 1959, 556

Dahl, R.A. 'The Concept of Power,' *Behavioral Science*, 1957, 201

Deutsch, K.W. 'The Future of World Politics,' *Political Quarterly*, Jan.–Mar. 1966, 27

Dickinson, E.D. 'The Analogy Between Natural Persons and International Persons,' *Yale Law Journal*, 1926–7, 564

Doty, P. 'The Role of the Smaller Powers,' *Daedalus*, 1960, 818

Draper, T. 'The Dominican Crisis,' *Commentary*, December 1965, 33

Durdenevsky, V. 'The Five Principles,' *International Affairs* (Moscow), 1956, 7

Dyer, P.W. 'Will Tactical Nuclear Weapons Ever be Used,' *Political Science Quarterly*, June 1973, 214

Emerson, R. 'Nationalism and Political Development,' *Journal of Politics*, February 1960, 22

Fenwick, C.G. 'The Buenos Aires Conference: 1936,' *Foreign Policy Reports*, 1 July 1937, vol. 13, 90

Ferrell, R.H. 'Woodrow Wilson: Man and Statesman,' *Review of Politics*, April 1956, 131

Finch, G.A. 'The Peace Negotiations with Germany,' *A.J.I.L.*, 1919, vol. 13, pt. II, 536

Foreign Policy Association, 'Information Service,' 27 April 1928, vol. 3, 72

Fox, W.T. 'The Management of Power: A Review,' *Journal of Conflict Resolution*, 1964, 300

Gasteyger, C. 'The American Dilemma: Bipolarity or Alliance Cohesion,' *Adelphi Papers*, No. 24, The Institute for Strategic Studies, London, January 1966

Gay, P. 'Rhetoric and Politics in the French Revolution,' *American Historical Review*, April 1961, 676

Glenn, E.S. 'Semantic Difficulties in International Communication,' *A Review of General Semantics*, 1954, 163

Griffin, C.C. 'Welles to Roosevelt: A Memorandum on Inter-American Relations, 1933,' *Hispanic American Historical Review*, 1954, vol. 34, 190

Halle, L.J. 'On Dealing With Franco,' *The New Republic*, 24 September 1962, 11; 'Does War Have a Future,' *Foreign Affairs*, October 1973, 20

Halpern, B., '"Myth and Idelology" in Modern Usage,' *History and Theory*, 1961, vol. 1, No. 2, 129

Hayashi, M. 'An International Machinery for the Management of the Seabed: Birth and Growth of the Idea,' *Annals of International Studies*, vol. 4, Genève, 1973, p. 251

Hershey, A.S. 'The Calvo and Drago Doctrines,' *A.J.I.L.*, 1907, 26

Hicks, F.C. 'The Equality of States and the Hague Conferences,' *A.J.I.L.*, 1908, vol. 2, 530

Hoffman, S. 'De Gaulle's Memoirs: The Hero as History,' *World Politics*, October 1960, p. 150

Hollands, E. 'Nature, Reason and State Authority,' *Philosophical Review*, 1915, vol. 25, 646

Hughes, C.E. 'The Monroe Doctrine,' *Encyclopedia Britannica*, London, 1955, vol. 15, 737

Humphrey, H.H. 'U.S. Policy in Latin America,' *Foreign Affairs*, July 1964, 585

Hunter, R.E. 'Power and Peace,' *Foreign Policy*, Winter 1972–3, 37

Jung, C.G. 'On Life After Death,' *The Atlantic*, December 1962, 40

Kelsen, H. 'The Draft Declaration on Rights and Duties of States,' *A.J.I.L.*, April 1950, 259

Keohane, R.O. 'Political Influence in the General Assembly,' *International Conciliation*, 1966, No. 557

Kennan, G.F. 'History and Diplomacy as Viewed by a Diplomatist,' *Review of Politics*, 1956, 170

Kissinger, H.A. 'Coalition Diplomacy in a Nuclear Age,' *Foreign Affairs*, 1964, 525

Korovin, Y., 'International Law Today,' *International Affairs* (Moscow), July 1961, 20

Landau, M. 'On the Use of Metaphor in Political Analysis,' *Social Research*, Autumn 1961, 331

La Feber, W. 'The Background of Cleveland's Venezuelan Policy,' *American Historical Review*, July 1961, 959

Langbaum, R. 'Woodrow Wilson: Tragic Hero,' *Commentary*, February 1959, 159

Levin, D. 'The Non-Intervention Principle Today,' *International Affairs* (Moscow), November 1966, 21

Lippmann, W. 'Second Thoughts on Havana,' *Foreign Affairs*, July 1928, 541

Lissistzyn, O.J. 'Western and Soviet Perspectives on International Law – A Comparison,' *Proceedings, American Society of International Law*, Washington, D.C., 1959, 21

Lockey, J.B. 'The Meaning Of Pan-Americanism,' *A.J.I.L.*, 1925, pt. I, 104

Magee, J.S. 'Structure and Substance: The Political Decentralization in the United Nations,' *Journal of Politics*, 1965, 518

Manno, C.S. 'Selective Weighted Voting in the UN General Assembly,' *International Organization*, Winter 1966, 37

– Majority Decisions and Minority Responses in the UN General Assembly,' *Journal of Conflict Resolution*, March 1966, 1

Marshall, T. 'The Supreme Court as Protector of Civil Rights: Equal Protection of the Laws,' *Annals of The Academy of Political and Social Science*, May 1951, vol. I, 101

Mendelson, M.H. 'Diminutive States in the United Nations,' *International Law and Comparative Quarterly*, October 1972, 609

Miller, F.P. 'The Atlantic Area,' *Foreign Affairs*, July 1941, 727

Mitrany, D. 'The American Continent,' *Survey of International Affairs*, 1938, London, 1941, 663

Monnet, J. 'A New Sense of Community,' *Nato Letter*, Brussels, March 1968, 2

Morgenthau, H. 'Beyond Nationalism,' *Saturday Review of Literature*, 16 July 1960, 36

Müller-Freinfels, W. 'Equality of Husband and Wife in Family Law,' *International Comparative Law Quarterly*, April 1959, 249

Myers, D.P. 'The Origins of the Hague Arbitral Courts,' *A.J.I.L.*, 1916, vol. 10. pt. I, 270

McNair, A.D. 'Equality in International Law,' *Michigan Law Review*, 1927–8, 134

Nieburg, H.L. 'Uses of Violence,' *Journal of Conflict Resolution*, 1963, 43

Nixon, C.R. 'Self-Determination: The Nigeria/Biafra Case,' *World Politics*, July 1972, 473

Orvik, N. 'NATO: The Role of the Small Members,' *International Journal*, 1966, 173

Parsons, T. 'On the Concept of Political Power,' *Proceedings of the American Philosophical Society*, 1963, 232

Piradov, A. 'The Principle of Non-Interference in the Modern World,' *International Affairs* (Moscow), January 1966, 53

'The Place of Law in Germany,' Anonymous, *Law Quarterly Review*, April 1943, 136

Pound, R. 'Philosophical Theory and International Law,' *Bibliotheca Visseriana*, 1923, vol. I, 73

Reynaud, P. 'When England Offered Everything to France,' *Saturday Review*, 16 March 1963, 26

Romulo, C.P. 'Little Brown Brother,' *Saturday Review of Literature*, 22 April 1961, 17

Roosevelt, F.D. 'Our Foreign Policy,' *Foreign Affairs*, July 1928, 573

Root, E. 'The Outlook for International Law,' *A.J.I.L.*, 1916, vol. 10, pt. I, I

Rowen, H.H. 'The Peace of Westphalia Revisited,' *Journal of Modern History*, 1961, 53

Samuel, Sir H. 'War of Ideas,' *International Conciliation*, New York, 1937, 473

– 'Looking to the Future,' *The Menorah Journal*, Autumn-Winter, 1960, 21

Schlesinger, A.M., Jr. 'The Failure of World Communism,' *The Post*, 19 May 1962, 13

Scott, J.B. 'The Sixth International Conference of American States,' *International Conciliation*, New York, June 1928, 277

Shub, A. 'Notes on C.V. Wedgwood's History of the Puritan Rebellion,' *Commentary*, June 1959, 531

Slessor, Sir J. 'Command and Control of Allied Nuclear Forces,' *Adelphi Papers*, No. 22, The Institute for Strategic Studies, London, August 1965

Smith, B. 'The Sometimes Baffling Mind of India,' *Harper's Magazine*, August 1962, 60

Spengler, J.J. 'Hierarchy *vs.* Equality: Persisting Conflict,' *Kyklos*, vol. XXI, 1968

Stein, E. and Carreau, D. 'Law and Peaceful Change in a Subsystem: "Withdrawal" of France from the North Atlantic Treaty Organization,' *AJIL*, July 1968, 577

Stimson, H.L. 'The United States and the Other American Republics,' *Foreign Affairs*, April 1931, Special Supplement, No. 3

'The Second Meeting of the Ministers of Foreign Affairs of the American

Republics,' September 1940, *International Conciliation*, New York, 1940, 263

'The Third Meeting of the Ministers of Foreign Affairs of the American Republics,' at Rio de Janeiro, 15–28 January 1942, *Internation Conciliation*, New York, 1942, 97

Thomson, C.A. 'The Cuban Revolution: Reform and Reaction,' *Foreign Policy Reports*, 1 January 1936, vol. 11, 261

– 'The Seventh Pan-American Conference, Montevideo,' *Foreign Policy Reports*, 6 June 1934, vol. 10, 86

Trueblood, H.J. 'Trade Rivalries in Latin America,' *Foreign Policy Reports*, 15 September 1937, vol. 13, 154

Ulam, A.B. 'Moscow Plays the Balance ...' *Foreign Policy*, Fall 1972, 86

Vernon, R. 'Rogue Elephant in the Forest: An Appraisal of Transatlantic Relations,' *Foreign Affairs*, April 1973, 573

Whitehead, A.N. 'Symbolism, Its Meaning and Effect,' *Daedalus*, 1958, 108

Willrich, M. 'The Treaty on Non-Proliferation of Nuclear Weapons: Nuclear Technology Confronts World Politics,' *Yale Law Journal*, July 1968, 1447

Young, O.R. 'Trends in International Peacekeeping,' *Woodrow Wilson School of Public and International Affairs*, Princeton, January 1966

Zilliacus, K. 'The League and the World Today,' *Problems of the Peace*, 13th Series, 1938, 257

Zolberg, A.R. 'Tribalism Through Corrective Lenses,' *Foreign Affairs*, July 1973, 728

Index

Lightning Source UK Ltd.
Milton Keynes UK
UKHW010002210722
406167UK00001B/210

9 781487 592394